Still Listening

Still Listening

New Horizons
in Spiritual Direction

———•◆•———

Edited by Norvene Vest

MOREHOUSE PUBLISHING
Harrisburg, Pennsylvania

Morehouse Publishing
P.O. Box 1321
Harrisburg, PA 17105

Morehouse Publishing is a division of The Morehouse Group.

Printed in the United States of America

02 03 04 05   10 9 8 7 6 5 4 3 2

Cover design by Annika Baumgardner
Cover art, *Land of the Midnight Sun,* by Diana Ong (b. 1940), private collection, SuperStock

Library of Congress Cataloging-in-Publication Data

Still Listening : new horizons in spiritual direction / edited by Norvene Vest.
     p. cm.
   Includes bibliographical references.
   ISBN 0-8192-1814-6 (alk. paper)
   1. Spiritual direction. I. Vest, Norvene.

BV5053 .S75 2000
253.5'3--dc21   00-056108

As spiritual directors, we ourselves are formed by many influences, not least of which is God's ongoing call to us to unfold in holiness. Yet no matter what other factors come into play, each of us is introduced to life with Mystery by our parents. During preparation of this book, four of the contributors walked alongside parents in the spiritual work of dying. We dedicate this book to all our parents and especially to them:

E. JANE DRISKILL,
mother of Joseph D. Driskill

EARL REED, SR.,
father of Juan Reed

GEORGE B. RUFFING,
father of Janet Ruffing

CARROLL WIGGINS,
father to Rich Rossiter's partner Perry Wiggins

Contents

Introduction

We welcome you to our volume on new horizons in spiritual direction, for which we have invited directors with special skills and interests to share their thoughts on cutting-edge issues in the field of spiritual direction. Writing about issues that may be surfacing periodically in their ministries, each author shares his or her insights about a challenge that has been the subject of their own deep reflection and prayer. We do not presume to be comprehensive but simply to speak of matters that each has found crucially important in practice. This book is not an overview of the spiritual-direction process, its definition and goals. Rather it is our hunch that "new" issues are arising frequently in the regular practice of spiritual direction, about which mature directors would appreciate a colleague's wisdom. We seek to address some of those issues fruitfully.

The chapters are divided into three sections. The first section contains reflections on the person who comes for direction. Always we know that the Spirit is embodied in the unique gifts and limitations of a particular person. Yet there are patterns of development that pose special challenges to the director, and these chapters intend to help us listen effectively in such cases. Tom Cashman considers the emerging field of spiritual direction within corporations, discovering how the Spirit is already present and strengthening the role of values at work. Joe Driskill sensitively explores concerns and opportunities in directing people who have been emotionally and physically traumatized. Barry Woodbridge spells out how addictive patterns permeate a directee's life. My own essay looks at the wary seekers who are returning to church through spiritual direction.

The second section speaks to special life issues that intersect with spiritual development. Howard Rice links the results of generational studies with spiritual-direction practice, and Margaret Guenther looks at spiritual direction as it assists on the threshold of death. Both Rich Rossiter and Juan Reed help us explore our own shortcomings in meeting persons who require that we grow in order to hear them into authentic speech: the marginalized and more specifically the sexually marginalized, the gay, lesbian, bisexual, and transgendered communities.

The third section locates the practice of spiritual direction within the environment around us. The section is titled "The Social Context" as a way of pointing toward broader, communal dimensions affecting the

moment of direction. Kenneth Leech reminds us about the essential connection between spiritual direction and justice. Betsy Caprio Hedberg
considers the dimensions beyond words that shape our spiritual lives, and
how the senses, especially the visual, can be brought explicitly into the
direction experience. Janet Ruffing emphasizes that a theology of incarnation must include a place for the passions of sexuality, and shows how
that need can be honored in spiritual direction. Sandra Lommasson shows
concretely how we can transcend our cultural bias toward individualism
by tending the communal soul of a congregation. Finally, Steven
Charleston asks where have we been and where we are going in this journey of the Spirit as a new century opens ahead.

The essays do not speak with a single voice, but with a diversity that
emphasizes the unity of our lives in God's Spirit. Yet unity never means
homogeneity, and we welcome authentic experiences of God emerging
from a variety of perspectives. Taken together, the essays invite us as directors to look more deeply and to pray more earnestly about our ministry:
in direction, do we seek primarily to "follow the lead" of the directee or
to challenge the directee to new ways of being? Stated another way, is
direction primarily contemplative or prophetic? When dealing with matters
of righteous passion in ourselves and our directees, to what extent is it
appropriate to rein in those passions by logic and system? When we
become aware of issues that make us uncomfortable, do we avoid directing persons with those issues, or can we invite God and our directees to
teach us new opportunities for conversion? As always, generalizations are
often inadequate in the search for fidelity to the Mystery called God, but
a genuine effort to struggle with difficult questions always helps to break
us open more fully to Divine Love.

May these reflections deepen the blessing of your important ministry
for you, others, and God.

Shalom, Norvene Vest

Section I

---·◆·---

The Person Who Comes

Chapter One

SPIRITUAL DIRECTION IN THE CORPORATE ENVIRONMENT

Tom Cashman

————— • ◆ • —————

The intent of this essay is not to offer a "how-to" process for doing spiritual direction in the corporate world. My hunch is that this environment is too complex and the directees too diverse for any general approach. What I share instead is how my ministry has developed in this area and how it continues to evolve. Ultimately, all any of us can share authentically is our own experience.

I question whether any of us ever sets out to do direction with a particular category of directee. Even if you are focused on doing direction a particular constituency, such as Roman Catholics or Presbyterians, the Holy Spirit often arranges otherwise. So we may be surprised to find ourselves journeying with clergy, or with gay and lesbian directees. Perhaps we are called to work with persons on the edge of the church, with only a toe or two still within it—not at all what we had in mind when we began to exercise this charism and calling. But if you are already working with corporate directees or are on the edge of this ministry, then perhaps my reflections will be helpful.

Some definition of "spiritual direction in the corporate environment" is important so that we are clear on the context.

To do this requires me to recap how and why I came to the ministry of spiritual direction. In 1983, people in my own congregation began coming to me informally for direction and spiritual companioning. I simply accepted this as a natural dynamic of parish life until my own director of that time, an Episcopal priest, Jack Gorsuch, told me of a program that he and several colleagues had started, the Pacific Northwest Spiritual Direction Training Program. He felt I had a charism for this work and, with his encouragement, I emerged two years later as a certificated spiritual director. In 1992 I went back to school for a B.S. in applied behavioral science, specializing in consulting and leadership. The degree gave me skills and some internal permission to leave the Fortune 500 company in which I had worked for nine years, and to begin to combine consulting, corporate coaching, and spiritual direction. One of my research projects for this degree led me to design a model for facilitating clergy-support groups. My work with two of these groups brought me into contact with a broad spectrum of clergy, and I found my direction practice gradually shifting to include an increasing number of clergy. It had simply never occurred to me that clergy might choose to work with a lay director.

By 1995, seven of my directees were clergy from a variety of denominational backgrounds. But I had met a few newer directees through consulting and organizational development. There was interest growing in some managers with whom I had connected in my corporate coaching work.

Just as my spiritual direction practice with clergy was a surprise development, that corporate managers sought to journey with me was unanticipated. The process by which this typically happened is worth explaining. Frequently I found myself coaching clients who sought discernment around spiritual issues and values. With awareness that I was making a shift in our work together, I would ask questions that touched on the clients' spiritual values and that sometimes evoked awareness of God moving in their lives within the corporate milieu. Similarly, I found myself bringing coaching dynamics into spiritual-direction sessions, often with clergy. When I mirrored segments of the narrative back to the one being coached or in direction, the person often was able to see the issue clearly for the first time. Next, questions, discussion, and/or suggestions helped the client develop alternatives and strategies for working with the issue.

These episodes greatly increased my awareness of the potential for overlap between the two disciplines and of the importance of understanding the differences. I needed to be aware what mode I was in at any given moment. I began to tell my directees and clients when I was making a shift from spiritual direction to coaching, or vice versa. It seemed important as well for them to be aware of my modus operandi, so they could hear and respond in an appropriate way. It was at this time through word of mouth that corporate managers began to come to me for spiritual direction. Over the last two years clients have asked to work with me in a mix of both spiritual direction and coaching.

Avenues into Spiritual Direction in the Corporate World

Let's look at the ways corporate managers come to seek spiritual direction. The entrée sometimes comes when a client in coaching or consulting is unexpectedly affected by a life crisis that colors everything he or she is doing.

Divorce, death of a colleague, or serious health challenge shifts perspective on the relative importance of work, career, family, personal goals, and a relationship with God. The window for discussion of spiritual direction opens. Often I would make referrals; some would ask me to work with them.

These events are not very different from the "trigger" issues for most new directees. But some crises specific to the corporate journey can open the typical successful manager, executive, or CEO to the need for a companion on the spiritual journey. Sometimes downsizing suddenly leaves the middle manager expendable in the new organizational chart. Sometimes acquisition by another company radically shifts a manager's role. She finds herself needing new skills and often feels disoriented and unsure of her own identity in this new constellation. Quite often the trigger is nothing less than success. A personal goal is achieved. Through the individual's vision and efforts the company moves into a new market successfully, or radically shifts the focus of its services. It is the corporate equivalent of winning the World Series, or running the four-minute mile. But the executive may find the moment of triumph hollow and without the sense of achievement he or she had imagined. In the sadness, in the postpartum depression that sets in, God calls. A yearning surfaces for the Transcendent, for the real, for that which is not transitory. In that moment, events can be seen from a numinous perspective that looks beyond the goals and yearnings provided so relentlessly by our culture and media. The need to know what is real, true, and ultimately important asserts itself. A window opens for a relationship of spiritual direction to begin.

Spiritual direction with clergy is perhaps a chapter for another book at another time. The task is quite different, yet similar in some respects, to work with corporate directees. There are some parallels that make the practice useful to mention. Both clergy and senior corporate managers feel the weight of the responsibility they carry. Both are highly motivated, capable professionals who expect much from their professional and personal lives. Often the spiritual journey is only slightly more conscious for clergy than for corporate executives. Clergy often have a strongly inculturated expectation that they are to be more "spiritual" than they find themselves in actual practice. They expect their prayer life to be more developed, more intense, and more intentional. They expect a more direct sense of contact with God through their spiritual practice. They expect themselves to receive significant and inspirational material for their sermons and counsels. Spiritual dryness for clergy is difficult to own and acknowledge.

By contrast, the executives with whom I have worked are somewhat astonished when our consultations take us into spiritual areas. Our culture tends to categorize persons as spiritual or as practical, pragmatic, professional types. Of course, we are all some mixture of those qualities. When a CEO first discovers that he has a functional spiritual gear on his psychic transmission it can be an amazing revelation. Often I work with a directee in "backtracking" over the significant events of life, opening the possibility of seeing God at work in and through those events. Then I may probe gently for some shape to the individual's worldview. What internal model of "how the world works" does this person carry? Where is God in that schematic? What God-image does this person carry through life? How might that image relate to parents and to family of origin?

Next we would explore the directee's prayer life. What prayer practice exists? What image of God is present in prayer? To which person of the Trinity does the directee pray? With what expectations is the prayer offered? Does the directee have any sense of prayer ever being answered? Does the directee have any sense that prayer is even heard?

Some individuals are unable to begin with these fairly traditional starting points for the journey of spiritual direction. For a variety of reasons, they may be blocked from directly addressing God in prayer, or even from consideration of God in their worldview and values. At the same time, there is still a yearning for God, for the Transcendent that seems to be in the very next room, but without a door for access. With these persons, nearly always men, I use a values-clarification exercise as our first work. With a set of eighty to one hundred value cards, I ask the new directee to select the fifteen most significant values. These are thoughtfully reduced to eight values. He is invited to reflect over time on their relative importance, and we discuss the process. Seldom have any of these executives previously come to grips with their core values. I talk them through the rationale behind the selection of each value, using each as an example of the executive's strong spiritual core that is being uncovered.

At this time, there may be flashes of insight. One executive burst out, "Good God! No wonder I fight with my staff over the shareholder reports. We are working from diametrically opposed values about what the shareholders are entitled to." Almost always this process is one of great affirmation. Almost always the directee is grateful and amazed to find that significant spiritual values undergird not only his relationship to family and friends, but also the action and direction of his professional life. The stereotype of life being compartmentalized into sacred and secular comes under examination. My premise that God is present in all aspects of life, that all is holy, all is sacred, and all is suitable material for the direction process may be difficult for these directees initially. Only after months of reflection and dialogue does this premise begin to resonate with the experience of the directee.

MAJOR ISSUES WITH CORPORATE DIRECTEES

Other issues surface with corporate directees that are similar to, yet different from, issues for lay directees with whom I have journeyed.

Preference for doing rather than being. While this is a cultural pattern for all of us twenty-first-century, white, urban, affluent Americans, it is far more pronounced in the corporate culture, where productivity is paramount and workaholism is endemic. High activity is not only important as a way of maintaining corporate image, but also bolsters one's own sense of worth. Perhaps only clergy receive more positive reinforcement for their dysfunctional workaholic tendencies than do corporate managers. When this fact comes to a directee's consciousness, I suggest that he or she begin to remember (or imagine, if necessary) what "being" time is or was like. Once that image is clear, preferably from that person's experience, they need to accept that this time is actual, valuable spiritual practice. The next step might be carving out time in the directee's personal schedule for regular "being" time. Last, and perhaps most difficult, is for the directee truly to own this practice as equal to the "doing" time that commandeers so much of our professional and private life. The ultimate gift may well become the rich experience of God speaking in or through "being" time in unexpected and significant ways.

Exploring one's prayer life. Even the term "prayer life" will often seem incongruous to new directees. Sometimes it's useful to help the new directee discover that he or she has an internal life that is as vital as the external life, and that prayer is part of that. Often it helps to characterize prayer as a conversation in which the directee takes responsibility for one side of the conversation. The response is received in various voices, tones, and movements; in the voices of others through whom God touches one's life; in and through events; sometimes through dreams and flashes of intuition that carry a numinous quality. Testing and interpreting the response is, of course, necessary and raises the topic of discernment.

Another aspect of prayer-life development is exposure to various prayer styles and practices. For new directees I suggest an exploration of contemplative practice, Franciscan, Celtic, and *lectio divina*. This step reminds me of a wine tasting, as it is highly individualistic and filled with the potential of significant discovery. There is delight when a directee finds a style of prayer that fits her personality. Too often in our liturgies and personal prayer traditions we have encouraged the individual to try to fit themselves to the given prayer, rather than attempting to fit the prayer to themselves.

Some directees are more comfortable with a diagnostic/prescriptive approach to prayer alternatives. If the directee's Myers-Briggs type is known, I use the excellent book, *Prayer and Temperament,* by Chester Michael and Marie Norrissey. The book's descriptions of each typology's spirituality and suggestions for prayer exercises to match each type are invaluable. If the MBTI is unknown or has never been determined, I use the *Gregorc Style Delineator,* which is quick and easy to administer. With results in hand, it is fairly simple to refer the directee to one of the four major approaches to prayer that *Prayer and Temperament* spells out.

Discernment. Dimensions of nuance and modality affect spiritual discernment in the corporate environment. Managers and executives exercise a kind of discernment constantly in their corporate roles. Decisions based on "running the numbers" are easy compared to decisions that involve many intangible factors. For example, a decision on how best to use people in building a project team is a classic example of right-brain function and creative discernment. This creative process is also at work in sensing how people are best motivated and rewarded within that team, and adjusting team process accordingly. The ethos or "feeling" of a team within a company, indeed, of the entire organization, is becoming a significant concern for corporate leadership. But being aware of team "feeling" demands subjective discernment rather than the process one might use in engineering. Technology fails to help us much when the data are "soft" and subjective. When working with clients with backgrounds predominantly in engineering, discernment at first can be a difficult leap in style. During one session with a manufacturing-process engineer, I casually used the term "hunch." That word galvanized him and the conversation that followed. Engineers, especially those who work in theoretical areas, are very familiar with the hunch or intuitive leap that often leads to a breakthrough, to new solutions. Asking the directee to "think about where that hunch comes from" takes us quickly into the spiritual arena in a nonthreatening way.

How spiritual discernment resembles what directees presently do, and how it is different, is often important bridging work. Integrating prayer, especially contemplative prayer and experiential spiritual practice, into the discernment process flows naturally out of that dialogue. Awareness that the directee is accessing and in some way "partnering" with the Holy Spirit in the discernment process may take a little longer. Sometimes a group-discernment episode in the corporate life of the directee has helped shape understanding. Remembering how the "new thought," whether God, Spirit, intuitive flash, hunch, or inspiration—however the directee best understands the idea at this point—changed the process and led toward discernment is always useful. Remembering what freed the group to get to that state may help. Ultimately, the goal is to enable the directee to engage in focused discernment with some assistance from the director.

Challenge of discovering God in all aspects of life. As a culture, Americans tend to compartmentalize life: This is sacred, that is secular. This is holy, that is profane. Because of my activity with Celtic Christian spirituality, I often refer to the worldview of Celtic times. All was holy. Everything was sacred because all came from the hand of the Creator. And so the Celtic Christians had prayers for all activities of daily life—churning the butter, carding the wool, driving the cattle to the upper pasture, and rowing the boat. There were even prayers for the daily routines of bathing and using the backhouse (outhouse). We can find a similar worldview in most Native American cultures, and in virtually all aboriginal peoples worldwide. It is only as we have become an urban people, a people of technology, distanced from the land, that we have lost this worldview. The sacred has become "other" and now needs to be sought with difficulty.

The corporate manager may need both encouragement and much "mirroring" from his director to begin to see God's presence and touch in professional events. Occasionally he will hear a significant message through the offhand or casual remark of a colleague. You can help your directee "unpack" that remark, to separate it from the person and the professional relationship and then to hear it as possible sacred content. "What struck you about this remark? Why does it seem significant in a professional (yet also spiritual) context? Or perhaps it is important for you in your personal life? Considering the content of the message, whose voice are you hearing? Are you hearing the voice of a particular person of the Trinity? Or is it a patron saint? Is it perhaps a guardian angel?"

Sometimes it is an event in one's professional or corporate life in which we are able to perceive God's touch or message. Great success or abject failure can be equally potent. I have learned to ask many of these questions from my own experience. If overwhelmed by a sense of failure when a creative leap or what I thought was an innovative idea falls short, is there something I am being taught? What might God want me to see as a result? Am I being led (through failure) to follow in Christ's footsteps for some larger purpose?

Success can be equally devastating. If success is suddenly mine, and I find it hollow and unfulfilling, what then? What am I to learn? What feelings come when I pray over this episode? (This question assumes the directee can differentiate feelings from wants and thoughts.) What direction does exhilarating success give to my life? What comes next? Where is God leading me? Or am I fooling myself? Is success a diversion from my real work, my true calling? Or is this event simply a happening without particular significance?

Discernment in this context is not only developing a sense of how God moves and speaks in events, but also developing an inner detection system for the numinous. Repeated exposure to the movement of the Holy Spirit builds sensitivity to its presence. A sweet alarm goes off when that grace is operating in proximity to my life. The marks of grace and the fruit of the Holy Spirit become more obvious over time, and I am able to see them more quickly.

Effects of corporate life on self-image. Those who have been in the corporate world long enough to ascend to a middle-management position or higher have been heavily conditioned in the way they perceive themselves. Many companies inculturate their senior managers to think of themselves primarily as members of the corporate family. Further, they are implicitly encouraged to place their prime loyalty with the organization, and in subtle or perhaps more overt ways to adopt its cultural values. Some of the cybertechnology companies of the Northwest have internal facilities for eating, sleeping, bathing, and recreating so that, except for extraordinary needs, the employee need not leave the premises. Over time this can condition the employee to consider as real family those coworkers with whom she spends the bulk of her time. The employee's personal identity shifts to the context of the company. Other connections and loyalties become secondary. Self-worth is determined by the perceived functional value of the person within the company. Obviously, this is a culture oriented toward the single, unattached person, able to work long hours and forsake most connections with the "outside world." These events may result in a relatively young, highly placed manager, whose rise to economic affluence has been rapid, if not easy, who is ready to move beyond economic survival issues and now to confront core values that may previously have been ignored. This stage, the seeking of the Transcendent in a transitional, shifting, technological world, tends to come at least a decade earlier than it did with my generation. Gail Sheehy in *Passages* wrote that my generation began to grapple with such issues in our late forties and early fifties. Today's cyber-cognoscenti may come to that point as early as their mid-thirties. Working with these younger directees has unique aspects and can be wonderfully rewarding. Generally, I have found the younger corporate leaders more open and adaptable than their older counterparts in pursuing the inner life of the soul.

Changing identities, changing priorities. One's priorities tend to align with the roles with which the self-image is constructed. If one's professional role is the primary identity, then work becomes the primary priority, providing intrinsic value and even justifying existence. For one whose primary identity is as father of a family, caring for that family becomes first priority.

One person I worked with admitted that his identities in order of priority were attorney, golf devotee, Phi Beta Kappa member, and fiancé. Becoming clear about that helped him come to grips with a key spiritual issue that had previously been buried. Eventually he decided that he wanted to change his identity sequence. With some encouragement, he began to pray for that change to take place. What seemed most significant in this process were three elements:

1. Being objective and honest enough to acknowledge, even to himself, his identities in order of priority;
2. Deciding that he wanted to change his identity and the priorities that came with it; and
3. Beginning to pray for that change, knowing that he himself was powerless to change by simply willing the change. As Keith Miller has aptly written, "He was willing to be willing."

So long as he saw himself as, above all, a professional trial lawyer, his priority was to be overwhelmingly capable, persuasive, and effective in order to have power over the courtroom process. He knew he wanted to influence the jury, to defer to the judge subtly as well as to engage the judge as a colleague, to crush the opposing attorney, and finally to engage and manipulate the collective emotions of the gallery.

As he brought this issue repeatedly to our sessions, this goal gradually shifted to becoming, in his own mind, a peer in seeing that justice was served. That this was his task along with the judge, jury, opposing attorney, and client grew slowly into prominence. To do this required acquiring humility along with a different perspective on his client relationships. The spiritual dimension of the changes seemed at least as important to him as the professional dimensions. Eventually, he was able to see his marriage as superseding his professional life and professional relationships. He was able to bring his relationship with Christ onto the same level and began to suspect that there was a core value in the "God stuff" (his term) that rippled through and enhanced every other aspect of his life.

The problem of making time. The pace of life hinders all of us from connecting with the numinous. The analogy I like to use is of electronic "noise" in urban areas which interferes with the effective use of radio telescopes. Thus, the scientific community builds radio telescopes in remote places. One of the most effective sites is in the Brazilian rain forest, far from even small towns. Radio telescopes need solitude in order to receive the faint information they seek from distant galaxies. Without that solitude, the faint signal is overwhelmed by the noise of "civilization."

Similarly, our senses are so overwhelmed by the noise and pace of contemporary life that the faint inner voice of the Spirit cannot be heard. The pace in the corporate world is fast and becoming faster. Commuting time used to be time for processing, thinking, reflecting. Now the cell phone brings the work world into the car, enabling the workday to begin hours earlier and end hours later than before. The typical manager or executive, conditioned by our workaholic culture, frequently takes work home. More of us also work from a home office, so that the previous boundary of place no longer separates us from the activity and "mind share" demanded by our work. It becomes easy for the corporate manager to find herself immersed, from waking to sleeping, in the flow of business. Time for prayer, contemplation, or other spiritual practice must be carved out intentionally and with difficulty. I encourage directees to make time for prayer and for solitude by scheduling it just as they would schedule any other appointment of their professional or private life. It becomes as necessary (and difficult) for the directee to protect that time from becoming preempted as she would any other business or personal item.

I have found *Living in the Presence: Spiritual Exercises to Open Ourselves to the Awareness of God,* and *Living Simply through the Day: Spiritual Survival in a Complex Age,* both by Tilden Edwards, to be very useful resources. They speak well to either men or women and can be modified to fit the most demanding lifestyle.

CONNECTING WITH CORPORATE DIRECTEES

The question is frequently asked, "How do you make yourself visible to corporate spiritual-direction clients?" I began this essay by stating that no one sets out to position himself as a director for any particular constituency such as business managers, clergy, or persons of a particular denomination. This process happens through the working of the Holy Spirit via networking and word of mouth and through other ways we cannot fathom. But there are appropriate actions if you find yourself sought out by corporate directees. I will assume that you already have prayerfully sought confirmation of that focus in your work and discussed it with your own director and/or supervisor. One option is to let a human resources director with whom you have rapport know of your ministry and the training you have undergone. Referrals might be appropriate if no boundary issues (see below) are involved. It may also be appropriate to give the same information about your ministry and training to parish priests and ministers who you believe have some understanding of spiritual direction, and who may wish to refer. This request should always be made with a personal visit, I believe. Don't just mail information about yourself and your training. Spiritual direction is a ministry of presence. Go in person to the one who would refer. Let the Holy Spirit build the bridges and enable the appropriate connections.

What are the boundary issues when you work for the same company as your directee? I often hear discussions of conflicted boundaries, in which a director works with members of their same religious community. How is working with directees from your workplace different from working with directees from your parish, diocese, religious community, or fitness club?

Some generalizations can be made. It is never appropriate to work with a directee that reports directly to you at your business or to work with someone to whom you report directly. Under certain circumstances, it may be workable to direct someone above you in the organization chart to whom you report indirectly. It is almost always inappropriate to be in direction with someone from your company that you also see socially. The literature tells us consistently that a spiritual director, in order to maintain a detached perspective, ideally should have had no prior or parallel relationship to the directee. This is so the directee can be heard without bias or the coloring of history. My sense is that the relationship stays healthy when neither the director nor directee is responsible to or dependent upon the other within the corporate culture. The principle is to allow for the spiritual-direction relationship to be, as much as possible, the only relationship between director and directee. As this is sometimes not possible or practical in religious communities, there also may be extraordinary circumstances in the corporate world. The Holy Spirit sometimes transcends such guidelines.

Use discernment. If a difficult decision presents itself, talk and discern with your own spiritual director or with your supervision group.

Another dynamic has increased awareness of the spiritual among corporate managers and made them more open to working with a spiritual director. That dynamic is the increasing acceptance of the spiritual dimension of work itself. Much has been written recently about the spirituality of work. Foundational writing has been done by Matthew Fox, Jack Hawley, Peter B. Vaill, and Geoffrey Bellman (see the bibliography at the end of this essay).

Many consultants in organizational development are talking openly with their colleagues about nontraditional (i.e., spiritual) tools and practices that they use in their work with organizations and corporations. They are also beginning to talk more openly with their clients about the same practices, and to look at the spiritual dimensions of reorganizing and restructuring corporate organizations. Both consultants and clients are now more willing to consider the spiritual aspects of change and development within the corporate organism. The trend toward spiritual practices in consulting and toward awareness of the spiritual functionality of corporations has been likened to that of "nontraditional" naturopathic and homeopathic medicine in health care. While we are a long way from universal acceptance of these so-called nontraditional approaches, they are being seen more often as acceptable. These alternative approaches are seen as needed balance to the scientific, left-brain traditions of organizational development and allopathic medicine. In fact, rather than being new and radical, the nontraditional approaches are traditions of long standing in this culture and many others.

Consciousness of the spiritual dimension of leadership in a corporation or public institution is growing rapidly. In a climate more open to the spiritual dimension of work and to the movement of the Spirit within an organization, it has become more acceptable (or at least less politically incorrect) for corporate leaders to examine the spiritual aspect of their leadership. Historical evaluation shows that it would have been unthinkable for a tribal leader to make a political decision without considering its spiritual implications. There was a time in the Celtic world, for instance, in both Christian and pre-Christian eras, when such leadership practice was a cultural imperative. No Celtic leader would consider important decisions without his anamchara (literally, "soul friend") at his side to aid in the discernment process. In this respect, by working as spiritual directors with corporate leaders we are simply revisiting and reclaiming a tradition of long standing. It is my hope that the essential nature of a spiritual director, companion, or guide for any leader—corporate, political, institutional, or religious—will be restored. But even now, many, from middle managers to CEOs, are looking for persons to travel with them on a journey that is spiritual as well as personal and professional. The Holy Spirit moves as pervasively through the offices and boardrooms of contemporary corporate America as it did through the early church in the Acts of the Apostles. Let us move with that Spirit.

REFERENCES

Bellman, Geoffrey. *The Consultant's Calling*. San Francisco: Jossey-Bass, 1990.

Edwards, Tilden. *Living in the Presence: Spiritual Exercises to Open Ourselves to the Awareness of God*. San Francisco: Harper, 1994.

———. *Living Simply through the Day: Spiritual Survival in a Complex Age*. New York: Paulist Press, 1977.

Fox, Matthew. *The Spirituality of Work*. New York: HarperCollins, 1994.

Gregorc, Anthony F. *Gregorc Style Delineator*. Columbia, Conn.: Gregorc Associates, 1986.

Hawley, Jack. *Reawakening the Spirit in Work*. New York: Fireside, 1993.

Michael, Chester P., and Marie C. Norrisey. *Prayer and Temperament*. Charlottesville, Va.: Open Door, 1984.

Vaill, Peter B. *Managing as a Performing Art*. San Francisco: Jossey-Bass, 1989.

Chapter Two

SPIRITUAL DIRECTION WITH TRAUMATIZED PERSONS

Joseph D. Driskill

———•◆•———

INTRODUCTION

The level of violence in the United States is staggering. We see daily in our newspapers not only accounts of homicides and handgun violence, but also reports of domestic violence; child abuse—sexual, physical, neglect; elder abuse; and the abuse of animals. Recent statistics for the United States indicate 969,018 substantiated cases of child abuse in a twelve-month period.[1] These statistics confirm our perceptions that large numbers of people are the victims of traumatic, violent acts that instill fear, diminish freedom, and thwart spiritual growth. While it is true that men are abused—often by other men—women are far more frequently the victims of abuse. Given this situation much of this essay will address the abuse of women. Many of the findings, however, apply to persons of both genders who have experienced trauma or abuse.

As people confront their own histories of abuse an important step in the healing process requires exploring the profound spiritual issues raised by such violence. Persons who have been victimized are left asking profound questions of meaning. Why me? If God is all-powerful why did God allow this to happen? What does this mean? Is it my fault? Such questions raise profound theological questions about the nature of God's power, God's grace, and the nature of a moral life.

The pervasiveness of violence raises theological issues not only for the victims of abuse, but also for communities of faith and the wider society. Faith communities address these issues both through advocacy programs intended to raise awareness of child abuse and domestic violence, but also through religious leaders who provide pastoral counseling and spiritual direction to traumatized persons. The issues of trauma and abuse raise a number of legal, psychological, and religious issues which require specialized attention. This essay begins with a brief discussion of the legal obligations of mandatory reporting and the value of a team approach to the healing process, including spiritual direction.

Spiritual directors who are committed to ministry with abused and trau-matized people need to understand how profoundly the dynamics of trauma affect directees' understandings and experiences of God. This essay will contribute to that understanding by identifying the psychological dynamics bearing most directly on the spiritual-direction process. Following this I will highlight religious and spiritual issues raised by the dynamics of abuse. Throughout I will suggest ways the spiritual director may contribute to the healing process. In this essay, when I speak of trauma and abuse I am lifting up dynamics and issues that most commonly describe sexual abuse and its impact on adults who have been abused as children. I also make ref-erence from time to time to the physical abuse of children and domestic vio-lence. While there are unique dynamics operative in each of these types of abuse, I will be discussing what they share in common unless otherwise noted. An annotated bibliography at the end of the chapter will point directors and directees to further resources.

Mandatory Reporting and the Ministry of Referral

Clergy are frequently the professionals first approached when people are in personal difficulty. That being the case, one may assume that a spiritual direc-tor may be the first person outside the family to learn that a directee is being or has been abused. In most states, if the directee is underage and the abuse is happening *at the present time* the director has an obligation to report this abuse to legal authorities. Mandatory reporting of abuse that happened many years ago is required in some states if the abuser is still living and has access to young children—for example, a grandfather who has access to his grandchildren. In many states this mandatory reporting is required not only of all caregivers and teachers, but of the general population as well. Many jurisdictions also require mandatory reporting of elder abuse. People who practice spiritual direction in any formal manner, either in an individual prac-tice or through institutions—counseling centers, churches, religious orders—need to know the legal obligations of their locale.

Spiritual directors may also work with people who are currently victims of domestic violence or who have yet to confide in others their history of childhood abuse. In either circumstance, mandatory reporting may not be required, but the spiritual director may serve a crucial function in refer-ring the abused person to additional professional assistance. Spiritual direc-tors will be well served to have a list of professionals from a variety of therapeutic fields who value and respect religion.

People who approach directors with occasional suicidal thoughts or vague suicidal intentions should be referred for therapeutic assistance. In cases in which the person seems intent on ending his/her life or has a plan to commit suicide, immediate referral is imperative and may require taking the person to a hospital emergency room for assessment. While the director does not want to become enmeshed in directee's patterns of rescuing and dependence, people who are actively suicidal or impaired in ways that could result in personal bodily harm to themselves or others need immediate attention. The wise director will want to err on the side of caution by seeking immediate assistance from other professionals.

Team Approach

People who have been sexually or physically abused at or near the time they are seeing a spiritual director will benefit from the services offered by a variety of health care professionals. While spiritual direction may assist in the integration of work done in other venues, the healing of abuse normally requires sustained and intense therapeutic work. However, making a referral does not preclude continuing to see the person in spiritual direction. Persons coping with the spiritual and emotional impact of trauma and abuse can benefit from the gifts of a variety of professions.

The team approach to healing is frequently superior to interventions by only a single caregiver. In my experience, spiritual directors usually recognize the importance of insights from other helping professions and are willing to coordinate with them in providing care. For example, traumatized persons may receive medication from a psychiatrist; engage in weekly talk therapy with a psychologist, social worker, or pastoral counselor; attend a group therapy session with others who have been abused; and meet monthly with a spiritual director to discern God's leading in the patterns of their lives. While it is not possible to prejudge the path along which any given directee may be called for healing and wholeness, some combination of the above treatments is likely to be beneficial for many people.

Directors can help their directees affirm the way in which God's transforming love may be working in a variety of therapeutic processes in which the religious dimension may remain only implicit. In contrast with other healing processes, spiritual direction provides a context in which the focus is explicitly on God's presence (or in some cases on what is experienced as God's absence). The desire to remain faithful to the presence of the holy in daily life is affirmed in spiritual direction. Here life's profound meaning and sacred depths provide the ultimate context for healing life's hurts.

PSYCHOLOGICAL DYNAMICS

The Stance of the Director

Spiritual directors who choose or are called to work with exploited and abused persons need to familiarize themselves with the psychological dynamics that typically interact with spiritual issues related to abuse. These dynamics often function at an unconscious level in the directee's life and in the directee's relationship with the spiritual director.

The spiritual director's knowledge of abuse and attitudes toward its significance may exercise a profound impact on the directee. Spiritual directors should neither inflame nor minimize discussions of abuse arising naturally in the spiritual-direction session. While the controversy around "false-memory syndrome" (Do adults frequently fabricate memories of childhood sexual abuse?) remains unsettled, we know that childhood abuse and domestic violence are widespread. Some allegations are false, but many are not. Physical violence and sexual abuse cross all social classes, racial/ethnic groups, and religious denominations. Perpetrators include but are not limited to husbands, fathers, grandfathers, uncles, dating companions, siblings, cousins, teachers, clergy, community leaders, mothers, and strangers.

Directors who attempt to avoid or minimize abuse issues raised by a directee will contribute to the harm previously committed by reinforcing the conspiracy of silence that leaves the victim alone with her issues and questions. Spiritual directors may feel a sense of discomfort around abuse issues. This discomfort may come from a number of sources, including their own lack of understanding of the issue, their own unresolved personal issues, or from disquiet around issues of sexuality. Directors whose lack of knowledge or personal sensitivities prevent direct discussions of violence and abuse when they emerge in direction should refer their directees to directors who are experienced in this area. The healing role provided by spiritual directors competent in this area is a gift that directees who have been abused deserve as they struggle with profound religious issues.

The Challenge to Trust

People who have been traumatized or abused as children frequently act out—especially in their relationships with authority figures—the unconscious psychological dynamics associated with the abuse they have received.

These unconscious attitudes emerge from the chaotic, hostile, and violent experiences of their childhood. In contrast to other children, the abused child "must find a way to develop a sense of basic trust and safety with caretakers who are untrustworthy and unsafe. . . . She must develop a capacity for intimacy out of an environment where all intimate relationships are corrupt."[2]

Adults whose primary relationships as children have been profoundly influenced by abuse will have difficulty trusting others, including those to whom they reach out for assistance. If the trauma has come as the result of sexual or physical abuse by a family member known and loved by the child (or a non–family member known and loved by the child) the directee may be especially conflicted emotionally. On the one hand, this authority figure—often a parent or close relative—provided love and support, while on the other hand he exploited the vulnerability of the child out of unresolved and unmet needs for control and intimacy. If the trauma was caused by a stranger, the trust issues may be present, but the feelings of confusion and ambiguity will be lessened.

The concerns with trust arise also from the person's relationship with the nonabusing parent. In most cases the child questions why the nonabusing parent did not relieve her distress and pain by providing protection from the offending parent or close relative. Children often believe the nonabusive parent knows about the sexual or physical abuse. In many instances the child's assumptions are correct. Thus even the nonabusive parent is perceived as a "bad parent."

The spiritual director can receive unconscious "bad parent" or "good parent" projections from the directee. Projections occur when one unconsciously attributes one's own feelings or attitudes to another. In the case of the "bad parent" the directee projects onto the spiritual director the feelings of anger, frustration, and confusion associated with the parent "who could not or would not see that the child was being abused and was suffering, and who failed to protect the child. . . ."[3] The directee cannot understand why this parental figure ignores the abuse. Often for the child this is construed as condoning the abuse; the child may conclude that they are "bad" and for this reason deserve the punishment.

The spiritual director may also be cast in the role of a wished-for "good parent." With this projection the directee unconsciously sees the director as a parent who would have protected the child by stopping the abuse. The adult who has been abused as a child has an immense need for protection and care as well as an enormous fear of exploitation and abandonment. "In a quest for rescue, she may seek out powerful authority figures who seem to offer the promise of a special caretaking relationship."[4] These authority figures, including spiritual directors who may be perceived as representatives of God, are idealized out of a desire for a safe haven. While on the surface this projection seems more benign than the "bad parent" projection, ultimately it is also problematic. If the spiritual director is identified as a representative of God, this may magnify the unrealistic hope that in direction one's unmet needs and hopes can be intuited and met. These idealizations, however, inevitably are shattered when the authority figure is unable to live up to the abused person's expectations.

Spiritual directors may find in the course of long-term work with a directee that they are alternately both the good and the bad parent. Recognizing the likelihood of being cast in these roles may help the director remain patient and consistent when responding to the directee. Responding genuinely as the people they are and not in accord with the emotional pull of the "good parent" or "bad parent" projections is essential for the directee's healing.

Fears Arising from Exploitation: Providing a Safe Environment

Driven by the fear of ongoing abuse the child learns at an early age to watch vigilantly for signs of potential harm. As a result, an acute sensitivity to the surrounding environment and the mood of the abusive parent develops. As a child seeking safety it was necessary to be aware of the actions of the abuser. For many children the abusive behavior follows an established, ritualized pattern. Certain locations in the house become the sites where the abuse occurs, the child's or parents' bedroom, a workshop, garage, cottage, car, or other secluded place. In addition, the child notices that the perpetrator frequently presents a particular mood just prior to the abusive acts. This may be one of anger, blame, or seductiveness directed toward the child. Abused children "become minutely attuned to their abusers' inner states. They learn to recognize subtle changes in facial expression, voice, and body language as signals of anger, sexual arousal, intoxication, or dissociation."[5] The child develops this skill rather unconsciously as a defense against attack. The child ultimately learns, however, that no matter how hard she tries to "be good," if the offending parent is in a certain mood the abusive acts will follow.

The adult who has been traumatized by sexual abuse will often unconsciously use these scanning skills in relationships with authority figures. By watching carefully they hope to keep the situation safe. When the "trusted" authority figure is upset or displeased in the most mundane way, the interpersonal dissonance "may provoke intense anxiety, depression, or rage"[6] on the part of the directee. Spiritual directors need to remember that their every move is being studied and evaluated when they are working with adults who have been traumatized as children. If the directee becomes upset at the director over a minor concern, the director may want to acknowledge the fear or pain that has been elicited in the directee, as well as to note God's willingness to hear the distress.

The inability to readily trust authority figures is addressed in spiritual direction not only by the relationship established between the director and the directee, but also by the structure of the direction session itself. People who have been abused have difficulty trusting not only other people but also their environment. An important aspect of safety is establishing appropriate and consistent boundaries not only within the interpersonal relationship but also in the spiritual-direction session. The abused person's need for a structured environment is as important in spiritual direction as it is in counseling and therapy. This structure over time contributes to an environment that is predictably safe.

The elements that create this safe space include meeting each time in the same location in a room whose furniture arrangement is established and predictable. Direction sessions should be arranged in advance and, when possible, for an established day of the week and time of day. The session itself should begin promptly and conclude at a mutually agreed-upon time. The elements within the session—for example, silence, prayer, conversation, guided imagery—should be mutually agreed upon and arranged in an established pattern on which the directee can depend. While this attention to form and structure may seem to limit the spontaneous movement of the Spirit, it is essential to remember that the abused person grew up constantly scanning the environment in an effort to avoid pain and violence. The Spirit is at work in helping the directee establish a trusting relationship in which genuine healing can occur. Attention to even mundane details is important for creating a safe space. Once the safe space has been created, it acts as a container for the deepest longings of the heart and provides a place for discerning the movement of the Spirit in the directee's life.

Self-Esteem: I Am Bad

The victims of child abuse are prevented by the abusive acts from developing positive self-regard. During their childhood years these children are repeatedly subjected to humiliation. Their weaknesses are typically reinforced by the abuser to "justify" the abusive acts. Many children are told from childhood that they are "bad." "Most abused children grow up thinking they are bad. . . . In the world of the child, to be hurt means that he or she is bad."[7]

The abused child hopes that she can overcome the abuse by being good. This creates in the child a willingness to be "good" by being obedient at almost any cost. Eventually the child comes to recognize the uselessness of trying to resist the physical or sexual violations. "Many develop the belief that their abusers have absolute or even supernatural powers, can read their thoughts, and can control their lives entirely."[8] Paradoxically, as the child recognizes that she has no control over the abuse, she works harder and harder to please the offending parent by being obedient.

As the child struggles to make meaning out of a world filled with abuse an existential crisis occurs. In order to avoid despair, the child tries to understand why she is being treated without love and mercy. She recognizes her dependence on her parents and struggles to understand their behavior toward her. The "child's psychological adaptations serve the fundamental purpose of preserving her primary attachment to her parents in the face of daily evidence of their malice, helplessness, or indifference" (Herman, *Trauma and Recovery*, p. 102). All hope would be lost were she to conclude that she is dependent on persons who are by their nature bad. "She will go to any lengths to construct an explanation for her fate that absolves her parents of all blame and responsibility" (101). However, in the world of the child the alternative objects for blame are limited. As a result, she usually concludes that she is a bad child and that she is responsible for the abusive acts inflicted on her. "Simply by virtue of her existence on earth, she believes that she has driven the most powerful people in her world to do terrible things" (105).

As a result of the abuser's reinforcement of what the child understands as her negative attributes and behaviors, poor self-esteem is fostered from an early age. The negative self-image and feelings of inadequacy are linked to the constant striving to be good (safe). In this environment the child develops an exaggerated sense of personal responsibility while concurrently believing that she has little to offer others. If untreated these patterns will persist into adulthood, resulting in a belief that one is worthless and unlovable.[9] This sense of worthlessness fosters an inability to value one's own needs. Adults who have been abused as children frequently are unable to articulate their needs. Often they do not even know what their needs are.[10]

Spiritual directors are frequently trained to help directees track and deepen their connection to their affective life as a means to recognize the movement of the Holy Spirit. Directors must remember that abused and traumatized people will not necessary have ready access to deeper levels of their affective life. Traumatized people who are just beginning the healing process will usually need to integrate anger, rage, fear, and terror as they explore their affective life. Spiritual directors who embark on this aspect of the journey with directees will need to be trained for the journey, to have supervisory support, and to be part of a network of allied professionals.

Retraumatizing: Unexpected Dangers

Many psychologists who work extensively with traumatized and abused people advise counselors *never* to touch their clients. They have learned in their work that what the counselor might think is an innocuous touch, patting on the arm or shoulder, may serve as a trigger for memories of sexual or physical abuse. The patterns of abuse are complex. For many children, socially acceptable, unobjectionable forms of touch were used by the offending parent as a prelude to the abusive behaviors. The child soon learned that these patterns of touch were in fact aspects of the abuse scenario. As a result, these seemingly harmless gestures became markers that could invoke fear and suspicion. Professional caregivers can retraumatize abused persons by inadvertently touching a seemingly innocuous area.

Spiritual directors need to be especially sensitive to this point. In the social culture and liturgical life of many Christian denominations, it has become commonplace to embrace or exchange a kiss or hold hands briefly during the passing of the peace. As religious groups have struggled to recognize that we worship not just with our spirits but with our bodies, efforts have been made to incorporate more bodily activity into our worship and prayer lives. A parting embrace of persons we have only just met is not uncommon when small groups conclude Bible study, prayer, or other religious function. As a result, for many who do spiritual direction a warm embrace at the end of a session seems a spontaneous and fitting way to part. A pat on the shoulder or hand are often supportive, caring gestures that a director might spontaneously offer. Those who work with abused persons warn that such acts may retraumatize the directee.

Directees who have not yet worked on matters of touch in their therapeutic process may be unaware of the many ways it can trigger their fears. There is a high probability they will not mention their internal trauma to the director since they feel shame knowing that it emerges from their own woundedness. In the direction process, if the directee initiates some form of touch or a closing embrace, the director may use this as an opportunity to discuss the safety issues surrounding touch. Respecting and honoring the directee's boundaries is essential for healing.

Patterns of Repetition

The recognition that many abusive parents were themselves abused as children can lead to the perception that those who have been abused will almost certainly become abusers. While a "small minority of abuse survivors, usually male, embrace the role of the perpetrator and literally reenact their childhood experiences,"[11] there is a much greater likelihood that the survivor will continue to be victimized as an adult. For the reasons listed above—difficulty trusting, an overwhelming need for safety, the inability to easily establish appropriate boundaries, low self-esteem, an attitude of obedience to those with authority and power, sensitivity to the needs of others—the adult survivor is likely to be further traumatized by victimization. "The risk of rape, sexual harassment, or battering, though high for all women, is approximately doubled for survivors of childhood sexual abuse."[12]

Spiritual directors need to be sensitive to the dynamics of repetition that may lead people to repeated victimization. This victimization may be severe; for example, with ongoing domestic violence it may involve being subtly taken advantage of as a result of unclear boundaries. Directors should be aware that men who have been abused may inflict a similar form of abuse on those over whom they have the opportunity to exercise power and control. Spiritual directors need to remember that they are obligated to report their directee's abuse of others if they learn that it is occurring. Helping the directee understand that such reporting is in the best interests of the family is a difficult and painful situation, but a moral obligation for those who cannot permit ongoing violence against children.

THEOLOGICAL AND SPIRITUAL ISSUES

The Role of Religious Language in Healing and Masking Abuse

Religious language has the potential both to facilitate healing and integration as well as to mask pathology and dysfunction. A skilled and faithful spiritual director needs to be capable of recognizing when the psychological dynamics associated with abuse are shaping pathological or dysfunctional understandings of God's activity in the directee's life. Without this knowledge the director can unwittingly help sustain a directee's wound by providing religious justifications that prevent healing.

For example, people who are in abusive relationships and seeking direction are surely being led by God's creative Spirit to find a means to end the abuse or they would not have sought help. However, if these same people are codependent—placing the needs of others ahead of their own while feeling a strong desire to help or rescue others—they may make excuses for staying with an abusive partner. They may insist that God is "telling them to stay" or requires them to be "faithful to their marriage vows." As a representative of a community of faith, whether formally through the office of priest or as a religious or informally as a lay member of a community of faith, the spiritual director is a witness for that community. It is difficult to believe that God would desire ongoing or escalating abuse for any of God's children. By making that theological affirmation the spiritual director may help a directee see themselves not as a victim, but as a person of value and worth who does not deserve abusive treatment.

Crisis of Faith: Can I Trust God?

Child abuse, domestic violence, rape, and other forms of physical abuse raise profound theological questions for those who have been traumatized and for those who are assisting in the healing process. Questions include: Why did this happen to me? Am I so sinful that I deserve this punishment? How could a good God allow this to happen? If God is all-powerful, how can God be loving and allow such horrors? Is the world a friendly or a hostile place? Does God offer any protection to those who are weak and vulnerable? Why did God let his own Son be killed? How does God feel about my anger? Will I be punished if I curse at God? In the process of spiritual direction, people who have been traumatized need to be allowed to raise the profound theological issues precipitated by abuse. The task of healing will require that people with religious backgrounds and concerns have a place where those concerns are honored and heard. Having these concerns heard not only by those in the secular helping professions, but also by persons typically viewed as representatives of God and the church, will be an essential element in the healing process. The abused and traumatized person who seeks to remain involved in the church will need to address these issues within the context of the community of faith if they are to reach a state of reconciliation and wholeness.

The ministry of spiritual direction is a form of pastoral care that offers abused people the opportunity to focus on religious needs and themes in the context of an experiential relationship with God. Given the psychological dynamics associated with abuse and the theological issues it raises, some people will seek spiritual direction to raise these questions. They may feel abandoned by God and cut off from God's love, and may wonder if a relationship with God is a realistic possibility.

People whose spirits have been shaped by traumatic experiences that create fear, rage, guilt, and shame often wonder if God can accept and transform these powerful—yet to them unacceptable—emotions. The experienced spiritual director knows from both training and life experience that God may be present in the depths of anguish and horror as well as in the depths of joy and delight. The director also recognizes that a person who is being subjected to violence may feel that God is absent. Questions and comments I have heard from those who feel estranged from God include: "Where was God when I was being brutalized?" "God was tortured once on a cross and died. I was tortured repeatedly and wished I was dead." "Where was God when daddy killed mommy?" In the face of such tragedies, Carlisle Marney, a well-respected, renegade Baptist preacher, said: "God has an awful lot for which to account."

The spiritual director, as God's representative, invites the directee into a deeper relationship with the holy. For this to happen the director needs to be able to hear the hurt, fear, shame, anger, and horror. If the directee needs to recount the episodes and the stories of terror or horror, the director must be capable of hearing the details of the sexual and physical brutality inflicted on the directee. For many abused people the director is a true confessor. The safety of both the relationship and the structured session permits the sharing of fear, shame, guilt, and anger. In spiritual direction the directee brings the hurts of her spirit to a religious setting, hoping that God can hear. The director's consistent nonjudgmental caring is surely a sign that God is present.

Victimization and Suffering in a Religious Framework

Perpetrators of abuse in religious households will frequently use religious language, symbols, and concepts to justify their abusive acts to their victims. Christian teachings on suffering are sometimes summoned to support violent acts. The assumption is that since God is just and merciful, suffering is the result of sin. It reminds one of Job's friends who tell him that his suffering must be punishment for his past sins. The abused child is led to believe that her suffering is punishment for her sins.[13]

These teachings may be used by the perpetrator to justify the ongoing violence. Such use is, of course, corrupt. Paradoxically, these teachings may also be used by the child as a defense mechanism. That is, the teaching gives sufficient meaning to the horror of abuse that the child is able to survive. In their quest to find a positive identity, children familiar with religious themes may identify with the sufferings of a saint who has been martyred. Children may learn the stories of virgins who are selected because of their beauty for sacrificial offerings to appease angry gods (usually male). The religious narrative is used to give meaning to the victimization and thus to permit survival rather than disintegration in the abusive environment.

While self-identifying as a victim can be a crucial defense mechanism in the child's life, for the adult it prevents taking responsibility for one's future. Adult survivors of violent homes who cling to narratives of victimization well into adulthood usually continue to see themselves as victims. They wonder if they can ever recover and worry that they will never be able to lead normal lives.[14] At some point in the healing process the person who has been traumatized needs to move from the passivity of the victim's role to one of action and personal responsibility.

People seeking spiritual direction may have used religious narratives or themes to cope with their abuse when they were younger. Depending on the degree of healing they have experienced these adults may seek spiritual direction in order to confirm the old narratives (if they have not yet worked on their trauma), or they may come seeking new understandings of God's healing grace (having given up old narratives, they are seeking new perspectives).

Directees can be helped by directors who make a theological distinction between voluntary and involuntary suffering. Voluntary suffering results when one is willing to endure pain for the sake of a cause or mission. People who engage in civil disobedience and are subjected to arrest or humiliation suffer because of a cause in which they believe. Parents can suffer if their child is ill and needs constant care and attention for a sustained period. These forms of suffering result from the voluntary commitments of those who suffer. Involuntary suffering, on the other hand, is not freely chosen; it is imposed on the victim. Such suffering does not emerge from one's commitments and seldom serves a greater good. For a child, physical and sexual violence are unquestionably involuntary forms of suffering. Such suffering is never justified.[15]

Socialization: Providing Alternatives to Obedience and Emotional Caretaking

There is ample evidence that women are traditionally socialized to be nurturing and supportive to those with whom they are in intimate relationships.[16] This nurture frequently involves being silent or quiet about claiming one's own needs. The socialization process often teaches women to take responsibility not only for the emotional needs of their children and spouses, but also for the emotional climate of their social and occupational surroundings. Women frequently attempt not only to meet men's emotional needs and but also defer to men's agendas, ideas, and opinions. Due to this caretaking of men, women have often been reluctant to hold men responsible for problematic relationship issues. In work situations, women who are sexually harassed often initially blame themselves. They worry that they have been too friendly or dressed too attractively.[17] These patterns of socialization between the sexes reinforce an abused person's assumption that she must be at fault.

Biblical passages are often used by fundamentalist and conservative Christians to legitimate women's deference to men. "[P]rescriptions for domestic order found in Colossians 3:18–25, 1 Peter 2:11–3:12, and Ephesians 5:21–33 are based on the patriarchal arrangements found in late-first-century Greco-Roman households with their hierarchy of husband, wife, children, slaves."[18] Popular—as opposed to scholarly—interpretations of the creation story in Genesis 2 suggest that due to women's creation from a man's rib they are subordinate and inferior. Ephesians 5:22–24 states that as Christ is head of the church so the husband is the head of his wife. The implication is that wives are therefore required to submit to their husbands' wishes. Little imagination is required to understand how such passages function in religious households in which domestic violence is commonplace.

Spiritual directors can offer alternative interpretations of these scripture passages by placing them in their historical context and by suggesting passages that illuminate God's concern for love and justice. For example, Galatians 3:28 describes the new relationships that occur in Christ: "There is no longer Jew or Greek, there is no longer slave or free, there is no longer male and female; for all of you are one in Christ Jesus." By emphasizing the mutuality and "oneness in Christ," directors can help traumatized persons reframe their understanding of human relationships in the light of God's loving nature. The spiritual direction may be a primary resource for biblical and theological reinterpretations essential to the healing process.

The Spiritual Journey: From Silence and Submission to Voice and Agency

Spiritual directors working with traumatized women need to understand how women's spiritual development may be shaped by the interactions of male paradigms of the spiritual journey and the psychological dynamics of abuse. Traditional understandings of spiritual development define a path that includes but is not limited to silence, deference, obedience, and disengaging from one's desires. This path of self-denial and quiet self-surrender characterized the spiritual needs of males in monastic life, who were surrendering the male privileges of their day for the sake of a higher good. Its appropriateness for those whose voices are marginalized by virtue of their gender must be considered.[19]

Women in general have not enjoyed male privileges and thus cannot give up what they have not had. The spiritual journey for women must be grounded in the lived experience of the spiritual life of women, not men. As a result, a woman's spiritual development involves, among other things, finding and learning to trust her voice,[20] reclaiming the body, and acting on the basis of experienced truth. Spiritual directors who recognize the gender-specific aspects of women's spiritual journeys will appreciate the significance of affirming the voices of women who have been silenced, not only by cultural sanctions, but also through the violence of abuse.

The path of spiritual development for people who have been abused leads through shame and guilt. The abused woman often wonders if God can forgive her for the things that have been done to her. Even as an adult, fear that she is responsible for what has been done to her may require asking if God can forgive her. At other stages in the healing process, her anger at what has been done to her and what has been taken from her may lead her to want to curse God. The director needs to help the directee understand that her relationship with God grows from her willingness to risk being absolutely honest with who she is, even in her expression of anger and rage.

The spiritual director facilitates the journey to the depths by being a reliable and compassionate companion. The directee is encouraged to avoid the silence of fear or obedience, to hear her own voice, to act in accord with her needs, not the needs of the abuser. Here in this place of darkness is the place of hope. This is when the deprivation of the desert makes possible the encounter with God in the whirlwind. Job received no answers; his trials were not justified. Yet in the encounter there was a sense of the holy that allowed Job to transcend his questions, to acknowledge his despair at life's injustices, and to move ahead with his life. Walking with the directee through the valley of the shadow is one of life's sacred tasks. Trusting that God will be there—even in the face of evidence to the contrary—is an act of courage and hope.

Spiritual practices that allow directees to enter into silence—not as an act of humility or for the sake of remaining silent—but to find the voice at the core of their being, where God is present, can be helpful to persons who have been abused and traumatized. However, the use of silence may be difficult for those who have yet to deal therapeutically with their abuse. Flashbacks and other traumatic memories may emerge in the silence. While finding one's voice may begin with naming the abuse, the emergent issues require therapeutic interventions. On the other hand, women who are comfortable using silence to gain voice will find that such practices honor their need to move beyond the deference and obedience of both their socialization and their plight as abused children. Finding God's love and mercy in the quiet places of spiritual disciplines allows a woman to find her voice, to identify her perspectives and needs, and to act accordingly. The director who supports this aspect of the spiritual journey will appreciate the distinctions between men's and women's spiritual journeys as well as the spiritual need abused persons have for voice, freedom, and self-direction, growing from an internal locus of control which at its depths is the voice of God.

Forgiveness and Justice

Those who perpetrate violence and trauma often manipulate church teachings on forgiveness to sustain their violent behavior. At a young age, children are introduced to the importance of forgiveness. "One has to forgive one's enemies, turn the other cheek, forgive seventy times seven or, as interpreted, always."[21] Men who batter their partners and people who abuse children may tell their victims that "if they are good people they will forgive them." Yet premature forgiveness allows perpetrators to avoid taking responsibility for their actions, and the cycle of violence continues.

Women whose sense of shame or personal failure may lead them to repeatedly overlook and forgive their abusers can be assisted by spiritual directors to recognize the nature of forgiveness and its relationship to justice. Forgiveness can be an important step in the healing process; however, when it is used to excuse ongoing abuse or to minimize the trauma that has resulted from childhood abuse it is not. People seeking forgiveness need to feel a deep sense of contrition and a willingness to take the steps necessary to avoid further violence. This requires being willing to shoulder both the moral and legal consequences of perpetrating abuse and seeing that the abused person knows how to seek professional assistance. Forgiveness goes hand in hand with justice. Attempts to seek forgiveness by asking the abused person not to report or to forgive "just one more time" do not recognize that true forgiveness requires both true repentance and a commitment to justice.

As the traumatized person works through the complex emotional issues that result from sexual and physical violence, forgiveness may for some people occur as one seeks to "let go" or to "get on with my life." Here forgiveness emerges from the abused person's deep sense of personal integrity and the realization that in order to be free of the past and open to life forgiveness must be granted. Marie Fortune explains what this means for the abused person: "I will no longer allow this experience to dominate my life. I will not let it continue to make me feel bad about myself. I will not let it limit my ability to love and trust others in my life. I will not let my memory of the experience continue to victimize and control me."[22]

The freedom that comes from this depth of forgiveness may take years for some traumatized people to experience. Spiritual directors should never try to push or force this move in the lives of their directees. When a person is ready it comes as a gracious gift in the healing process. Trying to encourage it even by gentle suggestion can be premature and may retraumatize the abused person.

Using Guided Images and Healing Rituals

People who have been traumatized through the repetition of violent acts require the healing not just of their spirits but also of their bodies. Guided imagery and rituals that support and effect healing can be created and utilized in spiritual direction. Guided images can be used in direction sessions, support groups, and individually. These healing exercises can be repeated as often as they seem helpful to the directee. Initially the directee may fear doing these alone and want the support of the direction relationship for safety. The use of guided images with people who have been or may have been abused should be done with great care. Abusive situations are often recalled in flashbacks. Sometimes past abuse is first recognized through an unexpected flashback. Such images are almost always emotionally laden and typically are frightening. Flora Wuellner offers guided healing journeys from a Christ-centered perspective both in print and on tape.[23] While these are not designed specifically to address the wounds of sexual abuse, the need to heal both the body and the spirit is affirmed. Wuellner offers careful guidelines for using the tapes. In my experience, guided images and guided journeys can quickly open deep spiritual and psychological wounds. Inexperienced directors should not use them with persons suffering from trauma and abuse.

Spiritual-direction sessions can create rituals for use in the direction session itself or in other settings. Such rituals may be as simple as lighting candles to allow light into memories of darkness. Rituals that symbolize cleansing old wounds or celebrating new beginnings may be appropriate. The director simply gives the directee permission to create rituals or in some cases may make suggestions that give the directee alternatives. In each case, however, the directee's voice and actions need to be encouraged and celebrated.

Conclusion

Spiritual abuse, physical abuse, and domestic violence raise profound theological issues. People who have been abused as children or who are involved in abusive relationships often come to spiritual direction wondering if God really cares about them. They search in the face of much personal evidence to the contrary.

Spiritual directors who work with traumatized and abused people should commit to learning the psychological dynamics and spiritual issues arising from abuse and commit to a team approach to healing. As directors they must stand with their directees at the face of the abyss. This spiritual companionship is a light in the darkness and, for some abused persons, the primary source of hope for a renewed relationship with the holy.

References

Bass, Ellen, and Laura Davis. *The Courage To Heal: A Guide for Women Survivors of Child Sexual Abuse.* New York: HarperPerennial, 1994. Will be of interest to both spiritual directors and directees. This edition has a new section addressing the "backlash" associated with "false-memory syndrome."

Davis, Laura. *The Courage to Heal Workbook: For Women and Men Survivors of Child Sexual Abuse.* New York: Harper & Row, 1990. Designed as a workbook for survivors. Practical, step-by-step approach to issues arising from abuse.

Fischer, Kathleen. *Feminist Perspectives on Spiritual Direction.* New York: Paulist Press, 1988. This book on spiritual direction in a feminist context contains a chapter, "Violence against Women: The Spiritual Dimension." A must for directors working with persons who have been abused.

Flinders, Carol Lee. *At the Root of This Longing: Reconciling a Spiritual Hunger and a Feminist Thirst*. San Francisco: HarperCollins, 1999. Seeks to reconcile women's spiritual development with their emotional and psychological needs. Demonstrates that women's spiritual development should be differentiated from men's spiritual development. Flinders draws on her knowledge of the saints to illuminate this important work.

Gil, Eliana. *Outgrowing the Pain: A Book for and about Adults Abused as Children*. New York: Dell, 1983. Excellent little book with illustrations for use with abused teens and adults. Does not directly address religious issues.

———. *Treatment of Adult Survivors of Childhood Abuse*. Walnut Creek, Calif.: Launch Press, 1988. This is a detailed scholarly work aimed at psychologists and other therapists who work with child-abuse survivors.

Herman, Judith. *Trauma and Recovery*. New York: Basic Books, 1997. Book recommended by those who work with Battered Women's Alternative. Explores the characteristics and dynamics of traumatic disorders, including captivity, child abuse, and terror. Also discusses the stages of recovery.

Lew, Mike. *Victims No Longer: Men Recovering from Incest and Other Sexual Child Abuse*. New York: Harper & Row, 1990. Intended for both abused men and their therapists, this work addresses the nature of abuse and recovery specifically as related to males.

Rosenbloom, Dena, and Mary Beth William. *Life after Trauma: A Workbook for Healing*. New York: Guilford Press, 1999. New workbook resource for those suffering from trauma, including sexual abuse and domestic violence. Exercises are offered with step-by-step guidance.

Chapter Three

SPIRITUAL DIRECTION WITH AN ADDICTED PERSON

Barry Woodbridge

————— • ◆ • —————

This essay explores the spiritual-direction relationship when the person receiving spiritual direction falls short of God's intent for them as the result of a form of sinfulness known as addiction.

Being human means we all miss God's intent for us in one way or another. In that respect, we are separated from God. That is what we call sin. One distinct form of that separation or sin is powerlessness over our own behavior because our time, attention, energy, and focus have shifted to fulfill some compulsive behavior. *Addiction* has taken on a technical meaning in psychology and to some extent in medicine. The word defines a compulsive behavior that removes human freedom and substitutes an almost ritualized repetition of a certain behavior, such as drinking alcohol, taking drugs, gambling, sex, or eating.

Spiritual direction, I believe, is one of God's provisions for wayward persons to find and embrace God's love and will for their lives more completely. In this essay, I explore what happens in the spiritual-direction relationship when the person being directed (a) is technically addicted but does not know it and is in denial; (b) is technically addicted, admits it, and is actively working on a spiritual program of recovery; and (c) is not technically addicted but manifests a "societal addiction" to some experience or substance. The term "societal addiction" means that they could modify or stop the behavior without intervention, institutionalization, or a structured program of recovery.

I should first name some of the presuppositions behind this discussion. First, I assume that, in the formal relationship of spiritual direction, the addicted person is the one receiving direction—is the one seeking another to help hold them accountable to their vision of God and God's vision of them. Although rare, the director could be the one with the addiction. This situation has occurred, but this essay does not focus on that possibility. As spiritual directors, we acknowledge that, because of our creatureliness, we are not exempt from the possibility of addiction. Insights in this essay about working with the Christian who is addicted hopefully will be equally useful should one director need to assist another with addiction. Admitting this possibility is difficult, because we usually think of a spiritual director as someone mature in their relationship with God; we expect that they would be discerning about their addictive tendencies and would seek assistance from their own spiritual director before these became compulsive behaviors. Yet while acknowledging that directors are not exempt from addiction, this essay focuses on the directee.

A second presupposition is that an addicted person has lost the freedom of will to stop addictive activity on his or her own. It could be argued that freedom of the will cannot be lost to that extent. Theologically speaking, people never lose 100 percent of their free will. But there are circumstances, including long-term addictive or compulsive behavior, in which the power of volition is surrendered to such an extent that one activity takes on a life of its own, becomes the path of least resistance, and renders negligible whatever freedom they may have. This is exactly what the term *addictive* refers to—one destructive action or activity that subjugates the will and becomes a higher priority than all conscious priorities.

A third presupposition is that addictive behavior is a disease more than a choice. Many works have argued the pros and cons of categorizing addiction as a disease. The intention here is not to offer a medical or psychological opinion, but to consider the relationships involved. As spiritual directors, we are invited to relate to the person under our direction as we would to one with another terminal illness. In fact, most authorities on addiction do consider addiction, if untreated, to be terminal. If the disease were cancer, we normally would not hold that person accountable for having acquired a terminal disease. We would not despise them for exhibiting its symptoms. We would instead open for them God's possibilities within the limits that the disease imposed.

The same approach is probably most helpful for the addicted. The symptoms of their disease and the choices they make may be distasteful and morally reprehensible to us. Yet God offers the possibility of viewing them as persons with a terminal illness; we should relate to them with the same kindness and gentleness we would show a person dying of cancer. What we receive from God for our part in the direction process is the grace to see the limited possibilities from which the addicted had to choose. Their bad decisions resulted from taking a path of least resistance. This trend has gained momentum so that their own will can no longer sway them by more than one-tenth of a degree. Here we experience with them the futility of self-guidance and the absolute dependence on God we both require for any good to enter our wayward lives.

A fourth presupposition is that spiritual direction is not the primary method for changing the addictive behavior. Spiritual direction should help the directee choose God over the addictive behavior, but it is never intended to be the primary means of recovery. Its agenda differs from that of intervention and recovery. For one thing, recovery from addiction usually involves one recovering addict working with another addicted person. So unless the director is in recovery from an addiction, the chances of helping the addict stop the addictive behavior are marginal. Second, recovery from an addiction usually involves participation with and support from a community of recovery. Spiritual direction is by its nature private rather than communal, so it alone is insufficient to effect and sustain recovery. Third, recovery normally involves replacing the time spent on the addictive activity with an equal or greater time in a recovery activity, such as participation in meetings and outreach to other addicts. Spiritual direction may again support and encourage this reallocation of time, but, it is usually limited to one hour once or twice a month. That would normally be insufficient to restructure one's time. By contrast, many addicts leaving an institutionalized program of recovery, in which they have spent hours each day in recovery groups and activities, must agree to a regimen of "ninety meetings in ninety days"—ninety minutes of recovery meetings every day—or risk violating the terms of their release from that institution.

WORKING WITH THE ADDICTED PERSON IN DENIAL

Working in spiritual direction with a person who is an addict is like aiming at a constantly moving target. Not that the person seems agitated—that may or be not be evident depending on what they are addicted to. The addicted person who does not think themselves addicted has learned to guide discussions away from the possibility of seeing their involvement with the substance or activity they are addicted to. Seeking spiritual direction may serve two purposes for them. It may express their subconscious hunger for a genuine relationship with God, as distinct from their actual compartmentalized relationship that may exclude or make allowances for the addictive behavior as a minimal aspect of their being. It may also strengthen the underlying hope that one is truly a good person making significant progress in the spiritual life. However, the addict's illusion is that one so dedicated to finding God and God's will would not be thought of as someone who would be involved with excessive drugs, alcohol, sex, or money.

Theologically, persons separated from God by addictions often are more driven than others by prevenient grace to find through religious means what is truly missing in their lives. They may seek elaborate spiritual disciplines, journal or write in a spiritual diary almost obsessively, seek confession and other sacraments regularly as a means of dealing with their guilt, attend retreats, write books on prayer and meditation, or help establish places and programs of spiritual development and growth.

Addicted persons bring a masked guilt to spiritual direction. They learn effective diversionary tactics to steer the discussion toward affirming them as persons of faith and integrity. For example, they may submit pages from their spiritual journals, dream logs, or prayer diaries and ask about the adequacy of their examen of conscience, their interpretation of some spiritual experience, their study of scripture, and so on. At first, a spiritual director may be delighted to serve someone so devoted to the process of direction. In the long term, however, the director must focus on more relevant instances from the life of the directed rather than presented material.

If a spiritual director suspects that material is being submitted in lieu of experiences that are being denied and hidden, it may be helpful to the director to recall three complicating aspects of the addicted life:

1. *Addiction survives by deception, including self-deception.* Without consciously wanting to defraud or deceive the director, the addict tends to present one thing as a substitute for another. They may state, "I found so much joy working in the streets, helping the homeless, since my last visit with you." That may be the evasive rendition of "I have been in the bars or back alleys hiding from my parishioners while trying to find enough alcohol (or cocaine)." They may report, "Our new program for abused children has really opened my sense of Jesus' compassion for all children and has been a blessing to me and our whole congregation." That may disguise the unspeakable message: "I must do something to show myself an advocate of children in case one of them reports me to the police and I am exposed. I need to create an irrefutable alibi as a known child advocate in the community."

Since the addict comes to believe and accept their own alibis as the truth, they may try to mislead the director and others by demonstrating concern for someone or something who reportedly has the addictive behavior they deny in themselves. That functions as another diversionary tactic. Who would expect that the chairperson leading the campaign against pornography stores himself lives day and night by the adrenaline of buying and viewing pornography from these same businesses?

2. *Addiction renders one self-centered and selfish.* Any compulsive, addictive activity is selfish and self-centered. In order to secure the time and energy addictive activity requires, one must deny other priorities and focus on one's own agenda. The illness is not rooted as much in the wrong of the compulsive activity but in the character defects that gave rise to it. For example, the addict might have felt anger and gradually chosen to deal with that anger by escaping the situation that he or she felt powerless to change; they instead sought a mind-altering state of drugged euphoria or sexual pleasure. An addict may initially choose the addictive behavior, feel fear over being found out, get away with it, and feel relief. That cycle is repeated until the brain anticipates the high of doing the forbidden and is reinforced by enjoying the high without being discovered. Gradually, the addict perceives a cloak of invisibility around the activity. No one has seen him during these repetitions, and he now assumes that no one ever will. The behavior, as well as its consequences, are distorted as minimal and as not affecting anyone, including the addict, who at this point still functions normally during his daily responsibilities.

But then those daily responsibilities are abbreviated or neglected to serve the addict's growing need for the substance or experience. Sometimes this deception goes so far that dual calendars, whether written or mental, are kept. One shows what one wants others to believe was done, and a second shows the priorities and appointments of the addictive behavior, scribbled in secret codes. The deception may include elaborate time-management reports, with daily, weekly, monthly, and annual tabulations proving the busyness of the addict. The second, hidden calendar, however, discloses that the addict's self has become the highest priority.

3. *At any hint of disclosure, the addict in denial minimizes the quantity and intensity of the addictive behavior.* The addict needs to perceive himself or herself as a normal and "good" person. To the extent that he or she acknowledges activity related to the addiction, those acknowledgments reflect the quantity and intensity of that activity in a non-addict's life. "We stopped by Las Vegas for a few hours on our way home from the regional conference" suffices for the "second calendar's" entry: leaving the conference a day early so that all day Friday through Saturday night could be given to a gambling binge funded by the entire year's allotment for education and travel. Or, in another situation, "I haven't gotten involved with <name> except for once a few months ago," may be the minimized acknowledgment that every waking hour has been spent in the company of or thinking about that person. A third person might relate that they

missed their last meeting with the spiritual director when they had been "under the weather" for a while and had slept through the appointed time. This account minimizes that they went on a cocaine binge and missed several days' work and appointments while in an altered state of mind.

Considering these three aspects of addictive behavior, how can the addict benefit from the spiritual-direction process? After all, honesty is at the core of direction. We seek who we are, and who God is for us, more honestly. From what has been stated, the addicted person is no longer capable of seeing themselves and their situation honestly. They have created a secret life so compartmentalized that they deny it exists or, if they do acknowledge it, they show the minor role it plays in their activities and emotions.

The first members of Alcoholics Anonymous discovered that the capacity for honesty was one precondition for recovery from alcoholism.

———— ·◆· ————

*Rarely have we seen a person fail who has thoroughly
followed our path. Those who do not recover are
people who cannot or will not completely give
themselves to this simple program, usually men and
women who are constitutionally incapable of being
honest with themselves.*[1]

———— ·◆· ————

The tension between truthful self-disclosure and self-deception characterizes everyone's sinful nature, but in the addicted person this tension may dominate the direction experience. The spiritual director who senses and verifies the suspected addictive behavior may need to state that no true spiritual direction can occur unless the directee first seeks help with a behavior that is beyond the scope of the direction process. Particularly if the director and the direction experience are highly valued by the directee, such boundary setting may function as a reality check and intervention, demonstrating that the addictive behavior is no longer cloaked. But if the directee continues to minimize the actions and does not admit needing help, the direction may have to be discontinued.

Suppose, on the other hand, that the person receiving direction admits that their behavior may have been only minimally disclosed and that it perhaps plays a more significant role in their life than they had been willing to admit. This would seem to open the possibilities for continuing the spiritual-direction relationship. If so, the director may want to require that the addicted person participate in a recovery group so that time spent in direction is not dominated by how to "stay stopped" from that behavior. The director may have no experience with the behavior, discussion of which diverts spiritual direction from its specific purpose of holding us accountable to our vision of the Lord and the Lord's vision of us.

This possibility brings us to a second topic in spiritual direction and addiction.

Spiritual Direction with the Addicted Person in Recovery

When the addicted person regains enough honesty to admit that their life is unmanageable by themselves, that their present form of spirituality has not been effective in restoring their freedom of choice, and that they compulsively repeat a behavior which is contrary to their own values and which they wish they knew how to stop, then spiritual direction may continue and be very helpful. However, neither the director nor directee should view direction as the primary program of recovery.

If the directee turns to a twelve-step program and begins to receive help from other addicted persons, she or he builds a trust and honesty in that fellowship that may transfer to the direction relationship. But the director needs to be aware that many twelve-step fellowships which adhere rigorously to the twelve steps of Alcoholics Anonymous will suggest to the addicted person that (a) they have a spiritual problem and not just a medical or psychological problem; (b) that the source of their spiritual dilemma is self-centeredness, along with anger, resentment, and several other character defects; and that (c) their present understanding of and relationship with God isn't functioning well enough to restore them to sanity and needs to be discarded in favor of a spiritual experience that returns their freedom of choice.

This last proposal may cause anxiety in the spiritual director, but this need not be so. First, the spiritual director may take affront that their role is being usurped by uneducated laity, untrained to guide someone spiritually. The director may feel that the spirituality implicit in the direction process and even in the life of the church is being challenged and threatened with replacement. This can be threatening, especially if the fellowship of recovery tells the addicted person not to spend time or to place trust in counselors or medical, psychiatric, or religious leaders. This process does not always occur, but some twelve-step groups revel in the testimonies of those who had seen dozens of professionals and never could quit drinking, drugging, or gambling until they started working the twelve steps. Such groups overcompensate by placing themselves outside the hope of other means of therapy.

The director should be aware that in its literature Alcoholics Anonymous, as the forerunner of all twelve-step movements, supports the role of both medicine and religion in the recovery process:

———•◆•———

*Alcoholics Anonymous is not a religious
organization. Neither does A.A. take any
particular medical point of view, though we
cooperate widely with the men and women of
medicine as with the men and women of religion.*[2]

———•◆•———

Should the addicted person in recovery raise the idea of discarding their present spirituality, the director should agree wholeheartedly. At stake is not the director's spirituality, which may be appropriate for the director. At stake is what the director cares about most passionately, the directed's saving relationship with God. That relationship has failed; separation from God in a pervasive aspect of the directed's life has thwarted spiritual progress. Rather than dismiss the directee who has to find a new spirituality, the director should congratulate them. With more honest self-disclosure, God now can reveal more valuable and relevant possibilities for living and serving, possibilities that heretofore had been obscured by self-deception, lies, and excuses.

In this sense, participation in twelve-step programs and in spiritual direction can be complementary as long as each understands its strengths and limitations. The twelve-step program, with its meetings, sponsors, and fellowship, holds that the purpose and power of God breaks the addictive cycle and offers the addicted person renewed freedom of choice. It creates a safe environment in which the addicted person can risk a new kind of honesty. It provides constant monitoring and support so that those who genuinely wish to stop self-destructive behavior can stop permanently. Its jargon and simple slogans ("One day at a time"; "Keep coming back"; "It works if you work it"; "Find God or die") provide practical tools which help replace the addictive behavior with what may appear to be a new, healthier addiction.[3]

The twelve-step program surrounds the recovering person with meetings and opportunities for service. Spiritual direction, on the other hand, helps the recovering person fulfill the eleventh step—"Sought through prayer and meditation to increase our conscious contact with God as we understood him, praying only for the knowledge of His will for us and the power to carry that out." Alcoholics Anonymous suggests a daily if not hourly spiritual discipline of seeking God's will, which exceeds the expectations of many spiritual directors because it comes under the urgency of death. The recovering person is told to find God or die. When the recovering person has gotten into this phase of their work,[4] the spiritual director can encourage them, clarify their spiritual experiences, and suggest ways in which they could improve in practicing the presence of God throughout the day.

Throughout this time, the director should recall the three aspects of addiction discussed above—self-deception, selfishness, and the tendency to minimize compulsive behavior. The addiction did not become ingrained or routinized overnight; neither does the program of recovery reverse these tendencies that quickly. One should expect the self-destructive behavior to stop immediately, with few, if any, recurrences, but the change in personality defects becomes the lifelong perfecting work of the Holy Spirit. As recovery continues, the directee should become increasingly open to exploring how their addictive personality shapes their experience of and response to God's grace in their lives. That is a fitting and proper topic of spiritual direction, as long as its pursuit does not veer into a counseling session and attempts to understand the origins of the illness. Discussion of the forms of inappropriate behavior is not necessary for effective spiritual direction; still, the directee should display increasing awareness and honesty about how divine activity is making it possible for them to deal with guilt and shame and to make amends for their past. The director walks a fine line here. She or he needs to strike a balance between a healing honesty about the past and perpetually labeling the person an addict. Recovering persons sometimes identify so strongly with their past addiction that it becomes counterproductive to embracing an image of God who sees them as much more.

SPIRITUAL DIRECTION WITH THOSE WHO SUFFER FROM A "SOCIETAL ADDICTION"

It has become popular to use the categories of the twelve-step movement to describe many types of immoderate behavior. So the pastor who indulges in chocolate is called a "chocoholic," and is warned to admit their powerlessness over chocolate and to seek a power greater than chocolate to restore sanity.

Any experience or substance can become the object of addictive behavior. In the twelve-step program, there is a pragmatic test of who is addicted and who qualifies as a member. If alcohol is the addictive substance, the prospect is told to try an experiment in controlled drinking at the nearest bar. Take one drink and walk out. If that experiment works, try it again. Then try not using alcohol for one month. Usually, a technically addicted person—one who has developed a reaction to a substance or experience such that they cannot stop using it—cannot pass these simple tests. Those who pass may have what is termed a "societal addiction." That phrase connotes an addictive tendency that is not yet out of control. It may not yet affect their ability to perform their job or family functions.

Societal addictions, according to Gerald May, can be categorized as either "attraction addictions" or "aversion addictions."[5] One may become compulsive about nail biting (attraction addiction) or have an aversion to dentists. May catalogs more than one hundred attractions and aversions and says that many may be beneficial, such as a mother's attraction to her children. Similarly, the natural expression of human sexuality is not harmful. Any of these experiences, however, is harmful when it becomes disproportionate or immoderate. That is the case with alcohol and the alcoholic. Appreciation of wine may be healthy for many individuals, but those in whom alcohol forms an immediate and addictive reaction cannot drink in moderation. Societal addictions reflect the tendency for addictive patterns of behavior to emerge around common and otherwise healthy behaviors.

One prevalent societal addiction is the consumer-credit mentality of buy now, pay later. Our culture encourages a need for instant gratification, whether in new spiritual disciplines or in getting photographs developed or in having credit approved within one hour.

These tendencies can also enter spiritual direction. Everything stated about the addicted person in denial and the addicted person in recovery is useful in identifying and responding in spiritual direction to emergent societal addictions. If a particular activity seems to be interfering with a directee's response to God or practice of spiritual awareness, the director may gently propose one of the experiments mentioned above. "John, your weekend excursions to the new vertical-marketing program and your 'building-your-business' efforts are all aimed at bringing you freedom from economic insecurity. It is important not to be anxious about your economic future. I notice that your retreat schedule has changed over the year so that you no longer spend much time alone with the Lord on retreat. I wonder what would happen if you performed a little experiment and took one of those weekend seminars and replaced it with one weekend on retreat. What would you think about trying that?"

If the person responds with a wry smile of understanding and a willingness to try the experiment, well and fine. Some balancing of priorities may result. If, however, the person insists that much morning devotion and sharing of spiritual goals happens at the vertical-market seminars and that their elected position prevents them from missing one meeting, there is cause to consider whether the activity has become a diversion. The director should tread lightly here and either release the avoidance to the Lord's time and timing or, if it appears to be affecting job, family, or health, suggest that spiritual direction may have to be suspended while that issue is dealt with elsewhere.

In all matters dealing with addiction, the director must wait for the guidance of the Spirit and not apply suggestions in this essay or elsewhere categorically. Yet there is a fine line between being spiritual friend and spiritual director. One wants to be supportive but effective as a witness to the Lord's leading. One wants to remain in relationship, yet may occasionally need to set boundaries for the relationship to continue. In all matters of "tough love," one deals first with one's own defects and submits them to the Lord for purging and transformation. Through such personal honesty, one may hope to speak words of hope and freedom to addicted persons.

Chapter Four

WARY SEEKERS: SPIRITUAL DIRECTION WITH CHURCH DROPOUTS

Norvene Vest

———◆———

While I was in college, I decided that I no longer believed in God. Many personal factors contributed to that somewhat precipitous decision, but in part it was also the time and my age. I was finding it difficult to reconcile the God of my childhood with the exciting new ideas I was absorbing at school, and like many of my peers in the 1960s, I opted for the liberal rationality of the Enlightenment instead of traditional religion. Today I might observe that the young adult I was felt the need to choose between two apparent opposites, instead of allowing herself to mature toward awareness of a deeper unity of reason and faith. But at that time I thought a decisive break was necessary, and I suddenly left the church. Since I did not soon have children to baptize I stayed away for more than fifteen years.

I marvel at the ways God worked with me in those years when my attention was stubbornly turned away. Somehow all my great spiritual energy and longing were carefully stored in an "inner room" I ignored, until one day a flyer arrived in my mailbox inviting me to visit an inner-city church. I reacted strongly, first eagerly reading the entire flyer word for word and then announcing loudly to my cat that *I would not* go back! But I did notice that my response seemed a little extreme, so a few Sundays later, I gave myself permission to sneak into the service late and to leave early, defying anyone to invite me to coffee afterward! How hungry I was, how rich my store of wonderments, and yet how insistently I fought myself and the persistent "hound of heaven." When a year later I moved back to a town I called home, I knew that one of the first things I had to do was to find a church home. Joining a confirmation class, I wept as I came forward for the Eucharist, so much like the prodigal child did I feel.

But how was I to make the transition with my whole self, mind as well as emotions, adult as well as child? I felt myself to be a battleground of "yes" and "no," knowing I could not simply revert to my earliest understanding of the gospel, but also knowing that I could no longer deny the part of me that loved God. A wary seeker, I asked the rector, "What must

I mean when I say the creed?" and he wisely responded, "Whatever you believe you mean." The acceptance warmed me while the freedom challenged me: what did I mean? Soon I was enrolled part-time in seminary, not to become ordained, but to find and learn to speak my own adult faith in Jesus Christ.

Who is the wary seeker?

I have deliberately chosen to name the wary seekers about whom I speak as "church dropouts," not to label persons as wayward, but to address the peculiar "in/out" status that many feel. Contemporary polls inevitably report a very high percentage who say they believe in God, but a much lower number who attend church regularly. Some of those non-attendees may have little or no previous exposure to church, but many have some church background coupled with a hesitancy about renewing church membership. Perhaps, as I did, they may "drop in" on a church service occasionally, but they have not yet found a faith home. I am particularly interested in those with some childhood training in and love for Christianity who at some time dropped out or away from church membership and commitment, but who now are feeling a renewed spiritual interest, coupled with reluctance to return to a faith they have "outgrown." My interest is with those quickened by a desire for a more "spiritual" dimension in their lives but not greatly inclined to seek it within the Christian church. I am not speaking mainly of persons abused by church dogma and/or church authorities, for their potential return requires a period of active healing that is beyond the scope of this essay. (See chapter 2, "Spiritual Direction with Traumatized Persons," in the present volume.) Bracketing such persons, we find a growing population of persons exploring widely and eclectically in the growing field of "spirituality," but who perceive the churches as places where doubt is the enemy of faith (rather than its active partner) and where dogma is more important than the experience of God (rather than its expression).

In my practice of spiritual direction, I frequently meet such wary seekers. The early and crucial question of our conversations is whether Christianity in fact has resources of value for them. I believe that Christianity offers an attractive and compelling faith home for wary seekers, and I find exciting the path we walk together as many of them rediscover the riches of the Christian tradition. However, special concerns, which invite the director's careful attention, surface with these wary seekers. This essay explores potential problems and suggests some paradoxes of engagement with such a directee, even as it also invites you, the reader, to be an active partner in this exploration.

THE MYSTICAL EXPERIENCE

Because the wary seeker comes as one not identified with the church (or only recently so), we may also expect them to be distanced from the experience of God. Sometimes, from inside the church, we tend to think that our task is to help directees have an experience of God's presence because we associate such experience with the spiritually adept. However, our wary seekers are often immersed in awareness of God's presence, though they may not have language for it. Many times they come full of excitement because they have had one or more mystical moments that they know to be gifts from beyond themselves. One benefit of the growing but amorphous popular field of "spirituality" is its clear message that the spiritual life is not limited to the discursive and rational. Contemporary seekers are deliberately opening themselves to mystical experience, and frequently do receive the direct touch of Spirit. Today the options for routes to the mystical are vast, ranging from time-tested practices of improvement in the flow of "chi" (also called "prana" or "life energy"), to the ecstasy of a sweat-lodge experience, to simple tears of gratitude for a friend's comforting presence. The market has no standards for screening such offerings to determine their intrinsic value, save that of "will it sell?" But, just as visions and voices have long been phenomena requiring careful discernment on the part of the church, we now find ourselves faced with many persons who undeniably are having direct experiences of the divine.

What do we do with "novices" who are mystics? Do we discount their experience because it falls outside New Testament language? Sometimes our human limitations as spiritual directors can blind us to the direct touch of God if it takes a form we do not recognize. And sometimes we may be reluctant to acknowledge an experience of God because we know how easily intense experiences can be distorted, even or especially when they are experiences with God. But even novice mystics know when they have encountered the living God, and, like all of us, they hunger for a resonating response of gladness and gratitude when they speak hesitatingly of the Holy. We can help the wary seeker name mystical experiences as the touches of God, affirming the blessing they carry. As directors, we constantly strive to ground talk about God in a specific experience of God. We know that the *first* step in spiritual yearning is always taken by God, who placed the desire in our hearts. How important that we help the seeker celebrate with thankfulness the very desire for God. From such celebration, we can see the deepening desire emerging in the directee to become more worthy of the beloved.

ACCEPTING DISCIPLINE

Soul friends have long understood that the tangible signs of God's favor are not the goal of the spiritual life. Often God thrills beginners with the gift of felt Presence as a means of deepening their attraction to a life requiring stability and fidelity over the long term. One essential part of the spiritual director's work is to help the directee learn to notice and build habits around practices that strengthen our receptivity to God's tenderness with us. We "train" ourselves for spiritual fitness, no less than for physical fitness, to increase our capacities and build our endurance. Our work, in the human-divine relationship, is to cooperate with the "enlargement of our hearts" (Rule of Benedict, Prologue 49) toward Love's ever-growing overflow.

Integrating mystical experiences of God with ongoing ascetic disciplines toward God is particularly difficult in today's culture. Accustomed as we are to information delivered in soundbites, we expect succinct explanations and rapid results in all endeavors. The array of spiritual options seems to invite an all-you-can-eat approach to the spiritual life, with a little dab of this and extra serving of that, requiring from us neither preparation nor cleanup. Our popular culture teaches us very little about how to develop and strengthen disciplined response patterns. It is difficult to move beyond this pervasive quick-fix mentality: we find it easy to believe that herbal remedies will make us healthy no matter what our regular diet; that physical fatigue can be alleviated by having professionals work on our bodies; that lifelong emotional traumas can be easily released in hypnosis or past-life therapy.

One formed in such a culture may well find long-term spiritual disciplines stressful, not trusting that God's response may be unfolding in relative hiddenness when signs are minimal in the short term. At best, our churches provide scripture studies and educational programs that to the faithful at least suggest alternative perspectives. But persons who have not had that long-term communal support will especially need help noticing in subtle interior changes and slight shifts in routine habits the signs that disciplines are bearing fruit. Whenever I recommend spiritual discipline to a wary seeker—such as adding five minutes of quiet listening to an otherwise rushed day, or reflecting on an event to discover God's presence—I am especially careful to set a context within which the discipline can be understood, and to discuss the inevitable temptations to discouragement and unworthiness. In subsequent sessions, we explore the directee's inner responses about the discipline, searching for possible negative self-talk and practicing realistic and believable alternative messages. When desirable, I point out that such practices were carefully worked out in the third- and fourth-century Christian communities of the Egyptian desert, even though they are often mimicked by the contemporary self-help literature. Our Christian tradition of prayer has long known that well-chosen disciplines are ultimately freeing. We can with confidence expect to notice and affirm the characteristic fruit of fidelity to discipline: the gradual emergence of a sense of personal authenticity united with an emerging confidence in God's care.

Pride and Trust

Classically, pride has been considered the principal sin that keeps us from relationship with God. This may be particularly puzzling for the wary seeker, who has been formed—as all of us to some extent are—by a culture committed to self-actualization. Indeed, in many places the term "Self" is equivalent to the term "Spirit," and ever-present New Age thought tends to emphasize a concept of God within. Repelled by the Old Testament images of an angry and jealous God, wary seekers may be noticeably hostile to any concept of God as Other, or God as over against humans. How are we to interact with such a stance?

Wary seekers frequently bring considerable understanding and appreciation for the contemporary values of psychological health. This is a definite gain for Christian theology and spirituality. At least since Aquinas's *Summa,* the Christian church has understood that nature and grace interpenetrate. What is good for the wholeness of the person is surely good for the spirit of the person, as Jesus made clear not only in his own life but in his ministry. The advances of the twentieth century in knowing how to strengthen healthy self-esteem contribute immeasurably to our understanding of the integrated spiritual life. Perhaps for the first time in history, we now have the opportunity to integrate the values of self-esteem and self-surrender in our growth to wholeness and holiness. We cannot ignore or set aside emotional health in our drive toward spiritual wisdom.

On the other hand, self-esteem alone is not sufficient for fullness of life. We have learned that meaning is discovered through committing ourselves to serve something greater than ourselves. When we remain self-enclosed, we ultimately will always encounter the despair of our inherent incompleteness. For, as humans, we are made to experience the elusive wholeness for which we long *only* when we freely choose to give ourselves away. In past centuries, such self-surrender was frequently misunderstood as suggesting self-contempt and humiliation. But we now have the psychological and spiritual insights in place to live into a deeper and more profound experience of self-surrender as the companion and completion of self-esteem.

The issue is not that of choosing between pride and trust, but instead insisting on their unity at a deeper level of awareness. The question is not whether this is God's will or my will, but rather whether I have courage enough to listen to my own truest desire, admitting that I can never provide for myself that which can only be received in love from an Other. When I insist on retaining control, I necessarily limit the possibilities to possibilities I can imagine. And genuine spiritual transformation is always well beyond the horizon of my imagination. When I insist on keeping my options open, I am deciding not to be anywhere in particular, and thus I separate myself from the gifts that can only come from particularity. Considerable humility is necessary to accept the human reality of limitation, contingency, creatureliness, death. Yet without such acceptance and surrender, we are never truly alive.

This discussion has implications for the way we function as directors, as well as for our theological foundations. As Christian directors, we consent not to be experts, even in our relationships with the wary seekers. We open ourselves in surrender to our directees, even as we value all we already are. The earnest probing of wary seekers particularly can bring us opportunities to revisit what we know about God, in order to discover it newly.

RELATIONSHIP WITH THE DIVINE

One of the more complex issues in dealing with the nonchurched is the matter of relationship with the divine. Who is God? Is it important that we have a personal relationship with God? Does it matter if we participate in community with others who do? Contemporary churches frequently give lip service to an expansive view of the Divine Being, aware that the image of God as Father, King, and Lord is an impediment for many people. Nevertheless, in worship itself, the language of scripture, prayer books, creed, and music tends to rely on ancient metaphors, to the comfort of those who are already attending church. But this comfortable language can be off-putting to wary seekers. Central as the Greek term *kyrie* is to the New Testament witness, most modern people have no direct experience of a "lord" and are often at a loss as to how to relate to such a being. Gender difficulties push many people away from the concept of a personal God altogether; many prefer to think of God as light or energy or spirit rather than to deal with the difficulty of figuring out whether God is male. Anyone who listens to the liturgy, however, will come away from church reasonably certain that God is male, no matter what is said to the contrary.

Church dropouts may raise important theological issues, felt as the cry of the heart. For example, many are deeply troubled by the question of why God the Father killed his Son, Jesus, on the cross, not as a flippant question, but as a serious concern about the role of violence and victimization in Christian thought. Genuine presence to such questions encourages seekers to believe that doubt can be the creative companion of faith. Honest struggle with foundational questions is indeed essential to personal appropriation of the good news, and much of our tradition is meant to puzzle and challenge us to see more deeply into God's reality. As directors, we are ready either to help the directee hear her own dilemmas with greater clarity or to propose alternative perspectives, whichever is most supportive at the moment.

Particularly for wary seekers, the question of God's being and nature is central. What is the nature of God? Why do bad things happen to good people? Even national magazines now probe such questions on their front covers. It can be helpful to verify that childhood images or parental experiences do indeed grow obsolete, but that God can encompass many images and embrace many doubts. While some seekers apparently want a faith community that will provide definite answers to every question, many of the wary seekers I meet are much more interested in someone who will listen to their questions, such as my own plea, "What does it mean when I say the creed?" As Elizabeth Johnson insists in *She Who Is,* language and symbol function and genuine engagement with the piercing questions of wary seekers may well test our own too-ready answers to questions about God's essence.

Can we as directors talk about what we believe without using the language of the New Testament, or of the early Christian centuries? Have we learned to translate our scripture and tradition into the language of our own life experience, so that we have ways of speaking simply about the ongoing validity of the witness? And how can we help our directees do the same? The language used by other ancient religions and insights is no less awkward than ours, yet sometimes wary seekers seem more receptive to basically unfamiliar ideas. It may help to point out to wary seekers that they may be more receptive to foreign ideas than they are to homegrown ones, encouraging them to apply similar criteria across the board. Christianity is rooted in the soil of Western culture, for good and ill. We know a great deal about its mistakes and abuses, and it requires courage and persistence to stand within a tradition we know to be flawed. Yet what tradition of faith is not flawed? As directors, we are invited to listen and to suggest language to share our experience of Truth, Love, and Beauty, not only in its mysterious complexity, but also in its utter simplicity.

We have several delicate but challenging tasks in hearing these wary seekers into faith. Some may come with no sense even of secular history, and thus no framework for understanding the human capacity to help concepts—even concepts of God—evolve over time. They may not realize that answers cannot be found for their questions until their "hearts have enlarged" enough to receive the true answer. Others may come with an unquestioned certainty that everything real has a literal and/or rational explanation. They may still wish to find answers stated in the simple cause-and-effect physics of Newton, fearful of the ambiguity inherent in metaphor and myth and symbol. My responsibility as director is twofold: On the one hand, I seek to offer responses at the level of the question, facilitating God's work in the person at the present. Yet on the other hand, I also desire to let questions continue to discomfit the seeker sufficiently to permit the seeker's breakthrough into the wholly new tomorrow that is the next step in their ongoing relationship with God. As the old saw goes, I want to comfort the afflicted and afflict the comfortable, and do both at once!

FEAR AND DESIRE AS COMPANIONS

Why are wary seekers here? Why are they seeking? What do they want in direction? What has changed to invite them to explore again that which once was rejected? These are good questions to pose directly at some time, and the answers are likely to revolve around the absence of something. Certainly my own return to the church was precipitated by a sense of loss, loss of something I had expected to find but had not. I had followed the path I thought would bring fulfillment in my life, only to discover a discouraging emptiness. I yearned for something more, something that I realized I was incapable of producing for myself. Desire led me.

Yet so did fear. I remembered the children's taunt to the lost: "You cannot get there from here!" I knew a great deal about how to accomplish things in the world, and I had no idea how to proceed from where

I was toward that unnamed thing for which I longed. I was afraid to give up control, even as I realized that I really didn't have control of the important things.

A terrible irony plagues the free-floating spirituality of our time. In a last-ditch effort to insist on ultimate personal control of life, many people have adopted the philosophy that everything happens for a reason. "Nothing is accidental," we are told, a sort of assurance that we are attracting whatever forces seem to be at play in our lives. If we fall sick, we brought it on ourselves. If we find a free parking space, God meant us to have it. We are even told that our wealth or poverty is caused by our own intentions and is caught up in the web of fates. Willy-nilly, seekers of many persuasions cling to this harsh vision of ultimate personal control rather than admit the reality of uncertainty and chaos.

Beneath this pervasive illusion lies the fear of living authentically. Experiencing life to the full inevitably means finding a share of tragedy as well as joy. By refusing to face uncertainty, we rob ourselves of the ability to name and grieve tragedy for what it is. The stories and images that nowadays surround us are full of terrible happenings, all of which are resolved at the last moment by the magic of technology. How can we learn to bear the terrible when we cannot even acknowledge it? In my earlier life, I strangled my desire for fullness of life. I knew that if I genuinely admitted my vulnerability, I would have to mourn all I had lost. But refusing to mourn was refusing to live.

The good news is that this inner territory of the soul is just where Christ is such a reliable guide. The central action of the Christian story, summarized in Christ's passion, death, and resurrection, is a message directly to the soul traversing this territory that we are not alone. There is One who accompanies the soul into hell, because the real stuff of life matters, even and especially to God. There is One who has prepared the way from death to life. When, as directors, we ourselves know the passage with Christ to be our own, we can enter again into the fearful places with those who come. We can offer hope simply because, with them, we are present to Christ. Gradually the community of faith itself, and its richly textured tradition of understanding, also becomes an unspoken but ever-present source of hope.

THE ROLE OF COMMUNITY

The final issue I wish to raise concerns this relation of spiritual direction to the community of faith. One of the important insights about spiritual direction that I learned early in my training was that Christian spiritual direction makes no sense apart from life in a Christian community. That wisdom suggests that meeting with another person periodically to talk about God is no substitute for the ongoing life of worship, formation, service, and support found in a congregation. However, as I think back on my own hesitant return to congregational life, I realize that before I could even think of church membership, I needed someone to listen to me unconditionally, someone to help me hear myself yearn for God. So, while I do believe that community is essential to Christian life, I am more often finding that I choose not to require it as a condition of offering direction. As director, I seek to be willing to consider that direction can be fruitful for someone who, at least for now, does not want to be part of a faith community.

On the other hand, one of the most serious issues for anyone in this culture seeking a closer relationship with God is excessive reliance on self-sufficiency. As Robert Bellah so convincingly demonstrates in *Habits of the Heart,* as Americans we have elevated individualism to a godlike status that seriously hampers our ability to make and keep commitments to one another. We are so fearful of eroding cherished personal "rights" that we habitually condition any commitment (even to God), at least subconsciously. We think of maturity as the ability to establish and maintain effective personal "boundaries." We believe ourselves to be "naturally" separated from others by our very consciousness. The tragic irony of such deeply ingrained yet deceptive habits of thought is that we fail to see them as the toxic blinders they are. Insisting on our individuality, we are perplexed by our loneliness, and suffer a distressing and seemingly unrequited desire to experience Love itself in a universe that is unified in that Love.

While as directors we desire to welcome the wary seeker as an individual hungry for God, we also seek to assist him or her to notice how true intimacy always changes the participants. The intimacy of love is always creative, bringing forth new life in ways not precisely controlled, nor even fully imagined, by the lovers. As always in the spiritual life, the "losses" incurred (of individual autonomy and control, in this case) are more than compensated by the "births" toward greater wholeness. It goes without saying that as director, I begin contributing to a reliable climate of trust, both in the integrity of the direction relationship as well as, more importantly, in the fidelity of God discovered in the directee's past experience. Gradually I reveal myself also as a person still growing in trust, also as one learning the disciplines and joys of greater reliance on God and on God's presence in community. As the directee and I become mini-community to each other, hopefully he or she will begin to seek additional opportunities for the communal support and challenge in which faith is lived fully.

Wary seekers have many gifts to offer the Christian church at large. They remind us of the value of doubt in keeping faith honest. New perspectives are always helpful in the mosaic of faith, and seekers' questions may help us toward sound critiques of existing thought and practice. Without them, we might neglect the foundational truths that engage us in lifelong growth toward God; with them, we are challenged to speak of Christ's impact on our lives in an immediate way. Too often as church, we find ourselves fussing over issues that have no real substance, while the world, in making the radical shifts required in the new millennium, cries out for a reliable connection with God. Wary seekers help us to remember and cherish that which is essential.

Section II

Special Life Issues

Chapter Five

GENERATIONS, OUR DIFFERENCES AND SIMILARITIES: HOW GENERATIONAL STUDIES ENLIGHTEN SPIRITUAL DIRECTION

Howard Rice

———— ◆ • ————

To engage in spiritual direction is to be conscious of how different we all are from one another. Each directee is unique and must be treated as such, yet there are similarities among them as well. Many spiritual directors use the MBTI (Myers-Briggs Temperament Indicator) as a helpful instrument; others use the Enneagram. Both are helpful tools to assist in understanding those who seek spiritual direction. Age is another important factor providing important clues about ourselves and other people.

Some scholars write that one way of explaining some of our most important differences is to see ourselves as part of a generation. Our common experiences of childhood, for example, give us characteristics shared with those who came of age when we did. Each generation has particularities that set it apart from other generations. One generation, for example, might have been overprotected as children; they remain cautious throughout their lives. Another generation is raised permissively and remains demanding. What is more, these generational changes seem to repeat.

Four generational types have repeated several times in U.S. history. A *civic generation* builds institutions in a crisis and overprotects its young, who are obedient but expend their energy trying to humanize the institutions and organizations left to them. This *adaptive generation,* in turn, tries to satisfy their children's every whim, producing a *self-confident generation* of idealists. The idealists tend to be so focused on themselves that they neglect their young. They raise a *reactive generation* that often is defiant and expects little from life. Adaptive generations want to give their children what was missing in their childhood—order and predictability—so they raise them in a fairly strict pattern of conformity. *In Generations: The History of America's Future, 1584 to 2069,*[1] William Strauss and Neil Howe examine how generations, lasting periods of eighteen to twenty-two years, seem to occur in patterns or cycles with amazing regularity. By examining the generations still alive in the United States today, we can discover what the pattern means to those of us who do spiritual direction. The pioneering work of Strauss and Howe has been examined from different angles but with essential agreement by many other writers. Among them are Gary McIntosh in *Three Generations: Riding the Waves of Change in Your Church*[2] and Mike Regele with Mark Schulz in *The Death of the Church*.[3] Regele maintains that by understanding generations in relationship to spiritual concerns, we see that the church has a choice: either to die as a result of resistance to change, or to die in order to live.

THE BUILDER GENERATION

The *GI Generation,* or *Builders,* were born between 1901 and 1924 and came of age during World War II. Members of this generation experienced the Great Depression as children or young adults and remember it vividly; they have been permanently marked by that experience. The most common characteristic of the Builder Generation is its enthusiastic patriotism and spirit of cooperation. This spirit came about because of their involvement in World War II, which more than anything else defines the Builder Generation. World War II was seen as a noble cause in which justice and goodness were on the Americans' side, and loyalty to God and loyalty to country were closely connected. Builders had tremendous confidence in their ability to organize and cooperate to solve problems. Perhaps because they have been involved in politics, Builders have voted for the winner in every close election since 1930. They gave us seven presidents, the first and last of whom were war heroes, John F. Kennedy and George Bush. As a generation, the Builders are loyal; because they value institutions, they have been joiners and organizers. They are represented disproportionately in Presbyterian, Methodist, United Church of Christ, and Lutheran congregations.[4] It is not surprising that they have remained in the institutional church through young adulthood and into their mature years. Having been forced into a spirit of cooperation by the crisis of war, they have continued to value cooperation highly. Builders are still the backbone of many congregations. Now, however, in their senior years, they have become more interested in material security and believe that they deserve some rest and relaxation. This generation, with age-segregated retirement communities, Social Security, and the GI loans, has given growing old new meaning. They have organized to protect their interests, with the American Association of Retired Persons (AARP) their most notable achievement.

The Builder Generation has been devoted to cooperation, achievement, and reason. Except for Jimmy Carter, Builder presidents have tended to be secular; some did not attend church. Builders are the generation most adept in science and engineering. They invented, perfected, and stockpiled the atom bomb in a relatively short time. They embodied the faculty of rationality and have had little thirst for spiritual questions. Even though they were loyal to the church, they wore this loyalty like their patriotism. They did not feel an inner emptiness; they were too busy building a new world, from the New Deal to the new world order. A congregation of Builders is not likely to have high interest in the spiritual life. This generation is extroverted and active. They have been doers all their lives and, although they have adapted themselves to retirement, they seek to remain busy as long as health permits.

Builders will probably go to their graves without asking aching questions about their souls. They are generally satisfied with familiar worship patterns and resistant to change. They are particularly resistant to any innovations in worship that involve showing feelings. They value the stiff upper lip and prefer to suffer in silence, especially the males, who value stoicism as an ideal and see expressions of emotion other than anger as a sign of weakness. Builders are regular church attenders, as health permits, and are active in some social groups in the church, but they do not ask for a great deal spiritually and are not likely to be candidates for spiritual direction. If they do seek counsel, it is likely to result from relationships with their children and losses they experience in old age.

THE SILENT GENERATION

The *Silent Generation* (born between 1924 and 1944) came of age during the Korean conflict, which was never really called a war; it was a UN military action. Korea did not inspire great feelings of patriotism. As children, members of this generation were overprotected by their parents from the chaos of war and depression, and they grew up as obedient children. They married early, had babies, and did everything that was expected of them. They were characterized as a generation with strongly middle-aged values. Terms such as "withdrawn," "unadventurous," "unimaginative," and "cautious" were also used to characterize this "gray flannel suit" group of young adults. The Silent Generation spent its years adapting to expectations of their parents.

In their middle years, this generation rebelled and began to ask serious questions about the meaning of life. This is the generation that invented the "midlife crisis." In midlife, many in the Silent Generation divorced and remarried; some changed careers, and many relocated. Up to this point the Silents were much alike, but they split into two groups after their midlife crisis. Some continued in their old ways with new vigor and persistence. Out of fear that the system they had faithfully served would pass them by, this subgroup began digging in their heels to stop progress. In the twenty-first century, the anxiety of these Silents will probably increase. They may very well "assist in the creation of the very thing they fear most—a world that will pass them by and forget them except as a filibustering bunch of indecisive blockers."[5]

Other members of this generation have sought to emulate their children in manners, speech, and clothing. Perhaps out of regret for the adventure they may have missed while trying to conform, many began to look inward and focused attention on their inner life. It is not possible to understand the strong emphasis on the psychological and therapeutic over the last twenty-five years apart from the soul search led by the Silents. Throughout the 1970s, this generation completed the shift from an elder-focused rising adulthood to a youth-focused midlife. This generation has often been caught in the middle, having to take care of aging parents living longer than before and, at the same time, to care for their own permanently adolescent young.

Its location between two dominant generations forced the Silent Generation to explore the depths of life while, at the same time, to maintain a sense of social obligation. Silents tried to humanize the technocratic world of their elders and thus are called an *adaptive* generation. Part of the task left by the Builders has been to work for change and justice. This generation produced nearly every leader of the civil rights movement: Martin Luther King, Jr., Malcolm X, Jesse Jackson, Cesar Chavez, and Russell Means, as well as feminists Betty Friedan and Gloria Steinem. The Silent Generation has voted consistently for the underdog; it preferred Nixon over Kennedy, Humphrey over Nixon, Ford over Carter, and Dukakis over Bush. It is the only generation never to produce a president. Yet, at the same time, it produced advisors to every president of the period—Pierre Salinger for Kennedy; Bill Moyers for Johnson; John Ehrlichman for Nixon; Dick Cheney for Ford; Stuart Eizenstat for Carter; James Baker for Reagan; John Sununu for Bush; and Leon Panetta for Clinton.

The Silents went from being defenders of institutions to becoming critics and agents for major social change. This generation has been involved in the search for deeper meaning, which for Silents has meant staying within the church yet seeking additional spiritual meaning outside. They are likely to show up dutifully for Sunday worship and, at the same time, to experiment quietly with nontraditional practices such as transcendental meditation or yoga.

It was the inner emptiness of Silents that sparked the most recent spiritual awakening. As Silents sought to understand their journey, they opened the gates of their feelings. They began the interest in spirituality and, serving as mentors to the Boomers, passed that interest to the next generation. Silents are represented out of proportion to their numbers in Episcopalian, UCC, Methodist, Unitarian-Universalist, and Jewish congregations.[6] They have intense spiritual issues, including their guilt for the moral chaos they see, and often ask, "What did I do wrong that my children don't attend church? How did we contribute to the misuse of drugs and alcohol? Did we spoil our children too much? Was our best just not good enough?"

The primary issue for Silents is the feeling of being left out, of being squeezed between two dominant generations who have grabbed the headlines and set the pace. Silents have worked hard to humanize the institutions passed on to them by the Builders, but they are tired, and many are retiring early just to catch their breath. The new century has dawned with the youngest Silents in their late fifties, but most have passed the reins of power to the next generation. They will, no doubt, remain the only generation in modern history not to elect one of their own as president. The closest they came was Michael Dukakis.

Silents are great candidates for spiritual direction. The same interest that drove them into therapy will move them to seek spiritual direction. They have a deep sense of their own emptiness and long for something more, which they have a hard time giving a name. They still go to church but they are not satisfied with traditional religion; they practice some New Age traditions but are not sure about these, either. They are spiritual seekers who may appear conventional on the surface. As directees, they cut to the chase: they are ready to settle down and get the help they believe they need. Their desperation may cause them to want help too much and to expect more than a director can deliver.

THE BOOMER GENERATION

The Boomer Generation (born between 1945 and 1963), so called because of their numbers, was highly visible from birth. They number seventy-seven million and account for nearly one-third of the U.S. population. Born during the postwar economic boom, they have continued to have more money than any generation in American history. They took center stage in infancy, demanded attention, and set fashions. As children they were overindulged. This is an important fact in understanding Boomers; their identity is shaped, in part, by their reaction against their childhood.

The parents of Boomers were not strong in setting boundaries and Boomers, as children and adolescents, were able to get away with much more than would have been possible for earlier generations. Having been raised by Dr. Spock, they were full of self-confidence. They were also full of idealism. This is the generation of the civil rights movement—the troops in the streets more than the leadership—and of opposition to the Vietnam War. Boomers have seen their mission not as constructing society but rather as purifying, or even sanctifying, it. Their idealism, though always changing, has been powerful. They have forever changed our world. One of the first Boomers now occupies the White House. There will no doubt be others to follow.

It has been said that Boomers make better preachers than builders, better philosophers than scientists. Their rise coincided with declining achievement in engineering, math, and science. They have excelled in occupations calling for creative independence, and the media has been their specialty. They control television almost completely and are the major players in film as well.

Boomers have been hard to please because they are constantly aware of the imperfections of all institutions. In spite of an upbringing that, in many cases, took religion for granted, they have expressed a great interest in deep religious questions. The generation appears to have stopped criminal drug use but has lost its spiritual trappings. Boomers moved from drugs and protest to the Jesus movements and evangelicalism, to New Age utopianism and a variety of millennialist visions. Most Boomers rejected the organized religion of their parents. As Boomers came to maturity, the mainstream Protestant denominations began to decline. Boomers found these churches cold and without fire, and they went in two directions: about one in two left organized religion altogether, while the rest moved into more conservative congregations where there was clear evidence of spiritual vitality.

Boomers serve as a transitional generation; their needs, desires, and worldview differ greatly from their parents. They are floaters who have a hard time making lifetime commitments, whether to churches, partners, political parties, or other organizations. Organizations of all types are in decline largely because of the disinterest of Boomers. Lodges, social organizations, and political-party membership have all suffered along with organized religion.

Boomers have been idealistic in the same way that the Puritans were. Such idealism has produced spiritual-renewal movements, including the Great Awakening of 1740, the transcendental awakening of the 1830s, and the missionary awakening of the 1900s, which sought to win the world for Christ in one generation.

This same idealistic desire to change the world for the better is markedly present among Boomers. Boomers joined every other idealistic generation in narrowing the gap between the genders. Boomer men began to take on nurturing values that had belonged exclusively to women as mothers and teachers, and Boomer women enjoyed secular roles once reserved for men: medicine, law, science, engineering, and the clergy. The last member of an idealistic generation to occupy the White House was Franklin Roosevelt, whose wife shared widely in his presidency. Comparisons between Eleanor Roosevelt and Hillary Rodham Clinton are not difficult to make. Both women were members of idealistic generations.

Largely because of the dominance of Boomers, we are living in a period of great interest in spiritual matters. Many people today are engaged in a search for depth and meaning. They are dissatisfied with achievements, material prosperity, and financial security. They are seeking what their materialistic culture was unable to provide: a sense of ultimate meaning, a feeling of wholeness, a relationship with God, however they define God. They carry on their search in a variety of settings, from twelve-step programs to the return to paganism of some feminist or men's-movement groups. They are also involved in the revival of Pentecostalism and are experimenting with the mystical in New Age activities. They are seeking wholistic medical treatment, eating meatless meals, and spending a good deal of time exercising. All of these activities are part of their search for meaning.

Regele and Schulz write that Boomers are found, out of proportion to their numbers, only in the following religious categories: New Age, no preference or no interest, Holiness, nondenominational, Jehovah's Witnesses, and Pentecostal.[7] Their religious interest is real, but their suspicion of institutional religion is equally real. They frequently have been called "believers without belonging." This renewal of interest in the spiritual life, without accompanying interest in organized religion of any kind, is a new phenomenon.

Above all, Boomers want to feel their faith. It must be a firsthand experience, for they are unwilling to trust authority figures, and certainly not the authority of their parents. As part of this distrust, they have rejected the denominational traditions in which they were raised. They are attracted by the God who is immanent, involved in their lives—a god who can be felt. In order to find this god they will chase after almost any guru, endure great privation and expense, allow themselves again and again to be deeply disappointed. They will do this because of the intensity of their desire for genuine religious experience. They are captured by visions of spiritual wholeness and authenticity. Whether in or outside the church, they seek their true selves and inner peace. They may move back and forth between a New Age or Eastern practice of meditation and a Pentecostal church, without seeing any logical conflict. Above all they seek experience and will try to find it where they can. They also want excellence and are turned off by a poor music program, unattractive surroundings, a less than spotless church nursery, or a stammering or what they see as a halfhearted preacher.

At the same time they are moralists. They cast every issue in their lives in moral terms, sometimes at the expense of subtle reasoning. If they are pro-choice it is with a sense of mission about a woman's rights; if they are pro-life it is a moral crusade of saving the unborn from murder. Whatever their position, they hold it with a vengeance. The last idealist generation (Missionaries) gave us prohibition. The current Boomer Generation tried to give us the prohibition of the 1990s—the eradication of smoking. Whereas the Silents are more likely to see the subtlety of issues and to show sensitivity to the feelings of others, Boomers have a hard time seeing areas of gray; they are sure of the rightness of their cause. Given that they are scattered and unlikely to vote as a block, thus far the Boomers' influence has not been in proportion to their numbers. Ultimately they will take charge of the nation. Dan Quayle, Bill Clinton, Newt Gingrich, Al Gore, and George W. Bush demonstrate the first signs of how they will use their political power by 2010. As Builders die and Silents retire, Boomers will have majorities in the U.S. Congress.

Spiritually, Boomers have reached middle age. As they begin to pass their fiftieth birthdays, the culture will be paying attention. Menopause will be given new meaning as an "in" experience. In midlife, Boomers will have to take responsibility for institutions; they will have the power that they have always criticized in others. They may use their power to destroy each other! Look how the Boomer-dominated media treat political and entertainment personalities.

Boomers are still idealists, still looking for the dream that has haunted them from the beginning. They seek anyone who can help or point them onward in their journey, which will have no end. Their God is to be felt more than understood. Because they have not rooted themselves in any tradition, however, they are easily misled. But they are not discouraged by false starts or even by false gurus. They will find a spiritual director who can help them come to terms with the need for rootedness, for some discipline in their lives. Spiritual directors working with Boomers need to encourage them to take responsibility for their lives, to become more than religious consumers. Boomers need religion to sustain them in their transition from coming-of-age adults to their mature years. They cannot hang on to their anti-institutional stance much longer. They need some connection to society, some institutional props to provide them with wisdom. They need mentors on whom they can rely.

THE SURVIVOR GENERATION

Following the Boomers has not been easy. The generation born after 1963 and before 1985 has been called *Generation 13* or *Generation X* or the *Buster Generation*. I prefer the term used by Regele and Schulz, the *Survivor Generation*. That this generation has no single name is a clue to its lack of clear identity. This generation came of age as teens during Watergate, the energy crisis, Three Mile Island, the Iran hostage crisis, and the threat of ecological catastrophe. They do not have memories of a hopeful society to sustain them and, as a consequence, they are somewhat cynical. Survivors quickly found out that adults in their lives are not in control either of themselves or the country. Almost half of Survivors are the children of divorce, and those who came from two-parent families were frequently latchkey children. They are mistrustful and cynical about their future. They have come of age in a time of reduced expectations, when they are told that they cannot expect to do better than their parents. No wonder they are depressed and, at the same time, have a spirit of recklessness. Boomers, in particular, have criticized the Survivor generation from the beginning. Michael Fay, caned for vandalism in Singapore, may represent this generation. A majority of Americans supported that caning and believe that the rest of this generation needs more of that kind of treatment.

The despair of the Survivor Generation is real. One can see it in their clothing; they dress in black in marked contrast to the Boomers, who dressed in a kaleidoscope of bright colors. Their depression is fueled by the breakdown of their families, by a lack of role models, and by a sense that things are getting worse, the streets less safe, the job market less secure. When Boomers were twenty-something, they were ready to save the world; Survivors feel barely able to save themselves. Survival has to be their goal. This generation in its music and language as well as its dress expresses a sense of hopelessness and futility about life. Survivors can articulate what is wrong with the world almost endlessly; what they need to hear is good news. Their expectations about authority figures are low, and their cynicism about institutions is high. Yet their volunteerism is also high. They would like to make a difference in the world.

Religiously, the Survivors are on guard. They have been let down almost from birth, and they are deeply suspicious. They have a low tolerance for what they perceive to be phony. Survivors are seeking authenticity in their leaders; they prefer truth to politeness. Unlike Boomers, many of them were not raised in the church, so they do not have memories of a religious upbringing to comfort or support them. They may look like they are confident, but a significant number describe themselves as stressed out. They lack positive adult role models. Survivors are looking for healing in their own scarred and wounded families. They seek community with near desperation, community that is safe, inclusive, and open, and in which people help each other rather than compete. They tend to see Boomers as fragmented and isolated. Survivors are very tolerant of difference. They contain the highest percentage of naturalized U.S. citizens of any generation in the twentieth century. They have a hard time with any effort to persuade them that their Muslim, Jewish, Buddhist, or New Age friends are going to hell. They grew up with television and rock music, and they want something more than the churches offer, something more visceral.

Survivors are pragmatists; they are more interested in how things work than in grand schemes to discover meaning. They ask fewer questions than Boomers, partly because they are on guard against falsity. They are religious cynics who have been let down too often to be taken in again. They tend to be the most conservative generation in matters of economics, but not on issues of ethics and morality. SAT scores are holding even as a higher percentage of students take the exams—close to 70 percent today. They are working hard at learning as a key to their survival; they do not believe that the Social Security system will work for them. They are lonely but afraid of marriage, because they have seen too much pain in marriages.

Like Boomers, Survivors are diverse religiously. But, unlike Boomers, Survivors are looking for anchors in a world gone mad. They are not as attracted to New Age spirituality or Eastern religion but are often found in theologically conservative traditions. They belong out of proportion to their numbers in the following categories: non-denominational, Jehovah's Witnesses, no preference, Mormon, and New Age. Part of the appeal to Survivors is a message that proclaims meaning without even trying to fit the framework of the modern world. Whether the Survivors will stay with these preferences is an open question. They are attracted to worship services with a beat, having been raised on MTV. They seek answers, but when the preacher or leader lets them down they are not shocked; they expected that anyway!

Survivors have been so deeply hurt by the world around them, so despised by the Boomer-led media, so let down by failed dreams, that they need, with desperation, a spiritual director who can point to possible achievement, who will be somewhat optimistic on their behalf and encourage them to dream. They need all the help they can to ward off depression and to see the light before them. The director working with Survivors will need to have genuinely high expectations of them and help them trust in their own ability. Survivors are looking for authenticity. In their discouragement they seek and need someone who will hold up ideals, who will inspire them. Above all, they need older people who will love them, accept them (tattoos and all), and treat them as valuable. Because of their desperation, they will turn to anyone who can provide these elements. They seek a God who is truth, understood and felt—a God who can point the way through the confusion that is their world. Because they are lonely, Survivors might be excellent candidates for group spiritual direction.

THE MILLENNIAL GENERATION

The final generation alive today has been called the *Millennialist* (born beginning in 1985), because they will usher in the new millennium. As these children have claimed our attention, the response has been different from our view of Survivors. The Millennialists are attracting positive attention, concern for their future, increased concern about the quality of our schools. Today nearly every politician expresses concern about the money we spend on education. This is the first generation to be dressed in school uniforms. Are these signs of a return to a generation that can build and cooperate?

If the theory behind generational cycles is correct, we will enter a world crisis between 2015 and 2025, when the oldest Millennials will be around thirty and the youngest about ten. Like the Builders before them, Millennials will be the right age to fill the ranks and to defeat the rising threat. They will rise to the occasion, organize, and cooperate. It is not a happy thought.

THE GENERATIONS AND SPIRITUAL DIRECTION

Many folks in several different generations are pursuing experiential religion, eagerly searching for some deep sense of God's reality. They are not content with religion which is correct, obedient, and intellectually demanding, but which lacks soul. A host of burned-out church members and pastors, who have grown cynical in the process of doing good, is witness to the human need for something more satisfying than duty. We have discovered the importance for our faith of what has come to be called "spirituality." We may call it by another name, but the search for a personal relationship with God is a common phenomenon of our modern society.

The longing for a sense of God as a present reality has caused some people, especially Boomers, to leave the church. They have seen the church as one more institution seeking its own survival. Pastors have not been educated to lead people in their search for God. They have not always been ready for the searching questions of their own parishioners. Because churches have been unprepared for the surge of interest in the spiritual life, they have been unresponsive, sometimes disdainful, of those who search. Using the generational model, churches are largely controlled by the Builder generation, which is thoroughly rational and uncomfortable with expressions of feeling. People in their seventies and eighties are disproportionately represented in the church sessions and councils that determine church policy. The Boomers and not present in significant numbers in most churches. They are not the decision makers, nor are they the ones making pledges. When they attend a church, to try it on, they are likely to be disappointed in what they see. Their desire for a sense of the holy is not likely to be realized in a highly logical, tightly organized, unemotional worship service. No wonder the Boomers and Survivors are found in various Pentecostal churches, especially those that are nondenominational or that play down denomination. They find there what they seek, a sense of being grasped by the holy.

Generational studies provides several insights to spiritual directors working with those involved in the institutional church or in flight from it. Note that in both cases these persons are in relationship to the church.

Builders have a big God who is transcendent and in charge. They do not want more than that. The crises of economic depression and war left them needing a God who could be counted on amid the insecurities of life. They have not greatly valued intimacy with God and now, as they have aged, some are asking important personal religious questions for the first time. They will ask how to face death with courage and dignity, or they may ask a spiritual director about loss, because that is their primary experience. They need spiritual directors who will help them express feelings they have bottled up, grieve their losses, and prepare to let go of life itself.

Silents are on the way, still on a spiritual pilgrimage. They have lived through tremendous change, and the ways that worked for them as children and young adults— staying within the lines, being good and obedient—have long since failed them. They want to know who they really are and what they have missed in life. They are ready for a more intimate God who will love them and hold them close. As they retire, they want to know that their lives have meaning and purpose. They need help to recover anchors they once had and to recast faith in new language. They are more open to change than Builders and are likely to value women in leadership. Above all, they need a sense of accomplishment to enable them to make peace with their origins.

Boomers are still idealists, still looking for the dream that has haunted them from infancy. They seek anyone who can point them onward in their quest. Their god is immanent, close at hand, and to be felt more than understood. They will keep looking until they find a leader who can offer them the vision they seek. Boomers need a solid religious tradition to sustain them in their transition from coming-of-age adults to their mature years. They cannot hold on to their anti-institutional stance any longer; they are becoming the wielders of power and the managers of institutions. Their spiritual directors should gently help them to distinguish between their religious ideals and their needs for community, order, and structure.

Survivors have been so deeply hurt by the world around them, so despised by the Boomer-controlled media, so let down by failed dreams that they desperately need. They seek spiritual directors who can point to hope and lift them out of their despair. Religious leaders must have integrity; Survivors seek authenticity above all. They also want leaders who will assure them that they are acceptable as they are. Survivors have ways of testing us—body piercing being one of the most obvious—to see if we mean it when we say, "welcome." They know that they desperately need community. The appeal of twelve-step groups is that they provide a safe place where a person can be called by name, upheld, accepted, and cared for. A spiritual director may encourage them to participate in group direction. They need community because, alone and unaided, they sense that they cannot make it. They want to relate to a God who can be both understood and felt, a God who can point the way through confusion.

The agenda for the spiritual director who seeks to serve fallen-away Silents, Boomers, and Survivors must include at least the following:

1. These people are nearly desperate for genuine community. Following the example of the twelve-step program, directors must enable people to be truthful about themselves without feeling defensive. Idle chat will not be sufficient. They may respond positively to small groups in which it is safe to expose one's real self without fear of rejection, in which they will find commonality with others who share some of their concerns for depth.

2. The new spirituality demands an emotional response. Boomers, Survivors, and their Silent allies want to feel their religion; they will not waste time on rituals that seem empty to them. Many Boomers and Survivors were not raised in the church; many others have left the church while in college. They have no institutional loyalty, no love of the old hymns, no experience with rituals that connects them with their own past. They need for a spiritual director to understand them without trying to "church" them. They also need a director who will be comfortable with their expressions of feeling.

3. Those looking for a new spirituality are always flirting with danger. Because they lack grounding in any tradition they lack the tools for sorting out what may be appropriate. They are ahistorical and lack the strength of a healthy tradition. They may find themselves deeply enmeshed in a cult before they have the wisdom to say no. These folks need in a spiritual director a nonjudgmental filter with which they can check their own experiences, test certain practices, and see what enhances and destroys their growth.

Traditional religion has an important role in our culture. Builders need religion to help create meaning as they accept loss and prepare for death. They expect and need the church to be solid and familiar. They resist and resent too many changes to what has sustained them throughout the years. Silents need the church to help them find new anchors as they prepare to let go of the power they now wield in business and society. Having worked hard, they now face retirement. The church can help them claim a sense of accomplishment, can provide needed community, and can enable them to come home. Boomers need the church to sustain them in their middle years. They need the church to provide them with accumulated wisdom. Survivors are looking for liveliness, authenticity, community, and inclusiveness. In their discouragement, they seek and need encouragement, someone to hold up ideals and to inspire them.

Interest in the inner life is difficult to sustain in our culture. What is sought cannot be produced quickly, easily, or unambiguously. Part of the appeal of the New Age movement is that some people see in the relatively simple and novel practices a way to achieve an experience of the divine presence without waiting or giving up very much—without discipline. I believe that spiritual directors can be significant for those searching for God outside the church. We may be a safe avenue they can use to express their distaste of organized religion and, at the same time, to explore the meaning of traditional symbols.

Chapter Six

SPIRITUAL DIRECTION WITH LESBIAN, GAY, BISEXUAL, AND TRANSGENDERED PERSONS

Rich Rossiter

———— ◆ · ————

*Today my pastor preached a sermon and said that I
am going to hell because I am a lesbian. He said I
am choosing to live in sin and can change myself
from being homosexual to heterosexual if I would
give myself totally to Jesus Christ. How do I make
sense out of what I heard this morning? I experience
myself as a deeply spiritual person.*

*I feel like it is such a special blessing to be gay. My
sense of compassion has been heightened. This
journey of healing I've been on has been nothing less
than transformational!*

*I am so angry at God for allowing the persecution
of my gay soul. I feel like I'm being attacked from
all of society, especially [from] my church and
family. God, help me understand this intense anger
that is inside of me.*

*My journey of coming out has been difficult but very
healing. I am now totally who I was created to be.
Light shines around me daily!*

———— ◆ · ————

God's lesbian, gay, bisexual, and transgendered children are one of
God's significant gifts to the human family. Increasingly, we are celebrating that we are a blessing to the earth. Amid the rhetoric and antitruth
about who we are, deep down we know we are part of God's plan for creation. If you cannot affirm as a spiritual director that same-gender love is

whole and healthy, that being lesbian, gay, bisexual, or transgendered is a healthy experience of human sexuality, and that our behavior and experiences are compatible with Christian values and ethics, then please do not accompany members of our community on the spiritual journey.

FACING OUR OWN HETEROSEXISM/HOMOPHOBIA

Spiritual directors who offer holy listening for lesbian women, gay men, bisexuals, and transgendered folk must be willing to confront their own attitudes toward same-sex orientation. As Larry Graham writes, "Without honesty about where one orients himself or herself among the range of opinion about the psychological, theological, and moral status of homosexuality, much harm can occur in caregiving and spiritual direction."[1]

On several occasions I have sat quietly with my sisters and brothers who have been damaged by others practicing this sacred art we call spiritual direction. I have concluded that those who offer spiritual direction to the queer community must undergo some special training and/or immersion in our community. Every spiritual director who companions a lesbian, gay, bisexual, or transgendered (l/g/b/t) person *must* have a solid working knowledge of this highly complex subculture with all its diversity. The spiritual director must embody the belief that being l/g/b/t is a healthy variant of human sexuality and that his or her life is compatible with Christian values and ethics. The director must also be willing to enter and work with the belief systems of l/g/b/t persons as well as to discuss sexual behaviors and attitudes. Recently, I entered a sacred discussion with one directee who wanted to talk about where God was present in the leather sex in which he and his partner experimented.

Unless spiritual directors confront their own internalized heterosexism (homophobia), it is easy for prejudice to blind us to what is present in the individual with whom we are walking spiritually. We all live in a homophobic society and are at best recovering from heterosexism, just as we are recovering from racism and sexism. We must keep central in our awareness that all persons who trust us with their spiritual journey remind us that God is within them and that they are within God! It does great harm to the soul when an ignorant director insists that "it" (our means of expressing deepest intimacy) is a "cross to bear." These and other beliefs impede the process into a spiritually vital and healthy relationship with God.

Please understand that l/g/b/t persons entering a relationship with a spiritual director will often suspect that he or she is heterosexist who will try to blame, criticize, or disrespect the directee. After all, most of us are representatives of the church—the same church that has historically shamed us and laid a myriad of antitruth into our laps. Whether or not a spiritual director is working out of a church or other religious institution, anyone in religious authority is suspect, for church has been the enemy for a very long time. My suggestion is that spiritual directors share rather quickly their own story—something about their experience in queer culture, or perhaps a bit about their own recovery from heterosexism.

Directors companioning the l/g/b/t community might consider visiting a gay-support group, a local Metropolitan Community Church (a Christian denomination with a primary outreach to the l/g/b/t community), or a gay or lesbian bar, or reading among the vast writings available about our community. Three excellent resources are Malcolm Boyd and Nancy Wilson's book *Amazing Grace: Stories of Lesbian and Gay Faith;* Chris Glaser's *Coming Out to God: Prayers for Lesbians and Gay Men, their Families and Friends;* and Heather Wishik and Carol Pierce's *Sexual Orientation and Identity* (see the reference list at the end of this essay). *Amazing Grace* comes with a sexual-orientation and identity-continuum diagram (foldout chart). You may also consider borrowing a book that has been helpful in your directee's coming-out process.

THE INTEGRATION OF SEXUALITY AND SPIRITUALITY

It is not possible to walk beside a l/g/b/t person and not deal with the inherent connection between sexuality and spirituality. If spirituality can broadly be defined as integrated wholeness in relation to self, God, and neighbor, including the larger society, then it follows that the character of our sexuality is in principle a foundation and expression of our spirituality. Our sexuality does indeed reflect and contribute to integrated wholeness. As James Nelson and Sandra Longfellow have taught, salvation is sexual; we are not saved from our sexuality but in, with, and through it.[2] It is through our sexuality that love is possible, estrangement overcome, and wholeness occurs. Sexual relatedness and wholeness are intimately related to one another.

Spiritual directors assist l/g/b/t persons to spiritual strength and wholeness by providing the space and perspective for them to discover the strength of persevering into God. This strength emerges from affirming one's sexual vitality and its capacity to empower personal affirmation and effective opposition to anything that diminishes it.

Spiritual directors are called upon to create a setting in which love, unconditional acceptance, confidentiality, vulnerability, and the search for meaning can take place for their directees. They are called to create a climate of shared trust in God, in the other, and in what is deep within. This is especially important for individuals who are infected and affected with HIV or AIDS. It seems almost impossible to find a l/g/b/t person who has not been touched by this pandemic. To work with queer persons who are struggling to prevent or to live with HIV and AIDS means one needs to be comfortable talking about sexual practices. It requires knowledge of AIDS research and community resources. Awareness of the psychological, medical, and societal issues is essential. Talking and finding God present in life, death, dying, grief, and loss will be called for. Some directees will be finding God's presence in new ways, as their current drug regimen has given them a second chance to live. Questions of the relationship of HIV and AIDS to God's will and goodness are central, and must be faced if spiritual strength is to emerge.

Directees themselves often are working on the integration of sexuality and spirituality. The need to help l/g/b/t persons overcome the internalized homophobia with which they are living is paramount. The coming-out process consists of one day after another of dealing with the antitruth that we have accepted. Often this exploration is lengthy, as we have been told for years that we are perverted, sick, and sinful. The experience is especially painful for those who grew up in the church and now no longer feel welcome or who are struggling with the dissonance between their self-concepts and the professed beliefs of church or religious institutions. When feeling hurt and alone, it is not unusual for some to blame and reject their natural soul, particularly if their religious beliefs were strongly conservative. Judy, who now lives in a committed relationship with her lover, is examining the verses in scripture that condemn her. She is slowly seeing and forming a different understanding of how scripture informs her life and ministry. Lisa's current prayer is that she can accept her sexual feelings and continue to find God in the loneliness she is feeling. If you care to reflect with a coming-out journal, read my book *Out with a Passion*.

It is important that spiritual directors be inclusive about the ways in which individuals can develop their relationships with God. If being in church brings up negative feelings, anxiety, or anger, perhaps the directee needs permission to leave the church for a while. Do not underestimate the power of giving individuals this permission, especially if you are working on behalf of the institutionalized church. Sometimes nature is a venue through which many l/g/b/t persons find meaning and solace. Many of my queer brothers and sisters are being fed by a doctrine of "co-creation," in which it is understood that diverse forms of life have emerged from God—and all are good. Eco-theological models are helping l/g/b/t persons affirm the goodness of diverse sexual orientations, combining modern science and Christian doctrines of creation and salvation to present an organic model of God's relation to the world.

DIRECTION AND THE STAGES OF COMING OUT

Each lesbian woman, gay man, bisexual, or transgendered person experiences the process of coming out in his or her own way. As there is no "right" way to pray, there is no "right" way, or one "usual" way, of embracing the soul. This journey is shaped by one's family of origin, personality, culture, and individual spiritual and religious history.

Within the social sciences, there is lively debate about models of coming out. Today most of these models come from gay men and need to be reexamined for lesbians. People of color and those from various socioeconomic backgrounds are bringing their own experiences to the discussion. The process I outline below takes as many variations as there are individuals. Each of us does our interior work at our own pace, works within our personal resources, and faces our own struggles along the way. In creating these stages below, I have drawn from my own experiences and from Craig O'Neill and Kathleen Ritter's *Coming Out Within: Stages of Spiritual Awakening for Lesbians and Gay Men*.[3] I highly recommend O'Neill and Ritter's book for every director's library, in which John Schneider's eight-phase model for transforming loss is adapted to lesbian and gay populations. Their focus is on motivation toward recovery and integration, and on loss as a stepping-stone to spiritual transformation.

Stage 1: Awareness of Being/Feeling Different

Adolescents and children who later understand themselves to be lesbian, gay, or bisexual usually experience themselves as somehow "different." Both boys and girls experience internal conflict about behaviors expected of them: dating persons of the opposite sex, using makeup, wearing gender-specific clothing, and so on. Almost always at this stage, this feeling of being different remains undefined and unnamed, as conscious words are not yet available to describe the feelings. The feeling is usually not attached to a gay or lesbian identity because sexual expression is not a part of the young person's experience.

Stage 2: Identity Confusion

Here the individual has a conscious awareness of stage one. The sense of difference takes the form of questioning. I believe the questions being asked at this point are the prayers of the person struggling with their emerging identity. Who am I? Am I really straight? Am I a gay man or lesbian woman? For today's young person, this stage often takes place during adolescence or early childhood; however, for baby boomers and older adults, this phase may take place at any adult age.

Societal stigmatization prolongs the period of identity confusion because it prevents people from discussing and exploring their sexual desires, experiences, fantasies, and feelings with others for fear they will be judged, fired, persecuted, or physically harmed.

At this stage, they may choose to avoid interests, people, or information relating to same-gender orientation. They may immerse themselves in heterosexual relationships to prove to themselves and others that they are straight. They may even adopt anti-gay political and personal values and verbally or physically attack those who are gay, lesbian, bisexual, or transgendered. Or they may avoid the struggle of identity formation through the use of alcohol and other drugs, numbing themselves to the conflict within the soul. Ted shared sexual intimacy with a colleague at age twenty-seven. At the time, he concluded he wasn't gay because he did not have an erection while sharing intimacy with the man. Fifteen years later he embraced his gay soul.

This is a stage of tremendous pain, grief, and depression. Their lives are carrying them forward into a new self-identity that is internally painful and externally judged as immoral and wrong.

Stage 3: Acceptance of Self and Emergence of a New Life Image

The third stage of coming out is acceptance. Here an individual begins to acknowledge that his or her feelings and behavior probably mean that he is gay or she is lesbian, or perhaps bisexual. In my experience, this is the stage at which l/g/b/t persons are most apt to seek spiritual direction. Often in this stage, one takes a fresh look at one's history, feelings, and life images, combined with new information about other gay men and lesbians in the community and in history. Here is the beginning of what we often call "coming out to myself." This is a roller-coaster ride of emotions, as the l/g/b/t person is beginning to develop a life image that will enable them to function from their deepest nature. Self-definition has begun, and questioning everything they have learned is right behind. As anguishing as this stage is, it is necessary for l/g/b/t people, who must lose the illusion that they can assimilate into a heterosexually defined life image. Thus the losses that the individual encounters are essential birth pangs for the emergence of a more personally viable life image. A new sense of self is emerging. One begins to embrace his or her authentic soul (self).

Stage 4: Claiming a New Self

Claiming an expanded self is the beginning of a more overt process we normally think of as "coming out." Persons at this stage affirm an identity as gay, lesbian, or bisexual. Often this is an attitude of toleration, not necessarily pride or affirmation. They work harder at connecting with the l/g/b/t community. They often experiment more frequently with same-sex partners and spend a greater amount of their free time in community.

Often at this stage, the director will experience in the directee an inner debate about whether they should come out or not, especially to their parents and family. The turmoil of when to come out to parents is always most significant. We often move forward to tell them, even though we are not convinced they are psychologically ready to deal with the issue. During this time, it is important to remind the directee that forcing the new identity is counterproductive. Still, directees may need to be encouraged to look at the antitruth they have accepted about homosexuality.

Thinking about coming out or actually coming out is a good time for directees to look at the relationships in their lives. Reflection on coming out to others can open up discussions about dependency and codependency. It may reveal their own inflexibility in their thinking that people should accept them. It may help them to see how caught they are in certain parts of the queer subculture, especially the more negative aspects of queer community. During this time a person may choose to examine the meaning of going out to gay bars, going to queer dances, frequenting lesbian or gay sections of the city, or enjoying homoerotic films.

Persons in this stage often have a weak interior world or, more accurately, a fragile connection with the inner life. During this stage, the directee is wandering through an area where they have not been before. Often they are alienated from an inner world because each time they embrace a new idea or person, their harmony and serenity is threatened. God may be imaged in terms of an external relationship, the kind one might have with a strict parent. This lack of inner connection most often means the directee is not very clear about their sexual orientation. Directors may be led to help the directee find an interior side to each of their exterior activities. I believe the main work of the director here is to help the directee avoid vagueness about what is going on and where God is in the process.

Many directors will find working with folks at this stage frustrating at times. Of all the stages of growth, this is the one in which there is the greatest resistance to God and growth itself. It is not immediately rewarding to work with people who have so little self-identity, yet we recall that all transitions offer a sacred time. It is a time when the directee is apt to be hard on him- or herself, when there is a great deal of self-depreciation, a kind of tossing and turning in the direction of life because they are taking their cues, most of them negative, from differing sources, both inner and outer. There is a sense of hopelessness or defeat because they feel they are predestined to act in a certain way sexually. The messages from churches generally confuse us more since most religious communities say we are good but what we do is bad. Because the directee has no inner authority to counteract the outer authority, the outer authority often wins.

This is also a time when feelings should and can be examined. A director may be helpful in distinguishing thoughts from feelings—this is essential for further growth. Growth takes place through clarification, and as long as feelings are expressed in a vague way the passage to the inner world is inhibited. In conclusion, this stage can be thought of as a rite of passage—an interior passage.

Stage 5: Rebuilding an Identity and Integrating and Reformulating Loss

Persons rebuilding an identity are beginning to feel healing and a certain peace with the past. The emotional intensity connected with loss is lessening. Often, the balm of time and solitude succeeds in softening the pain. This is an incredible time of growing self-awareness. Gradually, the l/g/b/t person is responding more to personal values than to group, church, or societal values. During this stage, the directee is expanding and increasing their powers for introspection and beginning to claim an expanded sense of self. The purpose of direction at this point is to help the directee rebuild their identity.

This is a vulnerable time. The directee is now aware of the movements of their interior life, but that does not mean that they can interpret them correctly. The director is called on to bring skills of discernment to prevent the directee from making decisions based only on what they think is the right thing to do.

During this stage, there is greater capacity for intimacy, because the directee is more acquainted with their inner terrain, and they are more able to differentiate among their feelings. There is also a willingness to work with God rather than trying to save themselves. God is now their God, and not the God of their parents or childhood church. God is now becoming personal. Prayer may become more affective; God is imaged as friend or lover. The more developed this stage, the more sexual feelings are diffused from the genital area throughout the person. During this time directors may encourage a weekend experience such as that offered through Body Electric of Oakland, California. The purpose of this organization is to help gay men and lesbians come home to their erotic body and energy, and to experience erotic energy as playful, sacred, energizing, and transformative.[4]

A great deal of deconstruction has gone on in the l/g/b/t person's life now. Much will have been and is being left behind. Again, O'Neill and Ritter, the two authors of *Coming Out Within*, describe the reactions in the fearful gay man or lesbian. They describe it as "holding on" or "letting go." They write that holding on often feels like foolish behavior, or not acting like oneself, usually to prevent being overwhelmed by grief (79).

The other reaction to fear is called letting go. This involves acknowledgment of the losses by denying something in oneself or one's world. Letting go is separating from the self that which was once valued. The authors tell the story of Jean and her first experience in a lesbian bar—it was a homecoming for Jean. After divorcing her husband, she began to spend a lot of time in the bar, where she was known for her earthy advice and capacity to make others feel comfortable. Over time, her newfound friends began to be concerned over Jean's excessive drinking. They agreed to confront her and encouraged her to seek treatment at a center that worked with lesbians. Rather than hearing that her friends cared enough to confront her, she heard rejection and judgment and told them to get out of her life. She moved away and, from time to time, felt intense remorse over rejecting her friends, but she was too ashamed to face them and reconcile (100).

Stage 6: Affirmation and Celebration, and Transforming Loss

Now being lesbian, gay, bisexual, or transgendered is embraced as a way of life. Long-term relationships often begin during this stage. A comment such as this may be heard: "I celebrate my sexual orientation and, in the context of spirituality, I understand it to be the essence of what I was created to be." There is a new sense of freedom, happiness, and contentment with one's soul. Individuals choose to come out to a much broader group of people, and even to let their sexual orientation be known publicly.

O'Neill and Ritter compare the process of coming out to the process of developing faith as described by James Fowler. "As individuals journey through loss, they experience an expansion of their vision that allows them to see more deeply, beyond the meaning of events and into the hearts of other people. Paralleling this is an increased intimacy with one's true self, with others, with the global community, and with the Spirit who weaves it all together" (179). With this emerging shift, there is a corresponding shift away from a solitary journey and toward reconnection with community. During this stage the directee takes even more interest in the spiritual journey—and not for some extraneous goal. This transition is marked by a clearer calling to social justice issues and a willingness to look at intimacy in their lives with increased honesty.

Throughout this process, the director may notice some of the special gifts that l/g/b/t persons often bring to direction. Many have a well-developed ability to see truth and hypocrisy in institutions—especially the church. Many see the value of meditative awareness and have the ability to be introspective. Some are asking deeply piercing questions of themselves and God: JoAnne is intensely examining the feminine aspects of Jesus, and has already integrated beautifully the masculine attributes of Jesus' and herself. It is also my experience that many l/g/b/t persons tolerate ambiguity, for we know that the absolute is often condemning and rigid.

Surviving the challenge of being l/g/b/t can enable strength to face the ups and downs of a spiritual life. Coming out while dealing with the rejection of church, family, and friends leads to the valuing of truth and self-discovery. L/g/b/t persons have had to explore deeply their feelings and perspectives in order to confront both their own and others' homophobia. We have struggled to reconcile our faith with teachings that said we were not deserving of the grace of God, or worse, that we had been damned to hell. Most are conscious of the ups and downs of the spiritual journey, aware that they are likely to continue. As Jay, a psychotherapist, said: "Coming out has been the deepest reflective period of my life. Examining my childhood and early adult theology has been hard work, yet healing. I know my spiritual life will continue to deepen as I give time and energy to expanding my sense of self."

THE BIBLE AND HOMOSEXUALITY

The Bible has been used from its beginning to substantiate various ideas, prejudices, and actions. "If the Bible says so, it must be true," has been the simplistic assumption of those not willing to do hard exegetical work.

Such persons take Bible verses out of their historical and literary contexts and use them to support the point of view they are trying to impose on others, or they dismiss all contrary evidence because they believe their interpretation of the Bible is the ultimate authority.

The Bible has been used to justify wars, the killing of witches, the execution of heretics, the acceptance of slavery, the persecution of Jews, the prohibition of African Americans from the priesthood, laws against interracial marriage, the superiority of men, the exclusion of women from leadership and clergy positions, and the condemnation and punishment of homosexuals. As a director, I invite people to embrace healthy skepticism when confronted by those who use the Bible to support their particular values and ideas, especially when these other views support nationalism under all circumstances, racial discrimination, violence against those of other religions, limits on the roles of women, and condemnation of sexual minorities. They are probably misusing the Bible by taking passages out of context and by ignoring information that might provide a different interpretation. I also remind directees that even if a particular point of view is clearly present in the Bible (such as patriarchy), they do have the right to disagree with the Bible!

When I companion a l/g/b/t person through scripture, the first task I invite them to do is to read the Bible and seek an understanding of what the Bible actually says. I encourage use of a current translation of the Bible, founded on the best biblical scholarship. I refer them to several modern translations to see how various Bible translators have chosen to translate from the Hebrew, Greek, and Aramaic into our own language.

The second task for the directee is to seek an understanding of the original intended meaning. Bible commentaries, dictionaries, maps, and cross-references are all helpful resources for discovering the meaning of a passage as it was intended by the writer(s).

I then invite the directee to reflect on the Bible passage as they have come to understand it and to test this understanding against the tradition(s) they are currently with, the experiences of their own life and the lives of others, and the best reasoning they can bring to bear. I encourage them to discuss their reflections with other l/g/b/t persons and with those who have very different life experiences. Finally I encourage the directee to arrive at a conviction that is right for him or her and those with whom they share community. I always remind them to be ready to revise their beliefs based on new information and life experiences.

Let us now together reflect on one or two primary ways some have used the Bible to condemn lesbians, gay men, bisexuals, and transgendered folks and/or the expression of their sexuality. Some people assume that homosexuality must be a major topic in the Bible. This is a false assumption. Homosexuality as a sexual orientation was not even known in biblical times. Only sexual behavior with persons of the same gender is addressed. The concept of homosexuality was not even introduced into language until 1869 by a Hungarian writer, K. M. Kertbeny (originally Benkert).

Some assume that many references in the Bible condemn sexual intercourse with a person of the same gender. This, too, is false. There are only six passages in the Bible that have been interpreted as speaking to sexual intercourse with a person of the same gender. Three references are in the Old Testament; three references are in the New Testament. Christians often assume that Jesus strongly condemned sexual intercourse between persons of the same gender. This is simply not true, as Jesus never referred to such behavior.

The Bible passages most often misinterpreted are Genesis 19:1–29, Leviticus 18:22, Leviticus 20:13, and Romans 1:26–27.

Sodom and Gomorrah—Genesis 19

The Genesis story is best understood by reading from Genesis 18:1 through Genesis 19:29. It is also helpful to know that the man, Lot, is Abraham's nephew and an outsider (alien) to the citizens of Sodom. Additionally, the phrase uttered by the men of Sodom, "Bring them out to us, so that we may know them," does not have to be interpreted in a sexual manner. It is possible to understand this as an intention of gang rape. Or it might also indicate an attempt on the part of the townspeople to find out the identity of these strangers staying at the house of a resident alien. By reading beginning with 18:1 one can compare and contrast the hospitality offered to the strangers by Abraham and Lot to that of the citizens of Sodom. This lack of welcome seems to be Jesus' understanding of the sin of Sodom as indicated in Matthew 10:14–15. Ezekiel 16:49 refers to the sin of Sodom: "This was the guilt of your sister Sodom: she and her daughters had pride, excess of food, and prosperous ease, but did not aid the poor and needy."

There is nothing in the story of Sodom that justifies condemnation of homosexuality. There is much in the story that suggests strangers should be welcomed and offered hospitality. How ironic that this story is used to condemn and to be inhospitable to lesbians, gay men, bisexuals, and transgendered folks, the "strangers" among us. Those who commit the sin of

Sodom are those who do not welcome the minority, the strangers. When l/g/b/t persons read this story they might identify themselves with the angels. They are received and welcomed by some, but others greet them with suspicion and contempt. Those who welcome them are also suspect. In the face of this reality, God commands that the strangers in our midst be welcomed.

The Leviticus Passages

The two Leviticus passages, 18:22 and 20:13, are similar. Their literal translations state that no male should "lie the lyings of a woman."

Leviticus contains the "holiness code" for the people of Israel, expressing the understanding of the world by the peoples of that time. It includes prescriptions for making atonement for sins so the offending Israelite can be forgiven. In addition, Leviticus includes prescriptions for maintaining ritual purity and holiness of many sorts. For example, Leviticus 12:2–5 states that a woman shall be ceremonially unclean for seven days following the birth of a male child, but if she bears a female child she shall be unclean for two weeks.

Leviticus 18 deals with sexual relations and identifies incest, sexual intercourse during the woman's "menstrual uncleanness," sexual relations with the wife of a kinsman, or a male lying with another male as with a woman as actions that defile the people of Israel and the land in which they live. The punishments are death. While much of the holiness code material in Leviticus is ignored by those who use the Bible to justify their condemnation of sexual relations between persons of the same gender, the particular verses that deal with "a male lying the lyings of a woman" are often quoted as authoritative.

However, it is important to understand the context of this prohibition. First, women had lower status than men. For a man to take the role of a woman in a sexual relationship was seen as beneath his status and confusing to the clearly defined roles of the genders. Second, during this period of history it was not uncommon for conquering armies to force their defeated enemies to submit to rape. This sexual act was one of aggression, dominance, and humiliation. The defeated enemy was treated "like a woman." Third, there was no understanding of homosexuality as a sexual orientation in which someone might participate in a mutually enriching and satisfying relationship. Fourth, same sex behavior was associated with the activities of those who worshiped other gods.

An important purpose of the holiness code in Leviticus was to create a people who were distinct and set apart from the peoples who had lived in the land before the Israelites. These people worshiped competing gods. Their idolatry and behaviors associated with their idolatry were called abominations. The Leviticus passages are an example of why it is important to know what is actually said, to know the historical context, and to disagree with the Bible when one encounters material opposed to the life experiences and reason of the contemporary directee.

Romans 1:26–27

This passage in Paul's letter to the Romans is seen as the most significant passage of scripture dealing with sexual intercourse between men and between women. It is also the only passage that mentions sexual intercourse between women.

To understand the passage it is important to keep it in context. Begin reading at Romans 1:18. As you read, notice that Paul expects his readers to know and honor God. However, he notes that some who know God have become ungodly and wicked. They have suppressed the truth and have worshiped false gods, images resembling humans or animals. As a result of their idolatry, Paul says, "God gave them up in the lusts of their hearts to impurity. . . ." "Because they exchanged the truth about God for a lie and worshiped and served the creature rather than the Creator . . . God gave them up to degrading passions. Their women exchanged natural intercourse for unnatural, and in the same way also the men, giving up natural intercourse with women, were consumed with passion for one another."

Continue reading through the end of 1:28–32, where Paul further describes these idolaters as being "filled with every kind of wickedness, evil, covetousness, malice. Full of envy, murder, strife, deceit, craftiness, they are gossips, slanderers, God-haters, insolent, haughty, boastful, inventors of evil, rebellious toward parents, foolish, faithless, heartless, ruthless."

It is appropriate to ask: do the lesbians, gay men, bisexuals, or transgendered persons whom you know fit Paul's description? Have they turned away from God and worshiped false gods? Are they acting out of wickedness, evil, covetousness, malice? Are they full of envy, murder, and so on? Even if only one of the l/g/b/t persons you know does not fit Paul's description, you might wonder if Paul is wrong in his analysis or is talking about some other category of people.

The "natural-versus-unnatural" argument is discussed in many books. In a nutshell, modern scholars believe that this description of male and female homosexuality is set in the context of Paul's discussion of idolatry as practiced in Rome, where worship was evidently directed to "images resembling a mortal human being or birds or four-footed animals or reptiles" (Romans 1:23). As part of these rituals, the worshiper had intercourse with sacred prostitutes, both male and female. The important point to note is that the distinction between natural intercourse and unnatural was a result of their participation in these pagan rituals. Paul seems to have particular kinds of people in mind as he writes his letter to the Romans. Certainly he does not have in mind the many Jewish and Christian l/g/b/t persons who today are living faithful, loving, responsible lives.

Of course, at times we may be called to remind a directee that it is possible for people to misuse the gift of their sexuality. Behaviors that deny the value and dignity of another, that use persons without regard for their wishes, that include violence, force, and coercion, are behaviors rightly condemned. Such behaviors may be present in both heterosexual and homosexual relationships. It is not sexual intercourse between persons of the same gender that is to be condemned. It is any wickedness or evil that is to be condemned.

In conclusion, the Bible has little to say about homosexual behavior. It says nothing about the reality of homosexual orientation. Those who use the Bible as the basis for their condemnation of all homosexuality and/or homosexual behavior do not have a strong basis for their position. Conscientious Christian and Jewish persons may disagree with those who use the Bible to label all homosexual behavior as sin. Many other Bible passages call for love, compassion, understanding, hospitality, and justice for all God's children. Nancy Wilson's book *Our Tribe: Queer Folks, God, Jesus, and the Bible* is an excellent resource for additional scriptural reflections for both directors and directees.

A WORD ABOUT TRANSGENDERED DIRECTEES

In closing, I wanted to say a brief word about my attempt to be inclusive throughout this essay by including transgendered people within the narrative. While I personally have had limited experience companioning transgendered Christians, I am aware that much more writing and reflection is needed by spiritual directors and pastoral counselors alike in this area. Gender issues and their relationship to identity are sacred and complex, requiring reflection and training beyond the normal bounds of the average spiritual director. A good starting resource for learning more about these issues is *True Selves: Understanding Transsexualism (for Families, Friends, Coworkers, and Helping Professionals)* by Mildred L. Brown.

References

Boyd, Malcolm, and Nancy Wilson, eds. *Amazing Grace: Stories of Lesbian and Gay Faith.* Freedom, Calif.: Crossing Press, 1991.

Brown, Mildred L. *True Selves: Understanding Transsexualism (for Families, Friends, Coworkers, and Helping Professionals).* San Francisco: Jossey-Bass, 1996.

Glaser, Chris. *Coming Out to God: Prayers for Lesbians and Gay Men, Their Families, and Friends.* Louisville: Westminster/John Knox Press, 1991.

O'Neill, Craig, and Kathleen Ritter. *Coming Out Within: Stages of Spiritual Awakening for Lesbians and Gay Men.* San Francisco: HarperSanFrancisco, 1992.

Rossiter, Rich. *Out with a Passion.* San Francisco.: Alamo Square Press, 1999.

Wilson, Nancy. *Our Tribe: Queer Folks, God, Jesus, and the Bible.* San Francisco: HarperSanFrancisco, 1995.

Wishik, Heather, and Carol Pierce. *Sexual Orientation and Identity.* Laconia, N.H.: New Dynamics, 1995.

Chapter Seven

CAN I GET A WITNESS?
SPIRITUAL DIRECTION WITH THE MARGINALIZED

Juan Reed

————•◆•————

In approaching spiritual direction with people who have been marginalized, the guiding metaphor I present for understanding the role of the director is that of a *witness*. A witness is one who is above all present. A witness *looks* as well as *listens*, sees as well as hears. A witness to the marginalized is present to see and hear those who are most often invisible and inaudible. Spiritual direction with the marginalized offers a ministry of witnessing, of "holy looking" as well as "holy listening." Such spiritual direction is listening with eyes wide open.

By "marginalized" I am referring to those who are not only different from the norm of the dominant, but who, because of the very aspects of their identity that distinguish them, are considered inferior.[1] They are those who because of one or more aspects of their identity are looked on as outsiders. The marginalized do not "fit in" and are pushed from the mainstream to the borders of the community.

The marginalized include people who are economically poor and physically disabled. Women have been marginalized as have been gay, lesbian, and transgendered people. People of color are marginalized. The elderly and children as well as single parents are marginalized, especially those who are poor. Men, women, and youth in prison are marginal. Homeless people are marginal. People with diseases, especially those stigmatized by society such as HIV/AIDS, are marginalized. The chemically addicted are marginalized. Often when an individual or group has multiple identifications that mark them as marginal, oppression is compounded. Thus already-marginalized poor people of color are placed even further on the margins if other aspects of their identity also mark them, such as sexual orientation, gender, disease.

The language of *margin* and *center* uses metaphors of space and place in understanding relationship. The center location is so considered because of its ability to enforce its dominance. Those at the margin, the borders, lack access to the center and its sources of power. Even though the language of marginality uses metaphors of space, those who are marginalized may be within close physical proximity to those in dominance, but remain "hidden in plain view," as one disabled woman described her experience. The marginalized who are more likely to present themselves for spiritual direction are not those on the far edges and borders of society but those who are *outsiders-within*.[2] These are people who possess the credentials for belonging, such as baptism, education, ordination, religious profession, socioeconomic status, and so on, but who because of other aspects of their identity, such as race, gender, sexual orientation, or disability, are excluded.

Outsiders-within are socially located at boundary spaces between the margin and the center. In and out at the same time, these are people who have an inside view of dominant society yet are denied full inclusion. They have characteristics of the marginal as well as the dominant. Assumptions of sameness are often made of them, and thus invisibility and muteness continues. Because we are so ill at ease with differences we may try to "equalize" everyone by ignoring the significant ways in which we differ. Examples of this are spiritual directors who say, "I don't see color, only the person," or, "To me she is not a lesbian but simply a human being." Statements like these and the attitudes they represent are ways of refusing to see and hear and appreciate the particular experience and identity of the marginal person. The normative experience of the dominant is superimposed and becomes the lens through which all are approached. Thus invisibility is maintained.

DANGERS FOR DIRECTORS

Because spiritual directors are often not familiar with the concrete lives of marginalized communities and individuals, when difference is acknowledged there is a tendency to go to one of two extremes. The first tendency is that the marginalized are seen as so foreign that they come to be seen as less than full human beings. The other extreme is that the marginalized are idealized and romanticized and seen, not as unique human beings, but only as representatives of groups. Their multidimensional experience and identity is flattened.

The first tendency can be seen in an example of a gay man in spiritual direction with a priest. The spiritual-direction relationship was well established so that there was trust between the directee and the director. The director knew of the directee's sexual orientation, and it had surfaced now and then in their sessions. However, when in one session the man spoke of the pleasure he took in sex with his life partner and how much their lovemaking meant to him, the spiritual director responded by telling him how foreign this experience was to hers. This ended the discussion, and the directee introduced a new topic. In a later peer consultation, the spiritual director mentioned how uncomfortable she was with her directee's discussion of taking pleasure in sex with his partner. I wondered with her what it was about this man's telling of sexual pleasure that made her so uncomfortable and made his experience seem so foreign to her. After some exploration she came to see that even though on an intellectual level she could affirm same-sex love and sexuality, this concrete and specific story of sexual love between two men threatened her. Her heterosexism caused her to distance herself from the directee and to put his experience of love in a less than human, that is, less than normative, heterosexual category. She came to see that she could indeed identify with this man's appreciation of his sexual relationship, as she enjoyed a satisfying sexual relationship with her husband. She was able to be present enough in a future discussion of her directee's sexual experience so as to reflect with him on the spiritual dimension of the sexual relationship.

An example of the second tendency, romanticizing and idealizing the marginal person, also comes from ignorance of their concrete lives and thus from seeing them as representatives of exotic groups. An African American man with advanced degrees in theology, which had been disclosed in initial conversations, was somewhat taken aback when the spiritual director expressed her appreciation of the man's theological insight by asking if he were self-educated. The director apparently had created an imaginary story of a man who had come to the theological insight he displayed by his solitary struggle rather than through the formal education of which she had been informed. Another example is of a Hispanic woman religious with several degrees from prestigious universities. The director, upon hearing of her educational background, remarked that she was a woman who obviously always got what she wanted. In both of these examples it is likely that if the directee were from dominant culture the directors would have admired them for their hard work and intelligence. Instead they were seen as romanticized representatives of their particular culture who came to their achievements through special privilege or heroic accomplishment.

It is important that the director be aware of and sensitive to the crucial role of the relationship in the spiritual-direction process. This is especially so when the director and directee are from different social locations. In peer consultation with spiritual directors concerning direction with marginalized persons, I have noticed a tendency of directors to overestimate their own importance in the lives of those to whom they minister and thus to distort the spiritual-direction relationship. I have heard directors, especially in long-term and at times intense spiritual-direction relationships, say, "I am the only one he has," or, "I am the only one who understands." But concrete assessments in exploration with the director reveal that their fantasies of rescue are based not on the directee's need and real situation but on the distortions of the director. Because spiritual directors are so often unfamiliar with the lives of the marginal, it is easy for them to overlook the rich relationships and sources of support and vitality that such persons may have in their lives. Even though a gay man may not be in a committed relationship, a rich network of friends may be what he considers family. A single mother may have rich and rewarding relationships and support with her children from community and extended family that the director may discount, even though the directee mentions them in sessions. A director's bias as to what constitutes family may blind him or her to other ways of being family.

When these distorted types of relationships are developed in spiritual direction, the focus shifts to the relationship itself rather than to discernment of God's presence in the person's life. The director can become very curious about this life that seems so different than his or her own. The directee in these situations is often ministering to the spiritual director's needs and may eventually leave spiritual direction because he is aware that he is not truly being seen or listened to. An overestimation of the spiritual-direction relationship and overidentification with the directee minimizes or destroys the opportunity for the directee to do what he or she came to direction for—discernment of God's presence and movement in their life. While there may be other relationships in which friendship and support are found, the gift of sacred time to focus on discerning the movement of the Spirit in one's life is missed if this is not kept as the clear purpose in spiritual direction.

In our day of heightened awareness of diversity and multiculturalism, our very efforts to include marginalized people can sometimes heighten a sense of invisibility and alienation. Physical proximity does not automatically address structural racism and injustice, nor does it insure understanding. In our postmodern awareness of multiple centers and of the relativity of the metaphor of margin and center, we often leave out issues of power. An awareness of how identity is formed by culture and of the multiple ways in which various cultures order and shape the lives of its members has led to the dismantling of claims to universality. All locations are equalized, while not addressing histories and current practices of privilege and oppression. Even though past categories have been much too rigid or used as ways of excluding people, history and current practice cannot be erased or changed with a change in abstract theory. People with certain characteristics are still excluded from mainstream locations on the basis of these characteristics. We abolish these categories in the abstract whereas, in practice, actual power relationships remain.

It is claimed that all stories are of value, and indeed they are, but all stories have not been valued. An increasing sense of the relativity of cultural and social locations has led to the idea of fixed identities and locations being questioned. Much of the questioning of fixed identity has come as marginal people move toward the center and claim voice and visibility. As they do so the power of their corporate voice can be negated by denying the very basis of their shared identity. The common experience of exclusion can serve as a basis both of identity and community. Without this sense of shared history and common struggle, marginal people are left isolated not only from relationships to those in dominant locations but also from one another, and thus are even more vulnerable and powerless.

Directors as Witness

Those who would be present as a witness in spiritual direction to those on the margin are, in some sense, themselves required to shift locations, or else the marginalized, even those within physical proximity, will remain invisible and inaudible. What one witnesses depends on one's location as well as one's openness to where one moves. It is not uncommon for witnesses to the same event to give conflicting testimony. Before moving social locations, or even grasping the need to move, one must first identify where one presently stands. It is easy to see others' social location without realizing that we too stand in a particular location. To begin a ministry of spiritual direction with the marginalized without first locating ourselves and, in some measure, shifting our location, may mean that our ministry simply maintains relationships of dominance under the guise of ministry, which means that we are bearing *false witness*. In such a case, the ministry of spiritual direction becomes a tool to enforce and maintain "business as usual." We do not deliberately have to choose the structures that maintain hierarchies of margin and center in order for us to participate in their perpetuation. Structures of dominance are so prevalent that they most often go unnoticed and, thus, unquestioned. They make up the very atmosphere in which we exist and are thus a part of our assumed world. A person raised in our society does not have to choose to be racist or heterosexist. We are born into and socialized into a world in which the rightness of these positions of dominance is assumed. On the contrary, the director who wishes to be a witness does have to be intentional in order to change practices that enforce these power-based biases.

I become aware of the lenses through which I view the world when I encounter someone who sees my world through different lenses. When I take intern ministry students through my parish and community, the students' questions and observations make me aware of just how much I assume about how things are done here. Sometimes my gut reaction to the interns' questions is, "How ignorant this student is." We all have our biases that lead us to the tendency of seeing our way as *the* way. The serious difficulty comes when those in positions of authority and power enforce their biases as the norm.

All spiritual direction begins with the director in a stance of listening and observation. This looking and listening is especially important in spiritual direction with the marginalized. Not only are those who present themselves to the director to be listened to, but it is also necessary that the director be listening to himself or herself in order to observe the lenses through which they view the other before them. Previous judgments are observed and then suspended as the person is listened to. The director listens with an awareness of his or her location, noticing how she or he is responding. The director observes the ways in which personal assumptions may devalue the person.

In the early spiritual-direction sessions it may be helpful to observe with the directee how the directee and director differ from one another in gender, race, culture, sexual orientation, or handicap. In an effort to seem open and welcoming, the director may minimize important distinguishing characteristics of the person. Do not overlook differences of race, class, gender, sexual orientation, or handicap, but use them as an opportunity to explore their meaning in the spiritual-direction process. Ask how the directee views coming to someone so different from themselves for spiritual direction. If the directee does not choose to explore the question at that time, at least they know that it is acceptable and appropriate to discuss these things in the context of the spiritual-direction relationship when they choose. They then know that it is not required to ignore important aspects of themselves in order to enter this relationship.

In listening to directees from marginal groups it is important to try to understand how the person understands the world. Rather than instructing the person on what spiritual direction is, consider asking their thoughts and sharing mutual understandings before negotiating how you will work together. The director may at first feel intrusive and indeed needs to avoid an excessive curiosity that objectifies the person. However, genuine openness and interest can provide the space in which the marginal person can tell their story from their unique perspective.

Those on the borders may be without voice, but they do hear and see. Genuinely witnessing eyes and ears offer the promise of revealing what they have heard and seen from the unique location of the edge. The perspective from the margin affords the ability to see and hear things not seen or heard at the center. Perhaps one reason it is difficult to see and listen to those from the margins is the possibility of their perception bringing our own view of the world into question. Directors can be threatened by the viewpoint of those whose lives are so unfamiliar. Opening one's eyes and ears, indeed opening oneself, is risky. Becoming witness to real pain and injustice may cause one to question, perhaps for the first time, the sense of the world as a just and orderly place. Looking at the injustice that pushes people to edges and hearing the voice of those at that location will change how one understands oneself, the world, and God. Drawing close to those who have been kept at a distance not only brings assumptions about the identity of the other into question, but one's own identity also becomes less sure. "An identity is questioned only when it is menaced, as when the mighty begin to fall, or when the wretched begin to rise, or when the stranger enters the gates, never thereafter to be a stranger: the stranger's presence making you the stranger, less to the stranger than to yourself."[3]

ALLOWING STORIES TO UNFOLD

Often in spiritual direction, those who are not used to being listened to will tell marvelously rich life stories, only to end with an apology for taking up time. Marginalized people know what to keep silent about and what to keep concealed. It takes time and practiced courage to release skills that have enabled survival, no less than shame and fear about "secrets." Beginning steps are filled with gaps and silences, and so much is left unspoken. But with practice and a developing trust the story takes on life as the person becomes more and more present and available to himself, speaking himself into fuller life.

Being a witness does not mean being passive. A discerning mode of asking and attentiveness is important. For the directee, simply to tell one's story and to be listened to is a healing and liberating practice. To have that story received with attentive presence can in and of itself be the beginning of a transformation of the story. We come to understand our lives by telling our stories again and again. In each telling we hear and see nuances that we may have missed before. In the telling and retelling revelation and meaning unfolds. But to tell our story we need ears willing to listen to us and eyes willing to see us. A story takes on life in the telling, and a life releases its meaning in the telling of its story. Our story makes us newly present to ourselves, to others, and to God. But an untold story is not a story.

We need people to see us into visibility and to hear us into speech. We need witnesses. In having someone listen to me, I listen more attentively to myself. Sometimes the director may feel very lost as the directee tells her story. There may seem to be a lack of cohesion to the story, or significant holes and gaps. This may be not only because of an unfamiliarity of the director with the lives of the marginalized, but it may be that the person has become a stranger to her own story. The director's attentive listening, exploration, and presence can witness to God's presence in the recovered story and to the ongoing mystery of the directee's being in God.

Those who have experienced trauma have the trauma magnified by the lack of witnesses to their experience. It is not uncommon in direction to hear people tell of violation and loss in youth and adulthood and to weep because there was no one there for them. No one who believed them, no one to see and hear them. Eyes and ears were turned away or closed. When others turn away from our experience, we are more likely also to turn from our experience. This is especially true in childhood, in which one of the roles of parents and adults in crisis situations is to interpret experience for the young. Even the most attentive parents and caretakers, however, cannot protect children from all loss and trauma, but they can buffer some of the pain by witnessing the child's distress, by their reassuring presence, and by rituals and stories that put the trauma and loss into context. The adult witness gives the assurance that this situation can be lived through. It is a presence that gives hope. Trauma and loss in youth as well as in adulthood are painful, but they can be unbearable if combined with the sense of being alone, the sense of no one understanding, no one seeing, no one believing, no one witnessing. "All you who pass this way, look and see: is there any sorrow like the sorrow that afflicts me?" (Lamentations 1:12).

Too often marginalized people, some who have experienced trauma, but all who have experienced not being listened to and not being seen, have this experience repeated in the present by spiritual directors who are blind and deaf to their experience. Opportunities for healing are missed by unempathetic questioning of the person's experience: "You're much too sensitive"; "Are you sure you're not just imagining racism?"; "Why are you so hostile?"; "I don't know what you're talking about, we're all Christian here?"; "You've got to be patient, it takes time for things to change." Such statements and questions do not open the directee to exploration and appreciation of his or her experience but bring their perception into question. The role of the director as witness is to listen and to look, not just at reported facts but also at how the person understands what happens in his or her life. This does not mean that the director ignores his or her own perceptions. But it does mean that the director stays with the unfolding story, not stopping, not offering premature closure or resolution. This takes patience and faith in the story one is witnessing come to life. Patient listening also provides the marginal person, who may be used to leaving out significant pieces of his experience to make it acceptable to someone else, space and time to speak his unique truth.

Sometimes directors may hear stories of profound suffering from trauma, loss, and oppression and yet full of references to God, spirits, and saints. This way of looking at experience may be very unfamiliar to the director and may move him or her to put the directee's experience into familiar psychological diagnostic categories. In the context of spiritual direction, use of these categories may not be very helpful, as they can prevent the director from seeing and appreciating deeper meanings to experience. The director may inaccurately see these stories as denial of extremely painful situations, whereas they are ways in which people seek to discover meaning in very difficult circumstances. Denial as a psychological defense protects one from fragmentation by not seeing what is before one, whereas the search for the meaning of experience explores the situation, looking for God's presence and purposes even in that which threatens one's integrity. As one woman threatened with serious disease said: "I don't know why I'm going through this but I know there is a reason." Upon exploration she said, "I am going through this, this is happening, but there is a reason for it." It is not a closing of one's eyes to what is before one; it is a way of seeing through difficult circumstances to deeper meaning. Job, who cannot accept the offered explanations for his suffering, still refuses to accept the world as meaningless and continues to search for deeper meaning to what has overcome him. In his suffering he affirms, "Even now, in fact, my witness is in heaven, and he that vouches for me is on high" (Job 16:19).

THE GIFTS OF THE MARGIN

Although there is pain and suffering at the margin, it is also home, also a place of joy and love. Marginal space, however, is always a site of struggle. A director's lack of appreciation of the life context of the directee can risk turning the directee's attention away from the margins she inhabits, and where the director assumes God to be absent. Spiritual directors can find themselves pointing the directee toward "the latest" ways of prayer and meditation in expensive workshops and retreats for which the directee has neither time nor money. Meanwhile, the presence of God in the life and struggles of the person is ignored. While everyone needs time and space for reflection, such "retreat" has as its purpose a return to where one lives with renewed awareness of God's presence. Once marginal space is seen as a place to be explored and not so much escaped, reflection reveals the margin as a place of rich possibility. Marginal space is no longer seen as a place where God is absent but a place full of divine revelation. Such space does not need to be romanticized to be appreciated, but struggle itself is revealed as a means of God's presence in the world.

The center is the place of the settled, the predictable, the routine, and, in some measure, the closed. Marginal space is desert space. With reverent exploration, space that is often viewed as the place of absence becomes not only a place of presence but also one of rich possibility not seen from the center. Those without access to the usual sources of power are open to alternate, new sources of power, unlooked for and thus unseen by those thought of as powerful. Perhaps this might be why Jesus could not perform miracles at home, but instead manifested his works and power on the edges, in the wilderness, with outsiders (Luke 4:22–30).

Spiritual direction with the marginalized has as its goal the discernment of God in one's life where it is actually lived. Direction is not an escape from the realities of marginal existence. If it is seen as such, then direction is the place to find solace and peace and the energy with which to cope with one's life. All of these are indeed fine qualities to discover in direction, but when they become the sole focus, the directee is prevented from accessing sources of power that may enable them to move beyond coping to participation in the transformation of all space. It is extremely important for directors with the marginalized to aid them in coming to a new awareness of themselves. If the director views the person in the same way as the dominant culture, then they are not only unable to assist them in the work of transformation but are a hindrance to that work and harmful to the welfare of the directee.

At times, marginal people, especially those in outsider-within positions, may incorrectly see themselves as the source of many of their troubles, when in reality the trouble may originate in their oppressive circumstances. A significant task for the marginal person is to reject dominant society's judgment as to what is and what is not of value. This is especially crucial in that marginalized people are of such little value to the dominant that internalizing the dominant judgment of oneself is self-destructive. It is crucial that the directee and the director are able to distinguish between transcending the self and destruction or negation of the self. Transcendence expands and takes one beyond oneself, even though it may seem to threaten the self. Destruction of the self diminishes the self and threatens to annihilate the self.

The arrangement of margin and center is not simply the result of conscious choices and actions by individuals but instead is systemic in institutional structures. Tragically, these arrangements are often so common that they are "invisible" to those in positions of dominance and privilege, and sometimes even to those oppressed by them. The struggle to identify and dismantle systemic oppression requires that the marginal person look at and speak about things ignored by others. It is a struggle that destroys false peace. It is not uncommon to hear from those in outsider-within positions, such as seminarians or members of religious communities who are in a minority, a resentment of extra work that their confreres did not seem to have to do. They found themselves having constantly to work at integrating multiple aspects of their identity for which their seminary or religious community either did not offer social support or devalued. There is a strong but invisible social pressure to keep silent about what one sees and feels. As one person in this situation said: "Everything is fine if I don't bring up the difficult subjects." A director who encourages "peace at any price," and who sees the source of conflict within the individual rather than in his encounter with oppressive circumstances, is in fact perpetuating these oppressive situations. At the same time, it is important for the director to realize that not every marginal person within dominant institutions has internalized the negative judgment of that dominant structure. It is crucial that the director witness the struggle of the marginalized and encourage the directee not to abandon the struggle through premature closure or by choosing one aspect of their identity over another. This intense inner work is the very place of encounter with God.

I have been involved in spiritual direction and Christian formation as a leader and participant for more than thirty-five years. I have been in spiritual direction with directors who not only did not understand my context but who also found it of little value. I also have been director for people from the edges, people of color, gay people, poor people, who previously had been in spiritual-direction relationships that did not value them and did them great harm. Once these people were in direction with a director who understood and valued their marginal location and its unique challenges, they made great progress.

I have also known and consulted with directors from dominant locations who can and do excellent spiritual direction with marginalized people. These are people who have purposely moved from places of dominance, from the center, to place themselves in the gaps where they witness what they could never have witnessed by simply remaining in their dominant locations. Such persons do the necessary hard work of repentance and conversion in order to have baptized ears and eyes. The real question is not whether people from dominant locations should do spiritual direction with the marginalized, but how they will do it and whether they will do it.

In Hebrew scriptures, God is witness to those who are oppressed and who have no other witness. In addressing Moses from the burning bush, God says: "I have seen the affliction of my people who are in Egypt and have heard their cry" (Exodus 3:7). To be a witness to the marginalized is to imitate God, who is witness to those who are otherwise without witness. God not only sees, but God responds to their cry: "I have come down to rescue them" (3:8), "I am sending you [Moses] to Pharaoh" (3:10).

Being a witness to the marginalized is also to align oneself with them as does God. The beginning is seeing and hearing what is most often not heard and seen. It begins in witnessing.

Spiritual direction with the marginalized must include developing practices of a just life and of advocacy on behalf of the marginalized. Witnessing demands testimony and participation in the struggle for justice. This can become a misunderstood role for spiritual directors, for spiritual directors do not speak for the marginalized but instead listen them into voice. This is a ministry of and to the church, for marginal people are needed by the church at large. The voices of those most often excluded are the ones most needed. Jesus reminds us that the rejected stones may well be the keystones, and he identifies himself with them.

Chapter Eight

COMPANIONS AT THE THRESHOLD:
SPIRITUAL DIRECTION WITH THE DYING

Margaret Guenther

———— •◆• ————

One of my treasures is a musty old prayer book, published in Philadelphia in 1856 and purchased at a country yard sale. After the usual intercessions and thanksgivings, its order for family evening worship concludes with a prayer for God's protection throughout the night, ending with this petition: "Make us ever mindful of the time when we shall lie down in the dust; and grant us grace always to live in such a state, that we shall never be afraid to die; so that, living and dying, we may be thine." There is something appealing in this matter-of-fact acceptance of death's inevitability and very comforting in the assurance that, dead or alive, we belong to God. For the faithful a century and a half ago, indeed for the faithful reaching back to the earliest days of the church, there could be no question that dying was part of the spiritual journey and that a "good death" was the goal of life. Even in my own childhood, death was an accepted fact, and I prayed nightly, "If I should die before I wake, I pray Thee, Lord, my soul to take." If death was not exactly a friend, it was a respected and awaited visitor. My grandparents died at home, in their own beds. It was a family affair. My grandfather was "laid out" in the little alcove just off the dining room; I still remember eating dinner just a few feet from his open coffin as if it were the most natural thing in the world.

Contrast this with our present time: despite our society's fondness for depictions of violent death in the name of entertainment, we live in denial that our own lives, *real* lives, are finite. Death happens on television, fictionalized or in the nightly news. Death happens to other people, preferably to those far away and unknown to us. Dying should take place offstage. If it is invisible, we can pretend that it never happened, or at least will never happen to us. The less said the better.

Despite the sensitivity and compassion fostered by the hospice movement, for many in the industrialized West at the turn of the century, dying has become a lonely and impersonal business, sadly disconnected from living. All too often it is seen a failure of medical technology and a defeat of scientific ingenuity, instead of an inevitable next step, the crossing of life's second threshold. This is all too often a silent passage: a lot of stories are never told, a lot of questions are never asked, a lot of words are never uttered. Yet the journey across the threshold deserves to be honored and celebrated. There is work here for spiritual directors!

But what are we talking about? As I understand and practice it, spiritual direction is a ministry, not a profession. It consists of one person's (the director) being prayerfully attentive to another (the directee) as together they seek to discern the action of the Holy Spirit in the latter's life. The director serves as holy listener and spiritual midwife, willingly putting herself aside and seeking nothing from the directee. Anything of deep concern is suitable material for the direction session, as there is inevitably a "God-component" in all human experience—which might, of course, be experienced as a (perceived) absence of God. This is a covenanted relationship, with meetings scheduled at regular intervals. Impeccable confidentiality must be maintained.

To be sure, this is a definition of traditional spiritual direction. Prayerfully attending the dying has its own distinctiveness. The "director" may be pastor, parish visitor, a hospital or nursing home chaplain, or simply a good friend. The relationship may never be identified as "spiritual direction" per se, but it is distinguished by the quality of loving but disinterested attentiveness characteristic of direction. This is not psychotherapy or pastoral counseling, but a ministry of prayerful presence.

Spiritual direction with the dying has its own time frame. Ordinarily, we think of the direction relationship as long-term, extending over a period of years, even decades, rather than months. We expect the relationship to develop slowly as trust builds steadily over time. Ordinarily, too, the meetings are spaced to allow time for the directee to reflect and do his own work. I never meet more frequently than once a month, while an interval of six weeks or even three months is acceptable. When we work with the dying, however, such an expansive use of time is an impossible luxury. Perhaps we will companion the directee for months or even years, but often our work must be compressed into a much briefer period. As death approaches, we meet more frequently, weekly or even daily. The meetings may be very brief, just a few minutes of conversation, prayer, or shared silence, but there is an intensity of focus that is absent from more leisurely, traditional direction.

One of the foundational truths of the hospice movement, as articulated by Dame Cecily Saunders,[1] is the fact that the dying are not dead, but *living*. This is so simple as to seem self-evident, yet it is easy to forget. The dying are not objects, to be minimized or patronized. They are infinitely more than their deteriorating bodies. At the same time, they are living in a very special way, poised on the threshold. In most areas of their lives, they have lost autonomy and have often become dependent on others for basic, often intimate services. They are inescapable reminders of Jesus' uncomfortable words to Peter at the end of John's Gospel:

———•◆•———

And further, I tell you this in very truth: when you were young you fastened your belt about you and walked where you chose; but when you are old you will stretch out your arms, and a stranger will bind you fast, and carry you where you have no wish to go. (John 21:18, NEB)

———•◆•———

This is part of the gospel message we would rather not hear and certainly not experience. Like Jesus given over to his captors and ultimately to his crucifixion, the dying have been "delivered up." They live in awareness of their smallness and impotence in the sight of God. They have entered a new place and are living in a new way. Just as we can read books and take childbirth-preparation classes to ready ourselves for the other great spiritual experience of birth giving, so we can study death and acquaint ourselves with its physical processes. But no amount of study or practice can replicate the actual circumstances at either threshold. The dying are in a place where we have not been. As spiritual directors, we approach them with reverence and respect.

As an Episcopal priest, I am writing from a Christian perspective. Spiritual direction is not the exclusive province of the clergy, however, and not all the people with whom we work will be faithful churchgoers. While my ministry now is in an exclusively Christian context, in the past I have worked comfortably with Jewish residents in a nursing home. Our mutual respect enabled us to achieve warm and candid relationships despite our fundamental differences. My point is this: death is a profoundly theological issue for all of us, not simply for the religiously observant. It is no longer possible to avoid questions of deep meaning. What is happening to me? Why am I suffering? Does my life make any sense? What about all my unfinished business, the things I never said or did or asked? What about the times I wish I had said, "I'm sorry," or, "Thank you"? Do I matter? What will happen next? What will it be like? Is there a God?

Whether we are lay, ordained, or members of religious orders, we are not likely to minister among people with extensive theological vocabularies. And even those so proficient verbally are likely to save the fancy words for easier times. We may minister to those who deny any deep faith and would claim only a nodding acquaintance with God. We might encounter some spunky agnostics and a few frightened atheists. It has been my experience that many good and faithful people tend not to value their spiritual experience, indeed the heroism of their endurance. They tend, rather, to see themselves as "ordinary," leaving the spiritual realm to the clergy, if not to identified saints and mystics. Most people have never had the opportunity to talk about themselves—their doubts, their fears, their faith. Whatever form it might take, spiritual direction when they are near death can open new doors for them and reveal new vistas.

The spiritual director can bring the gift of patience to the conversation. Although time may be short and death imminent, there should be no sense of hurry. Very sick and very frail people often speak slowly; indeed, even minimal speech may tax their strength. There may be long pauses, repetitions, or seeming loss of continuity. It is our task to listen carefully without revealing restlessness. Even the kindest caregivers are usually in a hurry: this is unavoidable since few patients have the luxury of round-the-clock private nursing. Even if we are in a hurry too, fitting our visit into a crowded schedule, we can create a sense of spaciousness. This may simply be a matter of posture. Just sitting down at the bedside, instead of hovering, implies that there is plenty of time. Our speech and our breathing, too, can indicate that we are comfortable with a slower pace. We must be willing to wait, comfortable in long pauses, and never guilty of rushing to complete the other's hesitantly uttered sentences.

This kind of listening is perhaps the greatest gift we can bring to the dying, for it suggests that we value the person we are with. It can be a prayerful activity even when no prayer is spoken, indeed when no words are exchanged. This is passionate listening, passionate because we care deeply about what we are doing. At the same time, it is passive, in that we are able to put ourselves out of the way, to attend carefully but not judgmentally. And it is compassionate, for we are not afraid to enter into another's pain, fear, and loneliness. A spiritual-direction meeting with a dying person is no casual visit, but an exercise of ministry even if we stay for only a few minutes.

So what do we talk about? As in more traditional spiritual direction, I come with no agenda, for part of the gift of passionate and compassionate listening is freedom for the directee to speak from the heart. When I am working with the dying, I take my cues from them. After a modicum of trust and affection has been established, most people are more than ready to talk about what really matters—especially if the spiritual director is the one person able to deal candidly with their impending death. Family members may be too grief-stricken to accept this reality, and too many physicians still see death as defeat, an enemy to be battled, not the next step on the journey. It is no comfort for the spiritual director to exude false cheer or to minimize the gravity of the situation.

It is important to let ourselves be guided by the dying person. The depth and quality of the conversation will vary from day to day and visit to visit. At times, denial may be all that keeps the patient going. Then the director is gentle, not enthusiastically supporting optimistic illusions, but quietly present. I am convinced that most dying people know that they are dying. If they want the respite of a little denial and pretense, it is not our task to hammer home the truth. Some days shared silence will say more than any number of words, and some days the conversation will stay at a very superficial level—pleasant and friendly enough but scarcely qualifying as spiritual direction. The dying person can control so little in his life at this point. We need to let go of any need to accomplish or achieve in our time together. Receptive presence is enough!

There will, of course, be occasions when the directee wants to talk openly of death. His death. Her death. In my experience, there comes a time when death is no longer the enemy, and the dying person is not so much defeated as accepting. Then we hear such statements as "I've lived long enough" or "I'm tired" or "I'm ready." Death is no longer so much to be feared as pain, degrading helplessness, incontinence, or loss of mental powers.

If the director is frightened by the fact of mortality and, most particularly, unwilling to confront the inevitability of his own eventual demise, he will find ways to avoid these conversations by missing cues or by failing to hear the implicit, but unvoiced, requests: "I want to talk about this. Ask me to explain the hints I've just dropped. Let's enter this conversational arena together—I've made you an opening." More crassly, the unwilling director will simply change the subject. Needless to say, such spiritual direction is no direction at all, and the dying person is ill served.

No matter how many books we have read or courses we have taken (or taught!), we are the neophytes here because the directee knows more about dying than we possibly can. We can, however, offer a safe place, where it is all right to weep and where *anything* may be said.

Not everyone is comfortable with "God talk," nor—as noted—does everyone have the vocabulary. Yet issues of deep meaning, the ultimate spiritual questions of life and death, can be discussed in ordinary language. Indeed, a specialized vocabulary can be an impediment, and stereotyped expressions can mask true feelings. If the directee feels the need to impress us with her exemplary piety, we won't get far. Her lips may say, "I know that God will never send me more than I can bear," but the prayer in the heart is one of outrage: "God, you bastard!"

We listen carefully, too, for what is not said, noting the great empty places. What is being avoided? Is it time for a gentle question; indeed, is a gentle question expected? Or should we bide our time until the directee is ready? There is no recipe here but, rather, careful discernment case by case and day by day.

Since dying is a part of living and living a part of dying, the directee will continue working toward wholeness right down to her last breath. Relationships with people long dead are not dead at all; there remains much to be resolved. This is a time for memories, joyful and painful. Childhood can seem as immediate as last week, and unhealed wounds continue to hurt. It is our task to be caring but disinterested listeners, open to everything and taking everything seriously. It is not our task to talk people out of their anger, disappointment, or fears. It is no comfort to the dying person to hear her story minimized, to be offered such shoddy comfort as, "That was a long time ago," or, "Surely that can't matter now—you can't still be angry after all these years." I have sat with aged people near death who were still dealing with childhood sibling rivalry, abusive or neglectful parents, and the tragic, untimely loss of spouse or child. The sense of time is distorted—or perhaps clarified—when death is near; and past and present melt together.

We will encounter dying people who have been deeply hurt by the church and feel themselves separated from God. They are angry with the church and often angry with God. It is easier to acknowledge anger with a fallible institution, however, than to admit rage at a (perceived) neglectful and punitive God. If the relationship with the spiritual director is comfortable and trust-filled, conversation can be candid. The directee has got past the place of saying what he hopes will please us, of using language that is not really his own. Now we can help pick apart the strands: what is lingering resentment at slights and hurts in the Christian community, and what is a deep alienation from God? Gently, we can remind the directee that God is infinitely more than the people and clergy of the parish. We may need to offer repeated reassurance: "The God to whom all hearts are open, all desires known, and from whom no secrets are hid already knows how you feel. The God who made you and loves you can take just about anything you can dish out. That God can absorb your anger just as a loving parent goes on loving a defiant four-year-old or a rebellious adolescent." Here the Psalms are a good resource. Almost everyone knows the Twenty-third, but it can feel like bitter irony to offer "The Lord is my shepherd; I shall not want" to the dying person who feels cast off, tormented, and deprived. Psalm Twenty-two speaks with quite a different voice:

> *My God, my God, why have you forsaken me?*
> *and are so far from my cry*
> *and from the words of my distress?*

> *O my God, I cry in the daytime, but you do not answer;*
> *by night as well, but I find no rest.*[2]

Psalm Eighty-eight is even more powerful, especially the closing verses:

> *LORD, why have you rejected me?*
> *why have you hidden your face from me?*

> *Ever since my youth, I have been wretched and at the point of death;*
> *I have borne your terrors with a troubled mind.*

> *Your blazing anger has swept over me;*
> *your terrors have destroyed me;*

> *They surround me all day long like a flood;*
> *they encompass me on every side.*

> *My friend and my neighbor you have put away from me,*
> *and darkness is my only companion.*

If nothing else, such psalms offer a strong reminder that scripture is not necessarily nice and that "negative" emotions have their place in prayer. Our hope, of course, is that the dying person move beyond this painful place of anger and desolation; but acknowledgment of hurt and rage is the first step.

More tragic and troubling than directees who are angry with God are those who believe themselves cast out and unworthy of love. They believe in God, even in the fact of God's love, but they are convinced that it does not include them. Sometimes they are burdened by guilt or shame from actions committed long ago. Often, though, they are filled simply with a sense of their own worthlessness—why should God care about *them,* flawed and fallible as they are? When we work with such people, we can try to make sure that they are able to believe in *our* love and faithfulness even if they can't be sure that they merit love from a most probably wrathful God with very high standards. We can mirror God's love even if the dying person can't believe in it.

In spiritual direction with the dying, we will hear confessions, regardless of our tradition and our ecclesial status. When I worked in a hospital before my ordination, I was scrupulous about offering to call a priest—Roman Catholic or Anglican—to celebrate the sacrament of reconciliation. Sometimes my offer would be accepted, but more frequently the sick person "just wanted to talk," to be heard without fear of condemnation. It was time to let go of a burden, carried perhaps for decades. The words needed to be said, aloud and in the presence of another. All baptized persons have the right, indeed the obligation, to declare God's forgiveness to the truly contrite. While this is not the same as sacramental absolution, it is an essential part of spiritual direction with the dying. For the person nearing death it is more than sufficient. As trusted friends and prayerful listeners, we are safe repositories of the story.

The fact of God's loving forgiveness may be difficult for the directee to accept. Just as we so easily feel that *everyone else* merits God's love, we can persuade ourselves that, however minimal our offense, we are beyond forgiveness. It is important for the dying person to be able to let go of the burden of the past. I find that scripture is a great help here, especially the story of Peter, whose sin of betrayal rivals that of Judas. In the last chapter of John's Gospel, his three denials of Jesus are balanced and eradicated by his three avowals of love. It is clear that he is forgiven. "Feed my lambs," Jesus says. "Tend my sheep. Feed my sheep. Get over it, and get on with it." The story of the prodigal in Luke's Gospel is also powerful: the prodigally generous father runs to meet his returning son before he has heard a word of repentance.

We need to listen carefully to discern the distinction between guilt and shame, and then to point out that distinction to the directee. We are guilty of our sins, willful behavior that separates us from God. Shame is something quite different. We may be ashamed of our own actions—stupid, silly, embarrassing, but not sinful. More commonly, though, shame is laid on us by others and is quite beyond our control. The most striking example of this is the nearly overwhelming shame felt by victims of sexual abuse. Both shame and guilt can be a ponderous burden; but it helps to know the difference, for the directee to be able to say, "This was my fault, and I'm sorry!" or, on the other hand, "This has felt horrible for years, but it's not my fault, and I didn't bring it on myself."

Most spiritual directors are kindly people and have a natural inclination to bring comfort by minimizing. So we say, "That's not really so bad, and I'm sure that you didn't really mean harm," or, "It was such a long time ago. Can't you just forget about it?" We must remember that anything that burdens the mind and heart of the directee over the years and decades, however trivial the offenses and hurts might seem to us, is to be taken seriously. If we do otherwise, we do not bring comfort, but diminishment.

Since spiritual direction is an act of worship framed in prayer, however much the traditional practices might be adapted for ministry with the dying, prayer lies at its heart. Prayer is what it's all about! So we pray together whenever we meet. Here, as always, it is good to let ourselves by guided by the directee. Some people are comfortable praying aloud; others feel anxious and put on the spot. For some a time of shared silence is all that is needed. Others look forward to prayer by the director, either healing prayers "from the book" or spontaneously. We quickly learn what is right for each person. I often ask, "What shall we pray for?" The answer is almost always for simple things—a night of decent sleep, an even modest respite from pain, the courage to face a new day, consolation for the loved ones. Simple things, but life at the threshold has become marvelously simplified.

I always pray for healing, even when death is imminent. Healing, after all, is not synonymous with cure. Rather, healing means the restoration of wholeness; and death is often the only restorer of ravaged bodies. So we pray for healing of body, which means respite from physical pain and deterioration, and for healing of relationships and memories, that all the old hurts may be let go and all the old wounds healed.

Old and familiar prayers bring comfort. Even people seemingly beyond speech join in the recitation of familiar psalms or the Our Father. When I taught in a seminary, I urged my students to equip themselves with a King James Bible and the 1928 *Book of Common Prayer*. That generation will die out soon, but there are still many faithful people who have the old words engraved on their hearts. In my nursing home ministry, many of the residents were Roman Catholic. When he was dying, Jimmy, a tough, working-class

Irishman, begged me to recite the Prayer before the Crucifix with him. I'd never heard of it, but a friend supplied me with a little book of popular devotions. When we said the prayer together, it was hard to picture Jimmy as a clean-scrubbed altar boy assisting at early Mass, but I was reasonably sure that he had not even thought of the prayer during the hard-working, hard-drinking years since then. Similarly, I came to love the Hail Mary from saying bedtime prayers with Anna, an ancient little woman whose body had simply worn out. At first, I winced when we said, "Pray for us sinners, now and in the hour of our death." That hour, for Anna, could have come before the dawn.

Old hymns are another path to prayer. Studies show that music reaches us when the spoken word does not. I don't sing well, indeed I don't sing at all, but I shall never forget a Good Friday nearly twenty years ago. I was on overnight duty in the hospital and stopped in to visit a man who was scarcely expected to live through the night. His grown children, neither of them observant Christians but brought up in the church, were with him. David, the dying man, rallied a bit and said, "I want you all to sing the *Nunc dimittis*."

Fortunately, it was an Episcopal hospital, and I was able to find a hymnal; otherwise, the three of us would never have managed the same tune even if we could recall the words. Together we gathered around his bed in the bleak, crowded ward and sang—reasonably in tune:

> *Lord, now lettest thou thy servant depart in peace,*
> *according to thy word;*
> *For mine eyes have seen thy salvation,*
> *which thou has prepared before the face of all people,*
> *To be a light to lighten the Gentiles,*
> *and to be the glory of thy people Israel.*

David didn't say anything more. I left him with his children and continued on my rounds. I am convinced that it was no accident that he died at dawn two days later. We had prayed the right prayer together.

The visible and tangible can bring comfort, especially when words are difficult or impossible. I learned this from Anna along with the Hail Mary. I never saw her without her rosary wound around her gnarled, old hand. She literally had something to hold onto and look at, even when the words escaped her. Small copies of icons, an inexpensive wooden rosary, a palm-size cross or crucifix are excellent presents for the dying, much better than teddy bears or bouquets of balloons—although these have their place as well, bringing a touch of childlike joy to the sickroom.

Prayer with the dying is a good place for gentle touch. We can lay on hands as we pray for healing. We can hold hands lightly, positioning our hand so that the directee can disengage if he becomes fatigued or uncomfortable. Sometimes a kiss of greeting or farewell is appropriate, but sometimes not. As always, we take our cue from the directee.

Planning the funeral or memorial service can be a prayerful, but not gloomy, undertaking. Family members may wish to participate, but often they are grieving in anticipation and unable to accept the reality that one whom they love is dying. With the spiritual director, the dying person can revisit favorite hymns and scripture. Identifying what speaks to us most intimately is a kind of mini-review of our theology—not that the spiritual director would ever name it so. Often our favorites are unknown to those closest to us. I am quite sure, for example, that none of my children knows that "Be Thou My Vision" and "What Wondrous Love Is This" are my choice for my exit. Nor do they know that Psalm 84 promises me all that I can want.

I have spoken of family and caregivers. If the spiritual-direction relationship has time to grow and deepen, we will almost certainly come to know the people who are daily present in the dying person's life. They are very likely stressed and fatigued. As I have noted they are grieving already in anticipation, unless they are simply unable to accept that death is near. This is a great burden for the dying person, who may well feel the need to keep up the charade and put on a brave front. Family members can offer him a great gift when they yield to the inevitable and are able to say, "It's all right. We know that you're tired. It's all right to let go."

The members of the household may have no one to talk to and certainly no one to listen to them. As spiritual directors, we can be present to them, but always remembering that our first loyalty is to the dying person. As in "ordinary" spiritual direction, impeccable confidentiality must be maintained. It is not our role to report on the dying person's words or wishes, nor should we serve as messengers or manipulators. This is a time for families to draw close together and say the things they have neglected to say—"Thank you. I'm sorry. I love you." Our job here is to do our best and then get out of the way.

All spiritual direction is serious work, a holy obligation to be undertaken reverently, but companioning the dying has its very special qualities. We know that, barring miraculous reversals, the relationship will end in death. To put it crassly: all our "successes" will die, indeed sooner rather than later. This is in sharp contrast to the traditional direction relationship, which can endure and flourish for years, perhaps decades. Work with the dying is rich, for life on the threshold is very real. Work with the dying is also poignant, for we cannot avoid being deeply touched.

This is very much an embodied ministry. Typically, my picture of a spiritual-direction meeting shows two reasonably well-dressed people sitting in a softly lit room tastefully decorated with a few icons. Bodies are well groomed and under control. The physical realities of dying change all this. To my knowledge, no one dies so neatly as Judith Traherne in *Dark Victory* or so graciously as Melanie Wilkes in *Gone with the Wind*. We must remain aware of the innate dignity of the dying person, prevailing over the indignity of a deteriorating body. Again and again, when death is very near and the dying has been very hard, I feel that I have had a glimpse of the crucifixion—not just the agony, but the shame of the merciless exposure that is part of dying. There is an old saying, "Naked we come into the world, and naked we depart." I know now that, at least at the second threshold, this refers to much more than literal, bodily clothing.

As spiritual directors to the dying (or to anybody!) we must face ourselves and know ourselves. We must face the fact of our own mortality if we are to minister to those who are facing death. So the first step is to look deeply into our own soul and our own self. We will need to deal with our own strong feelings as the relationship develops. I have found in myself something akin to "survivor's guilt," especially when I am companioning someone my own age or younger. I remember most particularly the months with Jim, a brother priest nearly young enough to be my son. Cancer was destroying his body, and at the end he could neither eat nor speak. He was fed by a tube and communicated—painfully—by writing little notes. After each visit, I felt cheap, as if I were abandoning him to get on with my own pleasant and active life. I was comforted by Henri Nouwen's concept of a "ministry of absence." He must have experienced feelings similar to mine when he wrote:

———— • ◆ • ————

I am deeply convinced that there is a ministry in
which our leaving creates space for God's spirit and
in which, by our absence, God can become present in
a new way. There is an enormous difference between
an absence after a visit and an absence which is the
result of not coming at all.[3]

———— • ◆ • ————

He goes on to speak of "the importance of being sensitive to the last words we speak before we leave a room or house." I've never quite lost my twinges of guilt, but I have come to see the twinges for what they are: a mixture of genuine compassion and a prideful self-assurance that God cannot manage without my physical presence on the scene.

Having one's own spiritual director is a prerequisite for all who engage in this ministry, but those offering spiritual direction to the dying are in special need of support. Always mindful of the sacredness of our conversations and the necessity for confidentiality, we need a safe place to talk and pray about the joys and burdens of our work. It is false heroism to think that we can carry everything and everybody *forever*. Our spiritual director and our spiritual friends can help us let go without ever abandoning the trust that has been placed in us. I have learned not to be afraid of tears—tears shed by the dying person, tears we have shed together, and my own solitary tears. They are a great aid in letting go.

I am also learning not to promise more than I can deliver—I haven't quite mastered this, but I'm getting better at not promising too much. Traditional spiritual direction can be done very much by the book, with neatly spaced appointments. Direction with the dying calls for more flexible scheduling, and we need to be careful not to commit ourselves to more frequent visits than we can manage realistically. At the very least, though, the directee must always be sure that she is carried daily in our prayers.

Perhaps most importantly, I am not afraid to say, "I don't know." Death brings some big questions: Why me? Why now? Why do I have to suffer? Despite a fair amount of study and pondering, I haven't found any satisfactory answers to these questions. One might even counter them with another question: Why not? Why not me, and why not now, and why not like this? But the dying do not merit such a harsh rejoinder, nor do they merit the usual platitudes that suggest that suffering is a sign of special favor with God or that "God never sends us more than we can bear." I cannot explain what I do not understand, but I can offer companionship as we sit together in the mystery.

Much of this essay is based on my work with those dying in a timely fashion, folk who have lived a full span of years and whose bodies have worn out. But there are others who do not fit this pattern. Cancer, especially, shows no respect for age or general good health. My first experience of such a death came a year or two out of college. Don had been the class comedian, kind and funny, never out of sorts. You couldn't imagine that death could touch him. Death would never catch him—death was just too serious for this lighthearted, generous young man. I last saw him in a hospital room a few days before Christmas. Bone cancer had ravaged his body—he'd always been a little bit plump, and now he was a skeletal old man. There were no more jokes. We both cried a little. I promised that I would see him again, but I never did.

I had almost forgotten Don, but recently he has become a vivid memory as the plague of AIDS has cut down a generation of young men. Their deaths, like Don's, anger and baffle me. Each time I visit a bedside or attend the funeral of a person much younger than I, someone whom I had expected to visit me in my old age, I ask myself the old questions. Why this person? Why this illness? Why such a hard and cruel death? Where is God? I have little wisdom to offer my young friends as they move toward death. All that I can offer is my friendship, my prayers, and my tears.

Thank God, we have become more sensible and humane in our understanding of this sickness. I recall my first visit to an AIDS patient over fifteen years ago, when the disease was just becoming known. Before I entered his hospital room, I was required to don a complete set of protective clothing including a mask. "Don't touch him," the nurse warned sternly, so I perched on a chair in the far corner of the room, probably looking like something from a science fiction movie. Now we know that the danger of infection comes from us, the allegedly healthy visitor: my harmless little cold, passed on, can play havoc with a compromised immune system. So long as we are healthy, we need not fear holding a hand or dropping a kiss. I still scrub my hands compulsively, though— before, not after the visit.

I have been privileged to have good friends in the gay and lesbian community during these years of plague. I have watched their care for their sick brothers and have been humbled by their faithful selflessness. I rarely hear about spiritual direction from them, but I see spiritual friendship lived out magnificently. There is something Christ-like about the willingness of these men and women to care tenderly for the dying bodies of their friends. This is not easy work. As they wash and clean and feed, they live with sights and smells that normally offend our sensibilities. There is a lesson here for the larger church, if we dare to let ourselves be open to it.

Spiritual direction with the dying—the very old and the tragically young—is a rich ministry. Our directees permit us to go with them in compassion and imagination to a place that is still beyond us. They are our teachers. In all humility, we can offer nothing more than our prayers and our friendship. And that is enough.

Section III

The Social Context

Chapter Nine

"Let the Oppressed Go Free": Spiritual Direction and the Pursuit of Justice

Kenneth Leech

———— •◆• ————

Now spiritual direction . . . is a witness against the
world,
and we commit ourselves to its testimony.
—F. W. Faber (1854)[1]

We're steppin' out of Babylon
One by one.
—Marcia Griffiths (c. 1981)[2]

What does spiritual direction have to contribute to a person who is deeply involved, entangled, even heavily compromised within the worlds of economics and politics? What is the role of the director in relation to the growing numbers of communities and networks of people committed to prayer and the pursuit of justice—those two features that Dietrich Bonhoeffer identified as being central to the vocation of the church in the coming years?[3]

Of course, we all are involved in various ways whether we like it or not, whether we recognize it or not, but in this essay I have two groups of people in mind. First, those who are deeply entangled within the structures of injustice and oppression, but who fail to see this, and who are inclined—and often encouraged—to keep their "spirituality" in a private, sanitized zone. Second, those who are social and political activists, conscious agents within areas of struggle and engagement, and those involved with guiding them. The needs of these two groups are often very different, yet there are currents—of self-deception and compromise, for example—that are common to both even though their manifestations are different.

This essay will be built around seven theses. In each thesis, I assume that the person with whom we are concerned is a practicing Christian. In each, I have in mind both individuals and communities: whenever, therefore, I mention a person or persons, I am also aware of, and include by implication, the community dimension.

1. The spiritual director, confronted by any Christian person, will need to stress the importance of matter, and warn of the danger of contempt for or abuse of material things.
2. The spiritual director will try to lead the person toward freedom.
3. The spiritual director will be concerned with the human fulfillment of all persons, and will point to those features that dehumanize and damage them.
4. The spiritual director will emphasize discernment and warn of the danger of blindness and illusion.
5. The spiritual director will point to the central Christian reality of death and resurrection, and will be suspicious, and encourage suspicion, of coziness and false security.
6. The spiritual director will emphasize the economic unit, the *oikonomia,* and warn of the danger of individualism.
7. The spiritual director will point toward eternity and warn of the danger of false treasure.

Dangers of "Spirituality"

However, it is necessary to begin by stressing the real dangers of the current culture of "spirituality," and of the widespread split between *spirituality* and *social justice*. Linked with this is the fact that spiritual direction itself has become part of the consumer market of the global economy. In saying this I have already identified a threefold problem. First is the problem of "spirituality" as a clearly identifiable compartment of Christianity, of religion, or of life itself. Of course, most of what is marketed as "spirituality" is not Christian at all, and makes no claim to be so. Christian spirituality is seriously underrepresented in most bookstores under the headings of "spirituality" or, as is increasingly common, "inspirational." (The latter seems to be a euphemism for "second-rate"!) Although much of it has Christian connections, it is not recognizable as Christian in any historic sense. However, most of it, Christian or non-Christian, seems to assume that spirituality is a compartment of life that can be studied, practiced, and talked about in isolation from other compartments.

This notion is both extremely modern and highly questionable. I believe that the idea of spirituality as a compartment has done immense harm already and is bound to do more. For this reason I believe that both the idea of "spirituality" and the function of spiritual direction need to be treated with extreme suspicion and critical scrutiny. It is precisely because they are so important that we need to recognize how easily they can lose their bearings and go off the rails. The main problem, in my view, is not that "spirituality" is being liberated from the church: rather it is being sucked into the values of late capitalism and the consumer culture, and is being sold as one more product on the (unquestioned) global market.

Second is the problem of the split between spirituality and justice. In spite of a mass of activity, including written material, to the contrary, it is still widely assumed that spirituality is only about the "inner life"—prayer, meditation, personal growth, and so on. It may have indirect effects on the state of the world, but the direct connection between prayer and politics is rarely made—certainly not by most of the publishing industry. Even when it is, it is often in terms of the need to "bring together" these dimensions, or of "healing the split." But perhaps the problem lies in the concept of spirituality as a "dimension" at all. I regard the "spiritual life" as the whole of human life, as viewed from the perspective of relationship with God. It is not an optional extra, and it is certainly not a "dimension": it is the whole of life viewed from its core, its very heart, its soul. As Tracy Chapman says, "All that you have is your soul." Theodore Roszak put it well almost thirty years ago when he said that "the fate of the soul is the fate of the social order": if the spirit within us withers, so will all the world we build about us.[4]

Third, there seems to be little doubt that spiritual direction is now a "growth industry,"[5] with accreditation, professional standards, and the paraphernalia of the professional identity—fees and all. Yet while various authors recognize this fact, few of them do more than allude to it, swiftly moving on. I find myself utterly alienated by this development, predictable though it was within the present state of capitalism. I believe that this important ministry is in danger of being absorbed and shaped within a political and cultural framework which is in fact hostile to gospel values, and it seems likely that some kind of "confessing church" movement will be needed to rescue the idea of direction—and much else in Christian life—from the captivity to professionalism and the law of the market.[6] A type of spirituality and spiritual direction that is itself imprisoned within the structures of injustice is a major part of our problem. If spirituality is to become part of the response to the problem, then it needs to undergo its own dark night of the soul, its own ascesis and purification.

Having expressed these presuppositions, I wish to reflect on each of the seven theses identified above.

Seven Guidelines for a Gospel Spirituality

1. *The spiritual director, confronted by any Christian person, will need to stress the importance of matter, and warn of the danger of contempt for or abuse of material things.*

That there is much unhealthy and deranged spirituality about is obvious. Much of it seems to be influenced by a concern for purity, and a desire to avoid contamination. Purity is a dangerous concern, and tends to become obsessive. If the spiritual realm is seen as a protected zone, a way of withdrawing from the complexity and mess of human life, then we are in deep trouble, and I believe that this is the case with much of the current interest in "spirituality." Many years ago Daniel Berrigan spoke to the appeal of a kind of pseudocontemplation, claiming that

———·◆·———

In the derangement of our culture, we see that people move towards contemplation in despair, even though unrecognized. They meditate as a way of becoming neutral—to put a ground between them and the horror around them. . . . We have a terrible kind of drug called contemplation.

———·◆·———

Such abuse of contemplation as a drug, Berrigan argued, has the effect that people practicing it "become another resource of the culture instead of a resource against the culture."[7]

The spiritual director who is committed to the pursuit of justice needs to be constantly aware that many people drawn to contemplation are being drawn away from the demands of justice in the world. Spirituality is seen as a private pursuit, disconnected from the ambiguities of material reality. Yet both a healthy reverence for the material order, and a healthy suspicion of those principalities and powers who seek to damage it, are essential elements of a materialistic spirituality.

"A materialistic spirituality? Is this not a contradiction in terms?" No, it is absolutely central to Christian praxis and understanding. However, this is not widely understood. Spirit and matter are still seen as opposites, and *materialism* is still used as a pejorative term. A central task of spiritual direction therefore is to rescue a commitment to materialism and material structures from the influence of the gnostic and Manichaean streams within our history. In spite of a venerable tradition of orthodox Christology and sacramental theology, the church has never quite shaken off the gnostic contempt for the flesh (wrongly identified with sexuality) and the world of matter, what the late Robert Lambourne called "the fear of flesh and politics."[8] We need therefore to stress that spiritual direction is about the material world and how we relate to it.

But once we have made this claim, we are only beginning the task. To recognize the importance of the material, to recognize the actual or potential sacramental character of all material reality, leads us to see that contempt for, and abuse of, material things are two sides of the same coin. The metaphor of coinage is, in fact, highly appropriate, as is the analogy with sex, since many of the problems associated with damaged spirituality are related to money and sex. If flesh and matter constitute the source of evil, then they are despised, but this often leads not to extreme asceticism but to promiscuity and irresponsibility (or to both at the same time!). To regard matter—money, for instance—as a source of contamination can lead not to lives of holy poverty but to financial exploitation and abuse, a phenomenon that we have witnessed in extreme form in recent years among the TV evangelists, though it is by no means unique to them. Similarly, the combination of a rigorous ascetical lifestyle and a (private) sexually promiscuous one is all too common, and Christian history is full of examples of this combination of "puritanism" and sexual excess. Spiritual direction gone wrong can aid and reinforce this process: gone right, it can be a force for wholeness and fullness of life.

I argue that a central task of spiritual direction today is to recover a right understanding of materialism, to recover the materialistic basis of the movements of the Spirit. This, at least, must involve taking our sexuality and our financial lives seriously. And here we run up against a problem identified by Peter Selby in his work on debt—the problem of the two languages.

———— • ❖ • ————

By seeing our debt to God and Christ's repayment of that debt as a spiritual truth (by which we easily mean, strangely for Christian believers, a truth that is not based in the material world), we are allowed to leave the financial world to look after itself and go its own way. We have made it possible for

> *ourselves to worship God (religiously) and Mammon*
> *(economically) by simply allowing ourselves two*
> *separate kinds of language, and not letting them*
> *interact in any way that would confront our*
> *dependence on the economy of credit.*[9]

———•◆•———

To begin or to restore the process of interaction is an essential part of contemporary spiritual direction.

2. *The spiritual director will try to lead the person or community toward freedom.*

In a sense this is obvious: spiritual direction has to do with spiritual freedom. Practitioners such as the desert fathers, Augustine Baker, and Ignatius Loyola—among many others—saw that spiritual freedom was the purpose of spiritual direction. The use of terms like *liberation theology* and *liberation spirituality*[10] should not blind us either to the oppressive character of much theology and much spirituality, or to the fact that *all* theology, *all* spirituality, and *all* Christian life should liberate, at both personal and social levels. This must include a liberation from the captivity to systems and to modern—and postmodern—forms of idolatry.

A key issue is the status of the individual as person and agent. Christian spirituality must insist that human beings are free agents, that they are capable of effective action and are not determined by immutable laws, economic or otherwise. The recognition of limitation and contingency should not lead us to that type of social determinism which sees human thought and action as no more than a reflection of one's social or economic position, a view that, in the words of the late David Nicholls, "one would be tempted to call 'Marxist' if this were not to speak ill of the dead."[11]

Spiritual direction is a process of "steppin' out of Babylon, one by one," but this assumes a consciousness of our captivity. It assumes our awareness that social structures can impede moral agency.[12] A key factor is the way in which Western Christians tend to be imprisoned within ideological assumptions that they assume are eternal truths, perhaps gospel truths. One of the biggest obstacles to economic justice, for example, is an imaginative failure in Western societies to conceive of the possibility of alternatives. This is not the whole story, of course, and there is evidence from many places that faith communities do provide places of alternative vision and hope, sometimes the only place. As the archbishop of Capetown noted at the recent Lambeth

Conference, "Only in our churches, our synagogues, our mosques, and our temple does it seem possible to envision a different world and a different economy."[13] The spiritual director must be concerned to inspire and nourish the imagination to see the possibility of alternatives, of a completely different way of life. Spiritual life is a movement of liberation from captivity toward the freedom of the children of God (Romans 8:19–21).

However, this movement involves cultivation. As Roszak has stressed, growth without careful cultivation produces no livable habitat, but only the deadly luxuriance of swamp or of jungle.[14] The creation of a "healthy ecology of the spirit," and the cultivation of disciplines, practices, and structures that support the spiritual work, is a major part of direction.

> 3. *The spiritual director will be concerned with the human fulfillment of all persons, and will point to those features that dehumanize and damage them.*

In this connection it seems to me that two kinds of danger need to be distinguished: the threats to spiritual integrity that come from the false values of the dominant culture itself; and the threats that come from the very struggle to resist and oppose these values.

First, the threats from the culture. They have been well expressed, in his usual disturbing way, by Alasdair MacIntyre. Writing of the value system of modern capitalism, he says:

————— • ◆ • —————

> *What constitutes success in life becomes a matter of the successful acquisition of consumer goods and thereby that acquisitiveness which is so often a character trait necessary for success in capital accumulation is further sanctioned. Unsurprisingly* pleonexia, *the drive to have more and more, becomes treated as a central virtue. But Christians in the Middle Ages had learned from Aristotle that* pleonexia *is the vice that is the counterpart of the virtue of justice. And they had understood, as later theologians have failed to do[,] . . . the close connection between developing capitalism and the sin of usury. So it is not after all just human sinfulness that generates particular individual acts*

of injustice over and above the institutional
injustice of capitalism itself. Capitalism also
provides systematic incentives to develop a type of
character that has a propensity to injustice.[15]

———— • ◆ • ————

If it is true—and I believe it is—that the capitalist economic order demands for its efficient functioning a type of person who is committed to, indeed trained for, the practice of the mortal sin of avarice, then, to put it mildly, we have a problem. "You cannot serve God and Mammon." This personification, by Jesus of Nazareth, of money as "Mammon" indicates that there is a real danger of worshiping a false god. Hence Christian writers from R. H. Tawney to Peter Selby are right to speak of the *idolatry* of wealth.[16]

Indeed, the entire history of the church could be written as a persistent attempt to worship God and Mammon, to do what Jesus says cannot be done. A spirituality that serves only to comfort or even to sedate people in this attempt must be confronted by a spirituality that warns that the acquisition of riches is a threat to eternal salvation. Thus MacIntyre, in a more recent contribution, claims that "to unfit our students for the contemporary world ought . . . to be one of our educational aims."[17] How do we see the role of spiritual direction here? Might it also be to unfit people for the contemporary world, to fit them, in fact, for the kingdom of God?

The second danger involves the threats that arise from resistance to the culture. It may be thought that, by the very fact of their involvement, those who work for justice in their communities are free from many of the dangers—antimaterialism, sectarian and elitist attitudes, and so on— that can affect spirituality. Yet it is necessary, in my experience, also to stress the goodness of matter in the face of a Manichaean streak in much political activism. This danger is not always recognized, nor is it the only danger that confronts political activists. So I need to add at this point that, in my opinion, those who guide and direct political activists need to be people with credibility, whose own commitment to the pursuit of justice is beyond doubt. Only such people can fully understand, partly because they recognize in themselves the particular temptations to which activists are prone.

Among the dangers of activism I would list the following:

(a) A neglect of inactivity, rest, and stillness. These are often seen as useless and escapist, forms of evasion, and diversions from "the struggle." To be "on the go" all the time is thought to be the mark of the true activist. To be unoccupied is the activist equivalent of a state of mortal sin.

(b) Neglect of close friends, and neglect of self. Friendship and close emotional ties are seen as luxuries that impede commitment. This, of course, can be true. However, this neglect often leads to a real personal decline, and political activists often become diminished human beings. As the British politician Denis Healey once said of Margaret Thatcher, they have no hinterland. No one saw this more clearly than the poet Denise Levertov, herself a political activist, but one who recognized the close connection between personal and social wholeness.

———•◆•———

The self will surely suffer if egotism leads a person away from the experience of the Human Community. And the commonweal as surely suffers if those who wish for its betterment are hollowed-out self-neglecters.[18]

———•◆•———

Spiritual directors need to encourage and help people see how we need one another, to stress the solidarity of the Body of Christ. They will find support in the New Testament, which speaks hardly at all about personal spiritual formation, but a great deal about the building up of the Body and its movement toward fullness.

(c) A life built on frenzy and compulsive busyness. This usually leads to a lack of focus, a tendency to accumulate more and more things, a collapse of reflection, and the cultivation of a personal culture of obligatory tiredness. This personal culture then becomes socially infectious, so that one may communicate little to others other than one's own exhaustion—not a very kind gift to people who may already have enough problems of their own. The spiritual director needs to warn people that they are capable of doing considerable harm, and to show that this realization can be the beginning of the activist's own healing.

(d) A constant sense of urgency and a lack of time. To stop or stand still is a deviation. So the activist is always on the move, never able to take time for people, always looking at his/her watch, always ready for the next thing, but in fact never totally ready for anything.

(e) A tendency to despise such things as beauty, joy, music, amusement, laughter, and dancing, and to see them as luxuries. Everything one does must have a clear point, a function.

(f) The commitment to pseudocertainty. Everything is clear; there is no room for doubt, perplexity, or uncertainty. So activity is determined by slogans, and by the mentality of the elite vanguard who know the truth and have the "correct line."[19]

(g) Because of all these features, a profound impatience with, and intolerance of, others who are seen as being too stupid to "see it as it is." So there arises a spirituality of indignation, frustration, and condescension that often turns to bitterness and pessimism in middle age.

In the face of these features, the director needs to stress the importance of stability, dependency on others, humility, cultivation of a capacity for doubt, internal struggle, and openness to learn new truth. This is hardly an easy task, but it is essential. The spiritual director is not simply one who comforts and reassures, pats one on the back, and cheers one on the way. The elements of challenge, confrontation, and questioning need to have equal place. This leads me directly to my next point.

4. *The spiritual director will emphasize discernment and warn of the danger of blindness and illusion.*

A central dimension in direction is the cultivation of an ability to see clearly, including the ability to see through, and to subvert, false and spurious claims. This "unmasking of illusion" was a key theme of Thomas Merton's writing, and he frequently wrote of the need for a ruthless campaign against delusions as the first stage in spiritual direction. At a time when the word *vision* has been so trivialized as to be almost unusable, it is necessary to recover a genuine sense of vision as involving insight, wisdom, perception, and penetration into the heart of things. What Christian tradition calls contemplation is not a simple clarity, or the "single vision" from which Blake asked to be delivered. It is a sharing in the darkness of God, a way of unknowing that subverts the simplistic nostrums of those who fear complexity and obscurity.

Merton saw that, if there is to be a deepening of vision and discernment, we need to restore the place of silence and solitude. Solitude is not hostile to communion but is necessary to it. "In solitude, in the depths of a man's [*sic*] own aloneness, lie the resources for resistance to injustice."[20] The encouragement of silence and solitude is particularly important for political activists, who are inclined to neglect this side of their lives.

The contemplative vision is subversive, as Berrigan memorably wrote,[21] and it is threatening to powerful vested interests, for it encourages and fosters a condition of sanctified dissatisfaction and discontent. The contemplative is always asking questions, always probing, motivated by that restlessness of spirit which is the source of creativity. And yet its sense of striving is rooted in a profound, and growing, sense of inner peace, of trust—an interior consciousness of our rootedness in God.

The spiritual director will not try to protect individuals from darkness. Indeed it can be argued that the point of direction is to bring people to the point of entry into the darkness, the *via negativa,* to that knowledge of God which comes through "unknowing" and which sets us free from captivity and blindness. If the eye is sound, the whole body will become full of light. But this illumination comes only through the shedding of illusions and through the gradual entry into the darkness in which God is encountered.

5. *The spiritual director will point to the central Christian reality of death and resurrection, and will be suspicious, and encourage suspicion, of false security.*

The Christian spiritual tradition does not only see the paschal mystery as historically the work of Christ. It sees the process of dying and rising as a constituent element in all Christian life and in the lives of cultures and societies. Christian spirituality teaches us to see in the painful process of disintegration and death the birth pangs of a new age. This is why all Christian spiritual direction arises from the baptismal incorporation, with its interrogations, its renunciations, and its immersion into and clothing with the Christ life. Baptism of adults—which will become increasingly the norm as the Constantinian era finally dies—is preceded by a catechumenal process, and is nowadays increasingly followed by further catechesis. It is a mistake to separate spiritual direction from this baptismal process, for it is from that process that direction derives its meaning and draws its life.

In baptism we enter into the mystery of Christ's dying and rising. Our only true security lies in that constantly renewed experience of being stripped naked, plunged beneath the waters, and raised up, and the condition of entry into that mystery is *metanoia,* a complete revolution in our lives. It demands that we let go of false securities and allow God to work His strange work upon us.

6. *The spiritual director will emphasize the economic unit, the* oikonomia, *and warn of the danger of individualism.*

Economy, *oikonomia,* the household, is a central concept in Christian spiritual theology. Spiritual formation is not about self-cultivation, but about building a community, a community in which equality and sharing are symbolized by the eucharistic celebration. It is no accident that the recovery of eucharistic worship and the renewal of Christian social consciousness were historically coincident. The eucharistic, and indeed the entire sacramental economy, undermines the divisions between spirit and matter, and between individual and collectivity, in a movement of "sacramental subversion."[22]

Indeed, the specific thrust of the Christian Eucharist is to bring together the holy and the common. "Holy communion" is not only the name of the central Christian act of worship; it also sums up the whole meaning of Christian life, which is the encounter with, and practice of, the holy in the midst of the common life of humankind. As we move into a new century of inequality and injustice, the authentic celebration of the Eucharist, and its testimony to equality and common life, will become more and more important. But it needs to be extended and made real in our social life: we need to become a eucharistic people.

In 1936, Michael Ramsey, in his pioneering study, *The Gospel and the Catholic Church,* opened a new era in biblical, liturgical, and social theology by his insistence that the church, the visible, material, embodied community, was itself an integral part of the gospel. Ramsey strongly attacked individualism as the opposite of Catholicity: "Individualism . . . has no place in Christianity, and Christianity verily means its extinction."[23] Since those days, the essentially social basis of Christian spirituality has come to be stressed by many Christians, not least those from an evangelical background. Even very conservative writers such as Brian Griffiths, former head of Margaret Thatcher's Policy Unit, see individualism as rooted in a profoundly anti-Christian vision.[24] Yet there is still a failure to see how deeply rooted individualism is in our consciousness. Thus in 1985, the Church of England's report *Faith in the City* complained that individualism had "crept into both public and private life,"[25] as if, having crept in, it could just as easily creep out. But the problem is whether this individualism is simply an aberration or whether it is so fundamental to our culture that the only hope for Christian spirituality is that of nurturing communities of alternatives and of resistance. If this is so, spiritual direction will assume a social importance beyond anything that its practitioners have hitherto considered.[26]

There is therefore a critically important question about democracy in relation to the ministry of spiritual direction. Don Cupitt has claimed recently that the future of philosophy and theology depends on their ability to democratize themselves.[27] In the same way, it seems to me, the future of the ministry of spiritual direction depends on its ability to democratize itself, to become a resource for all people, and to break with the elitist model which makes it a resource mainly for white, middle-class, leisured people. Every local "cell" of spiritual directors certainly needs to have an equal-opportunities policy!

7. *The spiritual director will point toward eternity and warn of the danger of false treasure.*

The threat of idolatry remains a real one, and the so-called other-worldly Christian is perhaps particularly prone to idolatry: for if the other world has no impact on this one, if it is "wholly spiritual," then there are no guidelines for our life within the fallen world order. It is not surprising that "otherworldly" Christians tend to be extremely this-worldly in practice. Yet there is a true otherworldliness that put its faith and trust only in God and in God's reign, that seeks to live now within eternity, refusing to be seduced by ideologies and systems that have no permanence. A rereading of the account of the fall of Babylon in the Book of Revelation would be a useful spiritual discipline at the present time.

Martin Thornton claimed that spiritual direction was our greatest pastoral need in the same year, 1963, that John Robinson wrote *Honest to God*. The time was not favorable to his view, but, by 1984, when Thornton's little book on spiritual direction was published and the year that Robinson died, the climate had changed.[28] Both Thornton and Robinson were prophetic figures, the former pointing to the coming importance of spiritual direction and the latter, through his New Testament studies, anticipating later work on the centrality of body and kingdom in our understanding of the gospel. Today we need to put Thornton and Robinson together and recover spiritual direction as a resource at the service of the body of Christ and the kingdom of God.

Chapter Ten

TENDING THE COMMUNAL SOUL IN A CONGREGATIONAL SETTING

Sandra Lommasson

———— •◆• ————

NOTICING THE COMMUNAL SOUL OR SPIRIT OF A CONGREGATION

The first set of alarms jarred members of the Davis, California, Fire Department from the deep sleep that comes in the early hours of morning; the second set of alarms was more human, but no less jarring. One by one, members of the Davis Community Church leadership, both lay and ordained, were roused from sleep with an ominous message: "The church is burning." As we rushed to the site from different sides of the city, the sky was far too bright for that hour, with flames shooting a hundred feet into the air over what had only yesterday been the nearly completed fellowship hall. We gathered in silence in the street, utterly powerless over the raging devastation that had consumed too much, and was now threatening both the sanctuary and the office wing. All we could do was to huddle together and pray.

When dawn came the fire was officially "under control," but its impacts in the communal body known as Davis Community Church had barely begun to register. Congregants gathered in shock, needing most of all to make contact with one another and to see for themselves what was left of the structure that had been their religious home. Individuals and clusters of grieving parishioners trailed through the smoke-blackened, water-soaked sanctuary. Others kept vigil outside the yellow Alcohol, Tobacco, and Firearms (ATF) tapes surrounding the rest of our building—tapes that signify a crime scene. In the weeks that followed we would have to absorb the truth that the $1.5 million dollars worth of damage had in fact been arson; someone had intentionally chosen to cause us harm. It's not an easy truth to digest.

The injury to the physical structure of the church, the "safe place" that had been revealed as so vulnerable, was like a tear within our communal body. This tear, however, was revelatory: the burned and broken exterior of our institutional life exposed in raw form the deep structure of our interior life, the communal soul or spirit, or what the Book of Revelation calls the "angel" of a church. Walter Wink, professor of biblical interpretation at Auburn Theological Seminary in New York, notes that in Revelation the seven letters to the seven churches are not addressed to the congregations as such, but to their angels: "The angel was the corporate ethos or essence of the congregation. This was the Biblical way of talking about the spirituality of the congregation. Each congregation had its own spirit, which was unique to [it]."[1] In his work *Engaging the Powers,* Wink speaks of the relationship between the external manifestation of institutions like Davis Community Church and their interior spirits:

———•◆•———

In the Biblical view [the Powers] are both visible and invisible, earthly and heavenly, spiritual and institutional. The Powers possess an outer, physical manifestation (buildings, portfolios, personnel, trucks, fax machines) and an inner spirituality, or corporate culture, or collective personality. . . . The spiritual aspect of the Powers is not simply a "personification" of institutional qualities that would exist whether they were personified or not. On the contrary, the spirituality of an institution exists as a real aspect of the institution even when it is not perceived as such. Institutions have an actual spiritual ethos, and we neglect this aspect of institutional life to our peril.[2]

———•◆•———

As designated spiritual director in and to the congregation in this critical and privileged time, I glimpsed aspects of this collective deep "soul" or "spirit" with a clarity that is difficult in more ordinary times. Trauma cracks open the usual veneers that cloud perception and frame reality. In the months following the fire, we were flooded with unhealed personal traumas that had been buried for decades within the lives of congregants, as well as a sense of released empowerment among lay leadership that had been traditionally reluctant to step forward. Somehow the two movements appeared to be related. As we listened, patterns of similarity in personal stories emerged, and we began to ask, "Is there something about this church that draws people with this particular kind of wounding and potential?" The answer appeared to be "Yes," as waves of new persons from a fifty-mile radius around the church simply appeared on our doorstep—individuals who again fit the pattern. We wondered aloud whether a "signal" of some kind about who we were (or who we might become) had gone out from the tear in our body into the extended community.

Similar to the night when all we could do in our powerlessness was stand in the street and pray, we gathered those who felt a call to pray for the church in simple openness to what the Spirit was engaging in our midst. Using the work of Flora Wuellner[3] as a touchstone, we introduced the notion of a Davis Community Church "angel" and invited people to pray for awareness of its/our central gift and shadow, need and desire, hope and wound. Those who responded prayed at home, returning weekly for sharing and group prayer. We were astounded in the gatherings at the similarity in reports of dreams, images, and themes that would arise from the weeklong prayer. In the span of one month, four different individuals, two from the praying community and two from the congregation at large, separately reported different variations of the same dream or spontaneous prayer image. In the imagery there were wounded children of all ages and both sexes hidden under the sanctuary floor or in concealed rooms of the church, wanting to come out and yet terrified of being exposed. These individuals, most of whom didn't even know one another, seemed to be touching an "inner spiritual reality" of the sort of which Wink writes.

Gradually we began to sense the presence of another fire, a "refiner's fire," at work in the interior space of our communal soul for healing, for purification, and for release into a greater fullness. In the dynamic interplay among spirits of individual members of the body, persons drawn to us from outside the communicant membership, and the corporate body of the congregation, our "angel" was becoming visible. It was a sacramental moment and graced awakening. There was a communal soul being revealed with its particular dimensions, as well as a distinct charism and call, and this soul was more than the aggregate of individual souls. The angel of our community was a distinct phenomenon, presence, and power, and was therefore a major partner in the work before us. The communal spirit being revealed in this passage was as much in need of conscious spiritual tending as any singular person or group within the community.

If we believe the Christian proclamation that "you did not choose me but I chose you" (John 15:16), it makes sense that a congregation is more than an accidental conglomeration of individual choices. We come together because we are called together: "Deep calls to deep" (Psalm 42:7) and the Spirit to spirit. Part of the resonance prompting response to the call is the recognition (often unconscious) of the essential God-seed, planted for grace at the core of both the person and the institution. If structures are given for grace to free us for love's purposes,[4] this is even more so of the church as the living Body of Christ. When individuals new to a congregation report a sense of "coming home," they mean perhaps that there is mutual recognition of the holy in the other, alongside the hope that "here I can experience my embeddedness in the vine, both receiving nurture and bearing fruit." The desire to come home to God is written into the cellular structure of the human soul: "As a deer longs for flowing streams, so my soul longs for you, O God" (Psalm 42:1), and one element of that homecoming is necessarily communal. It cannot be fully realized apart from participation in the community of "two or three" where the risen Christ dwells (Matthew 18:20).

The resonance between the communal body/spirit of a particular congregation and its individual members is, however, open to distortion as well as to the activity of the Spirit. Alongside the longing for authentic meeting and communion is all the human resistance to it. The structures are "fallen" as well as graced, and the history of the church over time reveals that this is as true of the "Body of Christ" as of other structural entities. It's no accident that Jesus' organic image of the church as the vine includes within it the necessity for pruning (John 15:2, 6). So it is that the sense of "coming home" can also signal a "sinking in" to what is merely familiar. The human capacity to replicate age-old patterns of wounding, self-protection, self-deception, and sin are well known, as is our propensity to seek out others whose patterns mesh with our own. Just as the miracle of the loaves and fishes can multiply God's bounty for all, so can an unholy sort of multiplication occur when our unhealed woundedness and egocentricities congregate.

Given this understanding of the living organism of the local church, with its capacities for both grace and distortion and its real spiritual power, it is clearly not enough that only individuals within the body are growing. Conscious attention needs to be given to the growth of the corporate entity as well. Spiritual direction is as appropriate and necessary for the communal spirit as it is for the individual person within the community. John Mostyn[5] notes that "directing the group spirit" is qualitatively different than "group spiritual direction." The first is tending the communal soul; the second is attending to individual souls within a gathered community. Both are beneficial, but the first is rarely practiced. Our cultural affair with individualism has led to the mistaken belief that it is enough to serve individuals who are part of a community, in the hope that their personal transformation will in turn transform the community. While one undoubtedly affects the other, growth needs support in both directions if it to sustain over time, and the power of the institution, which is real, can either contribute to or thwart that growth.

THE NATURE OF SPIRITUAL DIRECTION AND ITS COMMUNAL FOUNDATIONS

I believe that community—in the fullest sense, a place and all its creatures—is the smallest unit of health and that to speak of the health of an isolated individual is a contradiction in family or community or in a destroyed or poisoned ecosystem.
—"Health Is Membership," *Utne Reader*
(September/October 1995)

Spiritual direction or companioning is simultaneously individual and communal, simultaneously contemplative and prophetic. It is contemplative in the sense that its atmosphere is hospitable—there is a gracious space created for prayerful welcoming of a human entity and story, and for noticing together the ways the Spirit is already present. The contemplative attitude, which Walter Burghardt defines as "a long, loving look at the Real,"[6] is the container for the interaction and, in turn, becomes saturated by the long, loving look *of* the Real. The direction relationship is a holy holding space for the truth of another or An Other to enter and to be mutually contemplated, and in this mutuality to experience the self as knowing and being known. This knowing is of a different magnitude, however, than the simple connectedness of two human beings sharing a story—in the gathering of two or more in Christ's spirit, the indwelling, inbreaking Presence becomes manifest, and an actual experience of encounter can occur. This is the real experience spiritual directors often describe as "holy ground," or as being "brought to their knees" in sheer awe.

Spiritual direction is also prophetic. A prophet is one who "speaks forth" from and for the perspective of God, sometimes bringing a word of challenge, sometimes bringing a word of comfort or hope. Prophets are God's gift to and from communal bodies; there cannot be a prophet without a community and a tradition. A prophetic stance may well (and often does) create painful dislocation within and from a community, but this is still a stance in relationship to the community. A true prophet, even while on the edge of community, emerges from authentic, loving relationship to it. The practice of spiritual direction in its prophetic dimension may take both director and directee to the edge of communal sensibilities, because it supports the free movement of the Spirit both in creating structures and in blowing through them in ways that disrupt settled and contained categories. The Spirit will not be domesticated, even by our most earnest attempts to do so. Commitment to the Spirit's freedom to "blow where it chooses" (John 3:8), and to the directee's free response, is fundamental to the ministry.

Although encounter with grace and truth is present in both the contemplative and prophetic dimensions of spiritual direction, the communal aspects of truth are particularly lost to modern North American awareness: Truth is typically seen as the yield of the personal heroic journey. In its Germanic rootage, *truth* and its close cousin *troth* (as in, "I pledge thee my troth") are fundamentally related and relational. Parker Palmer notes that "with this word one person enters a covenant with another, a pledge to engage in a mutually accountable and transforming relationship, a relationship forged of trust and faith in the face of unknowable risks. . . . [I]n truthful knowing, the knower becomes co-participant in a community of faithful relationships."[7]

While the resurgence of interest in spiritual direction in our time recognizes the relational piece of conscious engagement as an essential container for growth in spiritual life, I believe that the communal dimension has largely slipped into unconsciousness, especially in the community of spiritual directors shaped by North American values. The newly adopted *Guidelines for Ethical Conduct of Spiritual Directors International* moves in the right direction in its concern with the communal context of the ministry. It is, however, a very different thing to uphold the need of the individual director to be communally connected, versus engaging in active, intentional, and mutual dialogue as a spiritual director with a communal body. The prevailing image of a spiritual-direction relationship continues to be the singular director with the singular directee; the implied hope is that this singular relationship multiplied many times will serve as the "leaven in the loaf" of the larger body of the church and of the society in which we live. It's time to reclaim more fulsomely the essential communal dimensions of our heritage, and to expand the image of spiritual direction to include tending the communal spirit.

DIRECTING THE COMMUNAL SOUL
OF THE CONGREGATION: PRELIMINARIES

Tending the holy in community has two broad, related, but distinct functions: the formation function and the soul-friend function. While the formation function is more broadly concerned with practices that shape the human spirit, the "soul-friend" function is explicitly focused on an intentional depth encounter with the Lover of the soul. The formation perspective recognizes that everything the church does shapes its members, consciously or not, and so engages its communal life and work together with as much care for form as for content. A directee who serves as a pastor recently commented on his concern that a search for director of music in his congregation be conducted carefully, because "The music of a congregation both reveals and shapes its spirit." His comment comes from the spiritual formation perspective.

The soul-friend function, or tending the communal soul, is more focused than the formation function, although it too is profoundly formative. It means nothing less than "directing the group spirit," which may also include working with individuals within the group. The two arenas of spiritual work are synergistically related, profoundly affect one another, and tend to travel together into or away from the invitation of God. The function of spiritual direction is as an interactive process of assisting another in noticing and responding consciously to the presence, movement, and invitation of the Spirit in lived experience. The "other" in this context is the communal spirit of the church. The director-directee relationship is covenanted, which means that both parties intentionally and mutually "sign up" for this work and focus.

One model of how this covenantal relationship might look is offered by Brother John H. Mostyn,[8] who through monthly two-hour sessions with staff directs the group spirit of a Catholic parish. As a contemplative listener he gathers the staff members with questions: "How are you coming to this meeting today? How has the Mystery of God been present to you in your ministry this week?" He takes notes as each person reports and then listens carefully during the staff agenda items that follow, tracking themes that surface throughout. His function as spiritual director is to listen for what is not being said as well as to what is being said—to notice and lift up for the group's reflection the times when there is energy and "hubbub" and the times when things get quiet. Both are important occasions for attending to undercurrents that would otherwise go unnoticed. As director, he is particularly attuned for the primary movements of God, and so he listens in the rest of the meeting for the relationship between what the staff first shared and the "business" of the organization revealed through its agenda items, budget, and process. After a break, the group moves to a different room. Following five minutes of silence, they reflect together on how the mystery of God has been present in the meeting that day, in both the time of personal reflection and in the structures of their life together as a ministry team.

The director can come from outside the community, as in this instance, or can be a member, depending on circumstance. The essential quality is that s/he has the freedom and ability to help a community take a long, loving look at its reality, and to bring to God and to each other what is noticed. I believe that it would be difficult for the designated leader of a group (or the senior pastor of a church) also to serve as its spiritual director, given the power dynamics and gatekeeping functions associated with leadership in this culture.[9] Even if s/he feels free personally, the models and definitions of leadership in the social context in which we live and work could muddy the relationship.

In addition to the basic charism for spiritual direction and formation in the practice, a director of the group spirit needs knowledge of and experience with group process to help create a safe environment that invites participation and depth. This individual must be a person of prayer who listens well, who trusts the possibilities for shared wisdom and leadership, and who practices a contemplative awareness in his/her own life. This awareness must be particularly attuned to the growing energy and passion in a communal body as well as to the constraints that seek to mute the epiphanies that come. The focus of the director is primarily toward the inbreaking awareness of the holy, so this person must have the capacity to name such movements as they arise and to invite the group to linger and to go deeper. The ability to be a nonanxious presence is essential and includes the capacity for self-relinquishment. The willingness to offer one's own perceptions in humility is crucial, as is sensitivity to the dying that signals conversion in a group. A director must be love-based rather than fear-based, and must value "truth-speaking in love" as an agent of health and freedom for the community. S/he is capable of directness when needed, and helps the group know where it is in the process. Most of all, while the director's focus is toward the yearning of God, s/he knows at depth that the choreography belongs to the Spirit and that outcomes cannot be scripted.[10]

As is evident in John Mostyn's vignette, when the director tends the communal soul the "directee" is most likely to be a leadership group within the congregation, or a subcommunity, such as a prayer group, that comes together with an explicit focus on the whole body. These specific, embodied microcosms of the communal spirit are the most accessible places to engage the covenanted interaction of a direction process, simply because of their discrete size. Although there is a way in which a congregation at large "signs up" for direction by virtue of its presence, there is a qualitative difference in interaction. While I consider sermons and similar vehicles important tools of congregational spiritual formation, even when there are "talk-back" opportunities, the interaction tends to stay at the level of discussion or reflection and not true dialogue. There is a quantum difference between discussion and dialogue, just as there is a quantum difference between decision making and discernment.[11] Dialogue and discernment, both of which are essential components of spiritual direction, take time, relationship, trust, truth telling, and skill, and so need a committed partnership in which to blossom.

The mutual work of spiritual direction has a context that frames and expresses the group spirit. A vital role of the director is to bring this context to consciousness, dialogue, and prayer. Ellen Morseth, B.V.M.,[12] names the structural elements of this context as the charism of the group, the cultures of group life, the edge to which there is energy, and the conversion to which the group is being called.

The *charism of the group* is the essence of its calling—"the place where [one's] deep gladness and the world's deep hunger meet" (Frederick Buechner). Much of the early work of the direction relationship is creating a space for the founding stories and deep history of the community to emerge, to be contemplated, and to be appropriated. A community needs to visit and revisit its initial founding charism and to look at how that initiating purpose is lived out today or is changing.

The *cultures of group life* are the influences that flavor the ways of being and doing together. How a community manages its business, handles conflict and negative feedback, and makes decisions are some aspects. Is leadership hierarchical or collegial? Is the rational/linear more valued than the intuitive/reflective, or vice versa? What do we have plenty of? What's missing? Again, the director is listening for what is not being said as well as to what is being said, and is helping the group notice its reality.

The *edge to which there is energy* is the creative edge where attraction, draw, and longing meet the longing of the Holy One for partnership in the ongoing creation of the realm of God. The edge might emerge out of a feeling that the group can do something better, or it might come from a sense of deep satisfaction in the mission already underway. A community must have energy to engage in its mission.

The *conversion to which the group is being called* is the invitation of the Spirit to the "More"—more wholeness, more truth telling, and more freedom to serve, all for Love's purposes in the world. A communal spirit will always possess shadows and "unfreedoms," which need healing and release, as well as gifts—and usually the two are closely related.

Directing the Communal Soul of a Congregation: A Case Study

What might directing the congregational spirit look like? In my own experience with Davis Community Church (DCC), an 850-member Presbyterian congregation, there were four major locations for exercising the "soul-friend" function: the staff community, the session (our governing board), called communities like the prayer group mentioned above, and individual direction relationships with persons in the congregation. This work occurred as a full-time lay staff member with the title of Minister of Christian Formation, in which my first duty was "to serve as spiritual director to individuals and groups in the congregation." Although I had particular skills and a role, pieces of the soul-friend function were sometimes assumed by other individuals in the church as well. Over time I awakened to the presence of the group spirit that lived through, around, and beneath the individuals and groups I saw, and began experimenting with ways of actively tending the communal soul. In my role as a spiritual director I served as contemplative presence, reflective mirror, encourager of dialogue, keeper of the communal memory, and holder of the sacred space.

The initial form of this ministry (pre-fire) was to meet with a variety of individuals in the church in a traditional, monthly, one-to-one relationship as a spiritual director. I would sit with perhaps thirty-five persons a month from the church and another ten or so from other churches or from the unchurched community around us. From the beginning I noticed distinct patterns of movement in the DCC group that seemed somehow synchronous, and that were not evident in the same way in other directees. Through the patterns I began to notice faint strains of a communal story seeking a voice and a hearing. The themes of the emergent story included a deep longing to be seen and heard, and a terror of it; a hunger to belong somewhere and a sense of incapability in finding and forming authentic community; experiences of profound early abuse and courage enough to reach out for connection anyway; a spiritual hunger and the sense that it was bottomless and would never be filled; a terror of judgment; a wound of trust such that each experience of connection with God or another would bring dread soon after the initial relief; and an emerging desire to discover whether one really had gifts to contribute to the building of God's realm in the world.

The themes would come in waves, as would the recoil that followed, in a rhythm that I named "The Draw and the Drawback." I sensed that these themes were in fact revealing a dance in the deeper structure of our communal life, between the spiritual energies of our church "angel" and the "Lord of the Dance." I am not suggesting that these themes were unique to us, but their prevalence, timing, and clustering carried the sense communally of a "body/spirit" wanting to be seen, heard, and touched, and yet strongly resisting such vulnerability. Something that I had heard at an annual church officers' retreat ten years before, when we were doing long-range planning, came to mind: "We're a friendly church," the refrain went, "it's just that nobody knows it." My system-wide journey of contemplative noticing, remembering, and making connections had begun.

The fire in October 1993 dropped us into chaos. Theories on the stages of group life are fairly unanimous in stating that a group must enter a period of chaos if there is hope for authentic community to emerge from the first stages of pseudocommunity, in which politeness, pretending, and getting along are the initial glue.[13] Although there is a major difference between chaos imposed from outside and the chaos that comes from people getting more "real" from the inside, any disorder opens set patterns to the fresh winds of the Spirit.

As the oldest Protestant church in a university community, we had once been the "right" church to join, and so appearances and "culture" were part of our heritage and were valued. Appearances crumble in crisis. I suspect that much of the human chaos resulted simply because our brokenness was on display. Every Sunday for the next few years, when we came together in worship the congregation faced the plywood boards covering a huge, blackened hole. The beloved stained-glass window that was the artful centerpiece of our sanctuary structure had been shattered; no matter how much we "pulled ourselves together," the wound was raw and visible. Southwestern lore says that Native American artists intentionally weave an error into their rugs so that the Spirit might breathe life into the creation. Perhaps the ever-present gash in the sanctuary served a similar function in opening our institutional body to the blowing of those same fresh winds.

One of the first places to feel the full weight of the fire was the staff collegium, which included lay leaders from the congregation. That year, in addition to the public breaking of our church, every person in leadership experienced some kind of break in his or her personal life as well. We were exposed to one another without masks and roles. As human beings in need of help we found ourselves drawn (driven?) to authentic, deep prayer as a subcommunity of the larger body. Desperation opens spiritual doors. As a spiritual director, I initially convened the praying community, structuring it as a contemplative mutual direction group in which I too participated. Much of the material shared in this group was personal, but I again noticed the resonance between the themes rising in members of the praying community and in other directees in the congregation at large.

Assuming the stance of contemplative listener is the first essential work of someone directing a group spirit, with the focus simultaneously specific—attuned to the concrete details that enflesh spirit—and global in looking for patterns across the community. Depending on the locus of the work, the next steps may involve simply naming what is noticed (the reflective mirror), or asking evocative questions that invite participants into prayerful dialogue with one another and with God. In our regular staff meetings I began to share (with permission) the cross-congregational themes I was noticing, so that we might wrestle together with their meanings and seek to discern the movement of God among them.

At one point, after hearing the imagery emerging about the lost and wounded children under the sanctuary floor (see above), the staff sensed an invitation of the Spirit to name potential places of communal wounding and to pray for their healing and release. One pastor preached a powerful sermon in Advent only two months after the fire, entitled "Shining a Light into the Darkness." The congregation was ready to hear it. A well-attended six-week adult series soon followed that opened discussion and reflection on "secret" things like the forms of abuse and addiction present in our church and community. As the conversations continued and deepened, a possible next step emerged into staff awareness; a "Service for Cleansing and Healing of the Sanctuary and Spirit of the Church Body" was created and performed. The ritual included naming the woundedness of the sanctuary and of the communal spirit of the people; speaking to and for the wounded ones, whose presence lives in and under the sanctuary;

prayers for cleansing and healing; prayers for infilling and protection of the sanctuary and people; and a ritual baptismal blessing and song.

Within a month, a woman who had grown up in the church, but who never attended because "it always felt so dark to me there," found herself drawn back to worship "for no apparent reason." She found her way afterward to one of the staff: "Something's different here," she said. "I don't mean the fire—everyone knows about that—but something else. It feels lighter in here somehow." She knew nothing about the healing service, but a new (or healing) spirit was evident to her through the atmosphere of our central gathering place, the sanctuary. The spiritual power for healing or wounding, contained in the mystical Body of Christ, is real. Because we are connected in the vine, tending the communal soul in an individual congregation affects the greater soul of the church and its far-flung parts, whether they know themselves connected or not.

Most of these initiatives came from the staff team out of the experience of communal prayer, which was opening the group spirit to our awareness. We wanted to tend its wounds. "We" however were also part of "it," and the shadow side of an obviously gifted staff team rose to awareness in the aftermath of the fire as well. DCC had historically been a staff-driven church, and happily so; it fit the academic and leadership culture of the university only two blocks away. The job of the church staff in this model was to be the take-charge religious professionals, and the job of the congregation was to let us. It made for a lot of freedom, but not for much lay partnership in leading the church. In my twenty-year connection with the congregation at that point, I had witnessed two generations of pastors struggling to get the lay leadership to "step up to the plate" without much success. People who were gifted leaders in other settings seemed to check those skills at the church door; the church staff would grumble, and then step into the breach. The staff was as stuck in its "All right, I'll do it," pattern as the congregation was stuck in its "Good, you're supposed to!" pattern. It was a partnership of sorts, only one without much authentic freedom. Something powerful seemed to lock the dynamic into place, so that energetic leadership that would surface now and again in the congregation would, at some point, typically burn out and disappear out the back door. The fire and its aftermath were clearly a conversion point in our communal life and spirit.

An odd gift of the fire was the overwhelming of the staff by pastoral, institutional, and personal loads. Business as usual became impossible. This reality, paired with the staff's intentional entry into its own personal and corporate work, was the beginning of a conversion. The deeper we went spiritually as a staff community, the more openings we noticed in the congregation. It was like someone pushing a finger on the center of a drum. The whole plane moved downward in varying degrees, from the edge to the center. The "conversion to which we were being called" built on our gifts (we valued collegial relationships) and addressed our shadow (we needed to open the collegium beyond staff to genuine inclusion of lay leaders). We perceived that the lay leadership body of the session was ready to take its own plunge, so it was a natural next step to take what we'd been learning about "directing the group spirit" to this newly energized lay leadership body.

Using the four practices described by Chuck Olsen in *Transforming Church Boards into Communities of Spiritual Leaders,*[14] we began the conscious integration of basic practices of spiritual formation into our regular session meetings. Remembrance of history and storytelling, biblical and theological reflection, prayerful discernment, and visioning the future provide the foundation for a distinctly Christian culture. They also engage the community in the contemplative stance toward its own life that is a crucial prelude to permeability by and responsiveness to the Spirit. As we began storytelling in our leadership gatherings, we mulled what it meant that the recent fire was in fact the third major arson fire in our shared history, and wondered together how that had affected us as a body. We told stories of today, too—in a modified "examen of consciousness" we would reflect together in board meetings on where we had experienced the most life and freedom in our common life in the previous month, or in our meeting that night, and where the Spirit seemed blocked.

Not only did the session step into leadership in the healing and rebuilding process after the fire, but within a few years it was ready to step out into a new level of spiritual leadership. After receiving a letter from a woman in the church expressing her deep pain over exclusion from full participation in congregational life, the session chose to wrestle significantly with one of the most volatile issues of our time: the ordination of gay and lesbian persons to leadership. Although this wrestling was undertaken with trepidation, an authentic dialogue began. A major task of the spiritual-direction function—creating a safe place for such dialogue among persons and between persons and God—had taken sufficient root to allow engagement of a potentially explosive issue. It was a remarkable movement in a congregation with a historical fear of "driving people away." After a two-year process, the session—and eventually the congregation—voted to stand in obedience to the Spirit (and ecclesiastical disobedience to the larger church body) in nominating and electing officers regardless of sexual orientation, even if it meant losing members and suffering disciplinary action. The communal spirit assumed the prophetic mantle that had previously been relegated to the voices of a disgruntled few at its edges.

During this process I felt moved to write the following letter to the session in my role as "reflective mirror":

———•◆•———

One of the images for church is that we are "the Body of Christ," and in the same way a physical body can register change in its health or makeup at an unconscious level, a spiritual body can also. That is why a slow, careful process of prayerful discernment such as you have engaged is so important—the impact of the spiritual office you exercise is real, and not just limited to the content of a specific issue or action. You have taken significant steps as spiritual leaders of DCC with great love and courage and integrity over the last few weeks, and the waves are rippling into the congregation even before a conscious awareness of anything concrete manifests itself.

———•◆•———

In the congregation, I am already experiencing an opening and movement in people similar to what happened after the fire. The best way I can describe it is that a number of people are openly bringing parts of themselves to church that they've always considered to be "contaminated" and outside the grace of God. At a deep level the sense that this church is a safe place to bring the fullness of one's being is spreading. Interestingly, the issues coming in over the last two weeks are not around homosexuality, but all of them have dynamics in common with homosexuality in the society and larger church: they are issues of deep pain and shame to the individual that have had the effect of making the person feel "on the margins" in some way whether with God, with others, or in themselves. And, they involve some sort of wounding for which the person needs and wants to enter depth relationship with God and others to engage the work of healing.

Many of these individuals are coming in crisis, because something is cracking open the habitual veneers that have covered the pain and allowed the persons to function, albeit in limited ways. I believe that "something" is the Holy Spirit, which you have released with new power in the congregation through the authority of your office in saying "Yes" to the call of God, as you have perceived it. The work of God is never to open such covered-over pain for its own sake, but for healing and freedom and release into the fullness God intends. Crisis presents both danger and opportunity—and so your continuing prayer work for the congregation in this time of spiritual opening is crucial.

It was a huge step into new terrain that enabled us confront our "demons" and to stretch our communal soul in new, uncomfortable, liberating ways. Our story is still unfolding because the initiating movements of God continue to reach out for us, and because we continue our own version of the dance I named "The Draw and the Drawback." We approach and we withdraw.

I write this essay during the anniversary month of the fire six years ago and note how much of this story has already slipped into communal unconsciousness. In an adult class recently, one pastor mentioned the fire and realized that most of the people there didn't know about it. The buildings have long since been rebuilt, and the miracle has receded into worry about how and when to complete paying for them. The plywood-covered hole in the sanctuary wall is filled with a new stained-glass window. The congregation voted for a more contemporary version of the old theme, providing perhaps an unintentional "window" into the ongoing tugs and pulls of the communal soul. We have settled back into patterns of normalcy, and I sense a profound challenge before us. Transformation is an ongoing work, not an accomplishment, and there is a temptation to solidify what was fluid response to the Spirit into forms that no longer connect with the living streams of the Holy. Movement is inevitable; the only issue is in which direction—toward the unfolding call of God who is always creating, or back into the familiar ways of being and doing with a new wrapping on top. There is a slow, silent, gravitational pull toward the familiar in the deep structures of any communal soul. The challenge is to continue the process when we don't think we have to; it will mean continuing personal and communal work as we confront new dimensions of our corporate soul, with its deep gifts and disturbing shadows. Like the Israelites wandering in the desert daylight after an extraordinary, adrenaline-powered flight through the darkness, we will need "the grace of remembering" the One who met us with such awesome power and love for freedom and fullness of life. Our group spirit will continue to need tending.

Tending the communal soul of this body or any other body is an awesome, privileged, holy, important ministry. Real encounter with the Mystery is risky, and needs support. Holding a safe, contemplative space for people to notice together the different dimensions of their corporate experience and nature enables the deeper patterns of the communal spirit to rise into view for celebration, conversion, healing, and empowerment. I believe the One who created the Powers "in, through, and for the humanizing purposes of God in Christ"[15] is inviting the worldwide community of spiritual directors to consider the communal dimensions of our calling. Let us listen together with discerning hearts for the new thing the Spirit is already creating among us.

Chapter Eleven

NOT WORDS ALONE:
SPIRITUAL DIRECTION WITH VISUAL IMAGES

Betsy Caprio Hedberg

—— •◆• ——

"One picture is worth a thousand words," we've been told . . . but does this old truism apply to spiritual direction? Let's explore the use of visual images in direction: ready-made pictures, directees' artwork, three-dimensional art objects, the sand tray, and other visual material.

Think, for a moment, of the role the pictorial plays in sessions with directees. We paint word pictures and refer to easily envisioned scriptural scenes. We may lead directees in prayer with guided imagery. These techniques elicit mental images, but they are basically verbal. Perhaps your directees enter a space graced with art of some sort—an icon, a cross, a powerful photograph, a carving. And they may, from time to time, bring pictures that have caught their attention, or you may produce news photos relevant to their faith journeys. Still, visual images usually play a minor role in spiritual direction.

What a shame this is, especially as we have inherited a wealth of art—sacred and otherwise—that can add much to the service we offer others. Few of us would dispute the soul-value of all the arts. We nod ready assent to statements such as the philosopher Hegel's that the purpose of art is to help us see what we might otherwise miss. We know, as Cézanne believed, that the arts can be a revelatory vehicle of Presence. Still, when it comes to our one-to-one ministry with others (and also in our own faith lives), words may be our major—or sole—rations. I begin my musing, then, with theory about why a picture truly may be worth many words, then explore practical applications to spiritual direction.

THE VALUE OF VISUAL IMAGERY

Many commentators have noted how the invention of printing and the rise of literacy, especially in Western Europe, diminished the role of the visual.[1] The word, born in human history long after the image, became the jewel in our crown, the proof of consciousness. As early as the sixth century C.E., the unique value of art began to be curtailed by both church and state. Later as the magnificent art of the Renaissance flourished, the official line often reduced it to a tool for educating the unlettered: "For those who can't read, here are some pictures." Allowing for numerous exceptions, we can still make the general statement that the increased emphasis on the verbal in Western culture, while hardly eclipsing the visual, gradually tended to diminish its prestige and quality. The arts became stepchildren, handmaids of a "higher" ethic. Among the people, of course, the pictorial never lost its dignity; folk art and sacred art worldwide was— and is—a flowing river of beloved imagery.

Toward the twentieth century, Western civilization's imbalanced valuation of word over image began to be redressed as photography, then film and television, and now the computer screen have refocused us on the visual (to the detriment of the verbal, say many educators). In the 1960s, researchers in education and psychology began to emphasize the complementary nature of both halves of the bicameral brain: the left side, suited to the linear pattern of words, and the right brain, at home with pictures. We learned, not for the first time, that the visual is not the second-best way of understanding, but is as necessary as the verbal.

In institutional religion, educators and liturgists paid attention, and have married word and image more richly than ever. Those of us offering spiritual direction can learn from the balance developed in the group-oriented ministries of education and liturgy. We need not, by omission of the visual, wrongly imply that words alone carry God's ongoing revelation, or that verbal windows into the infinite are the best windows. Directees' experiences as citizens of an image-saturated world have taught them otherwise.

Three disciplines provide the rationale for using more imagery in spiritual direction.

Aesthetics

Aesthetics is the branch of philosophy concerned with the arts. It tends to focus on two complementary functions of art: the expression of truth, and the transmission of beauty. The ancients asked, "Is not truth of all kinds beautiful?" and the corollary question, "Does not beauty open us to truth?" Even if we have not visited Aristotle or Plato for years, or never got around to Schiller and Kant, Nietzsche and Dewey, Bergson or Santayana, these questions with which they wrestled are important for the spiritual director. Some aestheticians explore the effects of image on the viewer or listener: art as teacher, art as healer, art as a pathway to freedom. Plato suggested that the contemplation of beauty enabled the soul to grow wings. Jacques Barzun wrote that art "offers a choice [of preferring] life to lotus-eating,"[2] and George Bernard Shaw said we need art to see our souls. Postmodern philosophers have moved from the Enlightenment's cerebral conceptualization of life through verbal abstractions toward phenomenological understanding through the senses and the "primacy of perception." Important considerations for the spiritual director? Of course.

World Religions and Sacred Art

The earliest peoples created religious art. Maria Gimbutas's work, among others, brings us images of the divine prior to 10,000 B.C.E.[3] For these peoples, as for their descendants, the purpose of art was to create a connection to the deity: to bring the viewer closer to heaven, and to coax the god(s) down to earth. Sacred art is, essentially, a symbolic bridge between two worlds. James Fowler's developmental stages of faith help us understand the power of symbolic images. His final stage, we recall, describes symbols as mediators of the transcendent in an intensely personal, ever evolving way.[4]

Prayer with images or kataphatic prayer has been a mainstay not only of Christianity, but also of the religions of India and Tibet. It is rooted in the doctrine of the incarnation: divinity has become incorporated into matter and, therefore, can be encountered with the senses. Praying with visual images helps sharpen our senses so we can recognize the "splendor in the grass," and see how "every common bush (is) afire with God." Some say that since God is completely Other, we can experience God through nothing (including images of the divine). But even among primarily apophatic or imageless religions, the visual has played its role. Think, for example, of the beautiful scrollwork of Islamic mosques and calligraphy, and the knotwork of the Celtic tradition. Even though Judaism forbade graven images, inscribing the Hebrew letters of the Torah has long been deemed prayer, and Jewish wives have long set beautiful Shabbat tables as a *mitzvah*. Shakers and Quakers may not have used many pictures but, instead, theologized about the invisible reality with the simple lines and polished woods of their meeting houses.

Paul Tillich explored the meaning of sacred art at length, and came up with four helpful categories of art:

- Religious style/religious subject matter
- Nonreligious style/religious subject matter
- Religious style/nonreligious subject matter

• Nonreligious style/nonreligious subject matter.[5]

Each of these four categories of images can be, potentially, spiritual—if not specifically "religious." Questions arise: Is a piece of art or a picture spiritual because of its subject matter, because of its creator's intention, or because of its effect on the viewer? Can each type of image have a place in spiritual direction?

Depth Psychology

Much newer than—but with roots in—philosophy and the religions of the world is depth psychology. In the mid-1800s, those working with the mentally ill began to note the vivid spontaneous artwork produced by some of their patients. These drawings, paintings, and sculptures often depicted hallucinations or delusions. The question was asked, not for the first time, "From whence come these images?" By the turn of the twentieth century, the work of Freud and then Jung had postulated the existence of a vast unexplored reservoir in the human soul or psyche: the unconscious. And the language of this "inner ocean"? Image. Words, they hypothesized, are secondary symbols, the language of consciousness, while the as-yet-unknown part of us uses primary symbols, the imagistic language not dependent on speech or cognition. In 1921, C. G. Jung wrote:

———•◆•———

*The primordial image expresses the intrinsic
and unconditioned power of the psyche.
[It is], thus[,] . . . the precursor of the idea.*[6]

———•◆•———

Those familiar with Freudian or Jungian work know how much the image is valued by these two schools. Dreamwork is a key component of each. Freud wrote extensively about artists, and Jung collected the artwork of his patients, much of it still on file in Zürich. Their great contribution is in helping us understand how much of ourselves is, as yet, untapped—and how the image can connect us to that hidden kingdom within.

Others who have explored the psychology of art are Edward Edinger, James Hillman, Erich Neumann, Otto Rank, André Malraux, Ellen Handler Spitz, David Freedberg, Leo Bersani, and, especially, Rudolf Arnheim. They ask questions about our identification with specific works of art, about how artists function as our eyes and voices, about art as a tool for social transformation, and about transference to works of art. Feminist psychologists have pointed out how linear, word-based modes of thought replaced visual gestalts and paralleled the rise of patriarchal cultures.[7] The entire literature of art therapy is, of course, relevant to our understanding of the psychology of art; the works of Shaun McNiff, especially, have a decidedly spiritual bent.

In 1911, the Russian painter Kandinsky wrote that the artists of his time were the spiritual teachers of the world. He claimed in his famous treatise, *Concerning the Spiritual in Art*,[8] that nothing can take the place of art for the refinement of the human soul. If he and the philosophers, spiritual thinkers, and psychologists mentioned above are correct, then how can images fail to enhance our service to those we companion?

Let's look now at some practical applications of these powerful theories.

INCORPORATING IMAGERY INTO DIRECTION

As always, any suggestions for spiritual direction have to start with the director's own interior life and the old cliché of "you can't give what you don't have." Many spiritual directors find visual imagery an important, even essential part of their own prayer lives; perhaps you, the reader, are one of these. If not, you might wish to experiment with some of these ideas. The more we mine this rich vein for ourselves, the more we will be moved to share its wealth with others.

Art Created by Directees

An obvious way to include visual material is to ask directees to bring in their own artwork. We can encourage them to draw and paint and sculpt. I remember fondly the young man who borrowed a truck so he could bring his eight-foot paintings to my office! Ideally, all of us would create our own art (if not on quite such a grand scale), but many directees refrain from sketching even the smallest stick figures.

Resistance to art-making by "nonartists" runs deep in our culture, often rooted in early home or school put-downs of childhood scribbles. The phrase "I'm not creative" is commonly heard by directors and therapists across the land. One way to help reduce this resistance is to invite directees to keep visual journals and dream logs. When writing about a topic in their journals (and we may want, also, to address "I can't write" or "I don't have time to write"), directees might also sketch or look for pictures to accompany their text. Collage is easy. It is helpful to have a facsimile journal at hand to illustrate this simple style of journal-keeping and dream-logging.

We might remember that copying not only text, but also images, was considered an important form of asceticism by medieval monastic scribes. Black-and-white line drawings lend themselves to copying or tracing, and this activity can be turned into a very simple form of visual prayer.[9]

The Artist's Way by Julia Cameron is a deservedly popular recent book.[10] I recommend it to everyone coming to our Center; even an exercise or quote from the book often can prime the pump. *Common Boundary* magazine for July/August 1998 published Lynda McDaniel's article, "Filled with the Spirit," a superior piece on how craft of many kinds can be transmuted into prayer. My spiritual director gave this article to me, and I've referred to it often with others.

Among many other writers whose work can help develop visual skills are Frederick Franck (see, among his works, *Art as a Way*),[11] Lucia Capacchione, Madeline McMurray, Margaret Frings Keyes, Betty Edwards, Judith Cornell, and Peter London. Chogyam Trungpa teaches about creating dharma art, the art of truth from the Tibetan Buddhist perspective.[12] All can help us, who are made in the image and likeness of a Creator God, tap into our own creativity.

Perhaps only a handful of directees will paint, draw, or sculpt. Still, visual material can be incorporated into sessions through many sorts of "ready-made art." The suggestions below are a sampling of ideas for the image-conscious spiritual director.

Images for Prayer

While the Christian church's attention to art at first focused on the decoration of communal worship spaces, as early as the eighth century artworks were sanctioned for private devotion. The Second Nicene Council of 787 declared that images of Jesus and of the saints could be displayed in homes as well as in churches. Later, Thomas Aquinas spoke of the value of images for awakening piety, wondering if pictures did not move the spirit even more strongly than words. Elaborate books of hours were commissioned for personal use by patricians of the Middle Ages, but even the poor could have a crucifix or their *biblia pauperum*, an early version of today's comic-strip Bible.

What kind of art (from any of Tillich's four categories) do your directees like? What is on their walls at home? Do they use these visual images in prayer? If so, can they tell us about this practice—even bring in pictures that touch their hearts? If not, can we open a door for them? What style of art do they prefer for religious subjects? If their taste differs greatly from ours, can we put aside our aversion to the sentimental religious art of an earlier day, or to Rouault, or to Francis Bacon? Do we display the art that moves us—perhaps in a small shrine, changing it with the liturgical feasts and seasons—then turn over its fruits to the ultimate Artist?

Perhaps, like many, you and/or some directees have been captivated by the sacred icons of the Eastern Christian tradition. Today these works of art are readily available, and iconographers are "writing" new images of contemporary saints as well. An icon is more than a picture; it is an object of veneration, thought to contain the spirit of its subject. If we have learned how to gaze on an icon and to allow it to return our gaze, we'll be able to help others who wish to pray with these time-suspending images. We could do no better than to learn from a master, Henri Nouwen, whose *Behold the Beauty of the Lord: Praying with Icons* is a classic.[13] And centuries ago—thirteen, to be exact—John of Damascus responded to the iconoclasts of his day with testimony to the power of iconic images for his interior life.[14] He still can teach us how to pray with these compelling works of art.

Then there is Britain's Sister Wendy Beckett of public-television fame, who makes a convincing case in her several books for the use of art—and not only religious art—in prayer.[15] The enlivening power of art, she says, saves us from "zombie life." The same theme was sounded earlier by Quaker sculptress Sylvia Shaw Judson in *The Quiet Eye*.[16] Directors who wish to incorporate fine art into their ministry will find excellent reproductions and stimulating leads in the work of both writers, echoing art historian Titus Burckhardt's belief that

———◆———

Art clarifies the world; it helps the spirit detach itself from the disturbing multitude of things so that it may climb again toward the Infinite Unity.[17]

———◆———

Fine art, however, isn't the only kind of visual image that can help the spirit climb. The religious folk art of many traditions is also part of our visual vocabulary. Do Native American sand paintings and carvings, or Southwestern santos, or Pennsylvania German fractura, or Shaker spirit drawings pluck inner chords for you or for directees?

Praying magazine, for years, featured photographs of everyday scenes as "prayer starters." We can follow its lead à la Karl Barth, suggesting that directees "pray with the Bible in one hand and the newspaper in the other"—especially pictures (and even cartoons) in the newspaper. We can pray with magazine and news photos in session. Directees can bring in other pictures that have caught their attention and led to prayer.

We can easily put together scrapbooks or albums of cut-out pictures on various themes: pictures of people expressing different emotions, pictures of scenes from scripture, pictures of archetypal symbols. These albums can be in a waiting area or beside our chairs, ready to move both director and directee into the world of image. "Life is frazzled, you say? Let's look through this collection of pictures of holy places, set-apart spaces. They're like oases that can help us get it together. Maybe there's one that will speak to you today. We can pray with it here, and you can take it with you in your heart." Better still, we can photocopy a picture that especially appeals to a directee and, together, consider ways to pray with it.

Accessing the Unconscious

Spiritual directors attracted by Jungian lights know there is a vast interior soulscape in each of us waiting to be explored. With training and care, they go there with their directees. How? Dreams are one kind of message from that world; we can encourage directees to sketch important dream imagery. The pictures described above can serve as conduits to the inner world.

Some spiritual directors use the wonderful modality of sandplay, eliciting images that are like waking dreams. In a tray of sand, the directee creates a scene using miniature figures: people, animals, vegetation, buildings, vehicles, bridges, rocks, driftwood, shells, gems (old costume jewelry), and other small items. The picture that emerges is like an intrasychie snapshot, a segment of the person's soul. Director and traymaker usually appreciate rather than analyze this three-dimensional assemblage; they may pray over it, then cover the tray so the scene's energy is contained.

Before embarking on sandplay work with others, directors should have their own experience of making a tray series and also receive training in this valuable way of accessing the unconscious.[18]

There are two special images which can be considered spiritual maps or soul blueprints. They are the labyrinth and the mandala. In the 1990s, thanks mainly to Episcopal priest Lauren Artress, we've seen a reemergence of interest in the ancient labyrinth. The design is appearing not only on canvas but also in stone in churches around the world. (The new

Roman Catholic cathedral going up in Los Angeles has plans, at this writing, for a replica of the Chartres labyrinth in its courtyard; the path will be wide enough to allow wheelchair navigation of the holy pattern.)

Few directors will have thirty-foot labyrinths at hand, but pictures of labyrinths (and even the table-sized labyrinth now available) can be traced meditatively with one finger. This could happen during a session, or be used by waiting directees as a way to shift gears. Also, labyrinth line drawings can be given to interested directees as prayer aids for home use, with follow-up on their effectiveness.

The other design for all seasons is, surely, the mandala. The centered circle (and the circle in a square, which shows the eternal energy grounded) has long underlain meditative spiritual art from Christian rose windows to Vedic yantras and Tibetan thangkas. While the labyrinth replicates the universal journey of life, the mandala centers us. It takes us to the still point within. C. G. Jung thought of the mandala as a map of the psyche or soul, and drew many throughout his life. Religion and New Age and Jungian sections of bookstores are rich in mandala picture books and, often, the experience of coloring and then praying with a ready-made mandalic design will move someone to create his or her own from scratch.

In considering ways of accessing the unconscious we can refer back to the concept of sacred geometry, which dates from Greece of the sixth century B.C.E. and underlies both the labyrinth and the mandala. Pythagoras, then Plato, deemed the geometric shapes we remember from high school—squares, circles, triangles, spirals, cubes, and so forth—to be the unchanging thoughts in the mind of God. These eternal forms, they said, were God's celestial building blocks, used to create terrestrially in the image and likeness of God.

Even more interesting to directors is the sacred-geometry corollary, which states that one way to realign with the Creator is to spend time with these shapes from the eternal realm: reflection on the heavenly prototypes, it is said, leads one back to first things. The art of all the world's religions has deep roots in the intentional use of sacred geometry to help earthbound souls conform to the patterns of God.[19]

Sacred geometry can enter the direction experience not only through labyrinths and mandalas, but also through any visual image containing the archetypal shapes. Icons in the Eastern Christian style are an obvious example; these are traditionally developed from underlying geometric grids and forms. And many American quilts are also classics of sacred geometry. In the Center for Sacred Psychology in Los Angeles, where I see people, there is often a quilt draped over a chair or hung on the wall; the quilt may even have a biblical name such as "Tree of Life" or "Crown of Thorns."

Recently we've posted large pictures of the mysterious crop circles surfacing worldwide in fields of grain. No longer dismissed as hoaxes, they appear primarily in England, contemporary versions of the old miracle of the wheat. These haunting "temporary temples" are marvels of intricate mathematical design. Questions about them have shifted since the 1970s from "What causes them?" to "How are lives being changed by these shapes?" The crop spirals and fractals are images of transpersonal reality, just like the smaller geometric shapes in icons and quilts.

Sometimes directees comment on a nearby "agriglyph" picture or icon or quilt. Once someone said, "That quilt is like my life—lots of odds and ends." My hope is that direction helps create a beautiful whole from bits and pieces, as does a quilt. More often these shape-based artworks are not spoken about but just present, providing who-knows-what portals into the primordial realm. One of the strengths of such nonverbal adjuncts to our spoken conversation is that they need not be analyzed; the image can work in silence, independent of our commentary.

Pictures That Teach

Directors may want to add to their picture collections specific images for the purpose of instruction. Again, often one picture will speak far better than a stream of words. Beside my chair I have a portfolio of such images. It was developed over the years as I found myself verbally trying to describe a basic point, or sketching little diagrams, or hopping up to pull books with clarifying illustrations off the bookshelves. Here are some of the images in this collection (the reader will note how they reflect my Jungian bent). They're among my most useful aids; I refer to them daily.

A "map" of the soul or psyche. Picture an island emerging from a four-layered ocean, each tier darker than the one above. The sun shines on the island, which represents consciousness. The layers are, from the top down, the personal unconscious, the family unconscious, the cultural unconscious, and the collective unconscious.[20] Using this scheme, I describe our joint efforts to directees, saying something like this: "You see how consciousness, where words reign, is such a small part of the whole picture. Our work helps lower the waterline so there's more consciousness. We do that by paying attention to whatever the unexplored part of the soul sends up (dreams, feelings, memories, etc.), and also by 'fishing' in the unconscious with its language of pictures and stories and symbols."

Sharing this chart with directees gives them a rationale for the use of image. If pictures are the language of the inner sea, then all can profit by learning to speak that language. Without this view, less visually oriented directees may dismiss the suggestion that they create their own art and seek out imagery, saying, "That's just your thing."

Pictures of seekers. I think it's helpful to have an image for living the interior life, and so have some pictures as starting points for directees who have yet to find their own. There's the deep-sea diver finding hidden treasure while watching out for sharks and other dangers of the waters. There's Jesus telling the apostles to let down their nets, an image for all of us who fish in the inner sea. These two pictures are natural follow-ups to the ocean chart, above.

If we change the analogy of the soul's layers from water to land, then two other images of the seeker work well. Picture an archaeologist who has dug down deeply and found . . . who knows what? And next, a miner hard at work in the dark. I'm still looking for a picture of oil drillers sending down a pipeline. In none of these pictures is the seeker alone: the diver is connected to life support, Jesus stands by the fishermen, the archaeologist has a team of colleagues, the miner has companions. The deep waters or the innards of the earth are best explored in partnership.

Another pair of pictures faces each other. On the left is John Climacus's "ladder of perfection," which can be found in icon collections. People are ascending the holy *scala* toward God in the upper-right corner, which is heaven, even as demons attempt to pull them off.

Opposite this traditional, dualistic view of the spiritual life is the picture of a pilgrim. He looks at a group of animals and people, each with a tiny image of God at its heart. The pilgrim does not have to go anywhere to reach the divine, but needs only eyes capable of seeing what is already present.

"What do you think?" I might ask, as people naturally gravitate toward the second picture. "Is the first picture your style? If so, do vestiges of that theology remain in your practice? How do you see spiritual growth?"

Attitudes toward spiritual practice. Here I use a Diego Rivera print. A group of laborers walks as if on a chain gang—backs bent, jaws tense, teeth gritted. With this picture I can ask, "What's the flavor of spiritual practice for you? Is it like this?" Usually the answer is negative; then I can ask, "If not this, then what is your idea of living the spiritual life?" Many directees come up with images of people in love; the thousand-year-old Christian version involves holy espousals or mystical marriage (e.g., the Catherines of both Alexandria and Siena becoming brides of Christ).[21] In alchemical language, these are images of the *coniunctio,* the union with the Other. The Star of David, also known as Solomon's Seal, which represents the marriage of earth and heaven, is a Jewish representation of this concept. China gave us the tai chi or yin-yang symbol to represent the same union of opposites.

Pictures of the inner family. Two favorite works illustrate this idea. Degas and Picasso both painted women gazing at their reflections in a mirror. In each case, the woman she sees is like herself, but shadier, less defined. Degas's *Madame Jeantaud at the Mirror* and Picasso's *Girl Before a Mirror* glimpse their shadows, to use Jung's term for a part of ourselves that is still in the dark (under the water, buried in the ground).

I also use sketches showing how people have depicted other members of the inner family: mother, father, child, and so forth. A photocopy of Jung's artwork is included, showing the wise old man, the medieval woman, the courtier, the prince of the church, and others he had met in dreams or projected form.[22]

Recording our spiritual biography. We have all seen pictures of the beautiful altarpieces of late-medieval Europe. Their central panels usually depict a saint in glorified (that is, heavenly) form. This panel is surrounded by small scenes highlighting key moments of this person's soul journey. Narrative icons are a smaller version of this "life-at-a-glance" idea.

A picture of such an altarpiece or icon gives directees a model for visually recording their own spiritual autobiographies.[23] "If you were creating your own visual soul story, what scenes would you put in the different sections? What have been the turning points of your spiritual life? How many spaces would you leave for things to come? How would you picture soul-events that were internal rather than external?" The altarpieces give us excellent clues. The clincher question is, "How do you suppose the central portrait of yourself might look?" We can make a line drawing of this art to give directees. They may make notes on the handout, or use it as a model for a collage of photographs or symbols or other artwork. A long-term project, this could become a twenty-first-century altarpiece, their own visual story of a soul.

In our office we have other sets of pictures. Most we have put together ourselves. Some are in scrapbooks or photo albums, some are on large index cards, some are taped in accordion-style foldouts, some are loose in boxes. For example, we have pictures of the story of the people of Israel and the story of Jesus. Scenes from the Hebrew and Christian scriptures can be viewed not only historically and theologically, but also psychologically; that is, we too can be led out of Egypt, and we too have been in agony in the garden. Directees can be asked, "Did any of these scenes ever happen to you?" Jung reminds us that "what happens in the life of Christ happens always and everywhere."[24]

Other picture cycles are of Mary's girlhood, shown with prints of Giotto's frescoes in Padua's Arena Chapel; scenes from Dante's *Divine Comedy* with the Doré engravings; the Taoist ox-herding pictures; illustrations of the nine Enneagram personality types; and an array of goddesses of antiquity. We also use contemporary maps of psychospiritual development, including those of Jung, Erikson, Maslow, or some gender-specific maps for women based on Carol Pearson's, Maria Harris's, and Maureen Murdock's work. All of these resources can be used to ask directees, "Can you find yourself in a picture?" (Do you think we had fun putting these sets of images together?)

The teaching pictures described also can be, of course, excellent channels into the inner worlds of directees, and they are often prayer starters as well. All three categories of ready made images have become integral parts of ministry for me, and directees often have echoed my conviction about their value.

POSSIBLE PITFALLS

There are problematic aspects to using pictures in spiritual direction. Let's look at a few of them.

First, if we are in love with visual imagery, we may need to monitor our enthusiasm. Having a stash of pictures at hand, we can find ways to integrate them into sessions when appropriate, but only when this flows organically. The bottom line with word or image is always, "Whose need am I meeting: the directee's or mine?"

Variety in imagery is important. If we add pictures to our repertory of spiritual-direction aids, we will want to be inclusive. With a multiethnic group of directees, it is essential to have imagery from each person's heritage. I still wince on recalling the African American woman who closed up after I offered her some Grimms' fairy-tale pictures. The wonderful characters she saw were not only all light-skinned, but also Teutonic, even Nordic. My unspoken, unintentional message to her was, "Your culture is not recognized here." We could and did talk this over, but our alliance suffered once I produced such exclusive imagery. (I have her permission to report this detail from our time together.)

Even if the only people crossing your threshold are Caucasian males, within each is the black man, the brown man, the Asian man . . . and who knows how many female inner-family members? Images should reflect transcultural diversity. The more than 1,600 submissions to the *National Catholic Reporter*'s "Jesus 2000" art contest strikingly reflected that diversity, and provided for many a twenty-first-century springboard into the eternal question, "Who do you say that I am?"

Variety is also important in balancing pictures of sweetness and light with distressing or upsetting pictures. If we have only the former, the implied message is, "There's little (or no) place here for sadness and pain." This, surely, is not the way we understand our ministry; we want to avoid visual omissions that suggest such an attitude.

Regarding pictures chosen or brought in by a directee, we can be tempted to leap to interpretation. The directee selects a picture from a group, and we are ready to analyze. But over-explaining art of any sort (again, words, words, words) can intrude on the experience of the artwork. One thinks of the rueful term *imagicide,* which means to murder the image by interpreting it too soon.

Although the history and symbolism of much art—fine art, folk art, everyday images—are fascinating, we should remember that interpretation and background information about a piece is only a supplement to its visual power. Too much input from the guide implies, wrongly, that the art cannot stand on its own. It also yanks the image out of the unconscious, which it has activated, and brings the energy into cognition too quickly. C. G. Jung often spoke of the troublesome intellect that aborts dialogue with the unconscious; in fact, he termed it "the devil"![25]

Even if we think we know what an image means to someone, this may be our own projection. Symbolic images can never be reduced to just one meaning, à la popular dream-interpretation books; symbols are, always, overdetermined. I may loathe snakes and have repulsive associations for them; a Freudian therapist may see them as phallic symbols; for someone else they may be the goddess's friend or the healer's totem animal. We may ask for directees' associations to an image, but will want to avoid contaminating these associations with our own.

We also want to monitor the ways we respond emotionally to a directee's choice of image. Be careful of evaluations such as "What a beautiful picture" or "Gee, that's gruesome." Such personal reactions from a director are another contamination. They can sway directees and hamper their freedom of choice in the future. "I won't bring Betsy this horrific picture I found of mass atrocities, even though it's haunted me all month," someone may think; "I remember how she recoiled when I chose that shot of the lion having a gazelle for dinner." Or, conversely, if a directee once brought joy to our face with her hearts-and-flowers artwork, she may want to continue to make us smile. After all, we work so hard, and are so good to others, and if she can brighten our day, etc., etc. This is a perfect setup for repressing the shadow.

Another pitfall involves suggesting a visual experience to a directee, who replies, "I'd rather just talk." Talking is fine—and maybe that is all we need to do. We might ask ourselves, however, if, skulking behind this statement, is the mistaken—and elitist—belief that imageless experience (especially in prayer) is somehow "higher" than imagistic experience. Some seem to consider apophatic prayer the truest form of prayer, thus demoting imaginal or kataphatic prayer styles to "less holy."

The history of spiritual theology tells us this is false. We know there are many paths to God (ways, as they say in Asia). The ultimate fruit of prayer may be infused contemplation, in which the soul is stripped and emptied so that it can be filled with God. However, we need not confuse this ultimate (and rare) end—which is a pure gift—with one of several means that predispose the soul for this grace. Apophatic prayer is one such means; praying with visual aids is another. The important question is, "What works for this person at this time?"

Finally, we know that spiritual directors need to be prepared for occasional emotional eruptions from those they see. Since pictorial material is a quick-acting catalyst for accessing our deepest interior caverns, it can also energize sea-monster-like memories or trauma that may be inhabiting those caverns. Imagery, even more than words, can be a potent trigger for eliciting a directee's unresolved issues. This is a plus . . . as long as we are prepared for it.

Our Image of Spiritual Direction: Metaphors for This Ministry

Let's consider the value to directors of images about our ministry. We have loads of words and mental pictures describing our work. Do we also have actual pictures to go with these? For years, I had a print of a Fra Angelico *Visitation* in my office. It spoke to me of how people came in, like Mary "full of grace," and how my task, like Elizabeth's, was to welcome them and to attend to the latest chapters of their faith stories. (It helps that my name is Elizabeth.) Directees saw the picture too; a few even said, "Oh, that's like us."

There are many beautiful ways to envision the ministry of spiritual direction. At one time we may be midwife; with another, fellow pilgrim on the road of life. Another time we may function as a co-sleuthing and recording Watson to directee's Holmes, or a Sancho Panza to questing Don Quixote. Some directors like the shepherd(ess) image. Paul wrote about planting and watering—spiritual director as gardener.

In the Sufi tradition the *murshid*, or guide, is likened to an oyster holding disciples within (and irritating them?) until they become pearls. There is the idea of director as "sign." Abraham Heschel urged fellow Jews not to have symbols, but to be symbols, to stand for the divine; Christian language for this is the person as icon. The director may be a dance partner, sometimes leading and sometimes being led as two respond in unison to the Lord of the Dance. There is even the image of spiritual director as yenta, the marriage broker between a soul and God!

Images of direction, which can nourish our service to others, spring from our own answers to two primary questions of the spiritual life: "What is my image of God?" and "How do I perceive my relationship to God?"

Living these questions moves me to ask, "If all is holy, if spirit saturates matter, if—as the scriptures and yesteryear's Celts and today's quantum physicists assure us—all of creation is connected in the web of life, then what visualization of direction best inspires me?" More and more, I feel akin to the view of the spiritual director who encourages others to test, soak in, and, eventually, to dive deeply into that all-encompassing ocean of love we call the living God.

This picture has been with me at least a quarter of a century. I still can see vividly the huge print of a swimming pool in the office of my own spiritual director. Lined up along one side, from deep end to shallow, are several persons in old-fashioned bathing dress. One or two have a toe in the pool. Another reaches in with her hand. In the center is a swimming coach (or maybe just a water-secure friend) encouraging them to "come on in—the water's fine." There are goggles and fins and life preservers at hand. In the pool are other swimmers. They splash and paddle, swim laps, or just rest and let themselves be upheld by the water. There are also a few high-board divers flipping gracefully in midair; the coach seems amazed by them and, clearly, is learning from them.

If indeed we are immersed in the divine, as Catherine of Siena imagined, then a parallel image of the spiritual director is a biblical one: that of the individual who helps to heighten others' senses so they can *truly* perceive. Eli tells Samuel to listen to God, the psalmist invites us to "taste and see the goodness of the Lord," Jesus wants us to have "eyes that see and ears that hear." In terms of an image for the altar in the director's heart (and on his or her wall as well?), maybe the guide is lighting a candle or turning up a lamp or screwing in a stronger bulb for greater clarity. Or does the spiritual director help fit others with ever-sharper glasses, the better to see how "earth's crammed with heaven" (director as optician)?

I have heard directees refer to their sessions as "tune-ups"—not as with a car, but as with a musical instrument. That is a good picture to inspire us, with ourselves as the fine-tuners even while heartened by the other's transmission of The Music. Another sort of tuning could show the director adjusting someone's antennae for better reception (directee as . . . Martian?). Readers fluent in cyberspeak will be able, surely, to come up with a computer variation on this theme.

Or how about the director as one who holds up a mirror so others can see themselves more clearly and with better perspective? For this metaphor, I'd like that mirror veined with gold; this way, it speaks to both parties of how the directee's life is shot through with the sparks of God, Holy Wisdom.

A related group of images could picture the director as one who helps uncover the presence of God, which wafts around and through us. We all tend to experience material reality as separate from spirit; the spiritual director can assist in dissolving barriers between seen and unseen, thus revealing that visible and invisible are one rather than separate realities. In Andrew Lang's *Orange Fairy Book* (1903), there is a wonderful picture of a man lifting a veil so a younger man can explore a sunlit area. The seeker's face is transfigured, as he (like Plato's cave dwellers) views a world "charged with the grandeur of God." Similarly, the director can be a porter who holds open doors or windows or gates into that infinity that is omnipresent—not another world at all, but one continually seeping into, saturating, and ensouling the mundane world. Pictures of any of the above could find a place in our consulting space, helping us to remember what we're about. We can change them as we change.

To put the above into theologese, directors cooperate in the continuing revelation of the incarnation of God—but Andrew Greeley says it better. Writing of the artist (and he could be speaking of the spiritual director), Greeley describes "someone who sees the hints of grace *lurking* in the world and in human life, and illumines them for the rest of us."[26]

Oh, yes!—and how might we do this very well? We know that the director's own spiritual life is the seedbed of this (and all) ministry. So, with the help of our own spiritual companions, we put on glasses that reveal how divinity irradiates and sacralizes all life. We discover our own doorways or windows into infinity and learn how to prop them open and keep them ajar. We seek out coaches to help us dive deeply into the ocean of love. Ripple effects flow into our ministry to others. Of course, the process often works the other way, as directees vault off a high board we didn't even know was there, penetrate The Deep . . . and open our eyes to what it really means to swim.

Visual images of spiritual direction itself, as well as pictures used to access the nooks and crannies of directees' souls, can coax God's shimmering presence into awareness in ways words alone can never achieve. The image is the gracious elder sister of the word, an enormous asset to spiritual directors of all persuasions. Now, having used several thousand words to make this point, it is surely time for a picture break. There's one waiting for me right now. Is one calling to you?

Chapter Twelve

"FLESH IS MORE THAN FLESH":
SEXUALITY AND SPIRITUALITY IN SPIRITUAL DIRECTION

Janet K. Ruffing, R.S.M.

———— • ◆ • ————

One winter night, Benedict's sister, Scholastica,
was awakened by a song bird. How can this be, she
thought, and she looked out the window of her cell.
Three naked men were dancing in the monastery
garden by the light of the moon. One whistled like a
bird and made her laugh. The men were fair to look
at, Scholastica thought, but she knew she needed
more rest before the first prayers of the day.

Kneeling by her bed, she closed her eyes and sleepily
said a prayer for the men—if they were men—that
they might find shelter, clothing, and rest for their
dancing feet,
and if (as she suspected) they were demons,
that they might return to from whence they came.

When she awoke, her cell was filled with the scent of
roses. Where the men had been dancing a rose bush
had sprung up and was blooming in the snow. It
bloomed all that winter, and it blooms to this day.[1]

———— • ◆ • ————

This is a lovely, ambiguous story of a wise monastic woman who could
hear the songbird of sexuality and laugh without having to repress either
its wildness or its strangeness. Like all good discernment, she prayerfully
waited to discover more about it so that the rose bush could bloom to this
very day. I would hope that as spiritual directors our directees would find
such openness when matters explicitly related to sexuality and spirituality
become part of their spiritual direction, as they most certainly will.

In order to help us reflect on the relationship between sexuality and spirituality in our practice of spiritual direction, this essay sketches a general theological, anthropological, and cultural framework.

PERSONAL EMBODIED SPIRITS

It seems to me that we might describe ourselves as "personal, embodied spirits." This anthropological assumption ought to condition how we relate our sexuality to our spirituality. As sexual persons, which all of us are, our sexuality always has a profoundly personal quality. It is never pure instinct, although there is much about our sexual experience that is rooted in mysterious survival. Because we inhabit our world in different embodiments according to gender and sex, our sexuality is always framed by our personhood, marked by our ability to choose how and when and in what ways we will express our desires in relationship with another, with ourselves, and with God.

As human persons, we are embodied. Our spirits do not exist without the graceful companionship of our bodies. It is in and through our bodies that we know and experience ourselves, the natural world, social life, and interpersonal knowing and loving. This temple of our bodies houses all of our spiritual experience, in which our spirit meets the Spirit and other people's spirits. Our bodies are the sacraments of our presence; this is the only way we have of presenting ourselves. Our spirits manifest themselves in and through our sensuousness and our sexuality.

I think that James Nelson's definitions are helpful here:

———— • ◆ • ————

*By spirituality I mean not only the conscious
religious disciplines and practices through which
human beings relate to God, but more inclusively
the whole style and meaning of our relationship to
that which we perceive as of ultimate worth and
power. This includes disciplines and practices,
but also myths, symbols, and rituals, informal as
well as formal. It includes the affective as well as the
cognitive. Significantly, spirituality includes the
ways in which our relatedness to the ultimate affects
our understandings and feelings of relatedness to
everyone and everything else.*

*By sexuality I mean not only physiological arousal
and genital activity, but also much more. While
human sexuality is not the whole of our personhood, it
is a basic dimension of that personhood. While it does
not determine all thought, feeling, and action, it does
permeate and affect all of these. Sexuality is our way
of being in the world as female or male persons. It
involves our appropriation of characteristics socially
defined as feminine or masculine. It includes our
affectional-sexual orientation toward those of the
opposite and/or same sex. It is our attitudes
toward ourselves and others as body-selves.
It is our capacity for sensuousness. It is all of this.*

*The intimate relation between sexuality and
spirituality is evident if one believes, as I do, that
sexuality is both a symbol and a means of
communication and communion. The mystery of
sexuality is the mystery of the human need to reach
out for the physical and spiritual embrace of others.
Sexuality thus expresses God's intention that people
find authentic humanness not in isolation but in
relationship. In sum, sexuality always involves much
more than what we do with our genitals. More
fundamentally, it is who we are as body-selves who
experience the emotional, cognitive, physical, and
spiritual need for intimate communion,
both creaturely and divine.*[2]

———— • ◆ • ————

GRACE IN THE SENSES

If we draw on another often poorly understood theme within Christian tradition, our sexuality is one of the ways through which we experience that particular "grace in the senses" that we signify by the term *incarnation*. God becomes flesh that we that touch the holy in and through our senses.

Sometimes, I think women know this grace in the senses more intimately and pervasively than men because our sexuality, "by its very nature, is a total sensory experience, involving the whole body (not just the genitals). . . . A woman does not even need a partner or a significant one-to-one relationship to be in touch with her sexuality."[3] Many women describe these total sensory experiences as sensual or ecstatic rather than "sexual" because women's bodies are programmed at the cellular level to respond to such grace in our senses. "Sexual energy is the life-force (Eros) that permeates all of creation and is part of the joyfulness of creation."[4] Because some of us do not associate this rich sensuality with "sexuality"—when taken in its more limited sense as exclusively genital—some women may not explicitly connect such experiences with sexuality at all.

Contemporary women nature poets with a mystical bent evoke this diffuse sexuality and sensuality as it rises in consciousness in response to nature and to one's own inspirited incarnation. Mary Oliver and Pattiann Rogers offer excellent examples in their poetry.

I find it common in retreat direction that God literally makes love to us in and through our sensuousness in response to the beauty and even terror of creation. It is equally common in my experience that directees describe these experiences without conscious reference to sexuality, because these are usually experiences that happen alone, without specific genital stimulation.

Yet these responses lead us to another neglected theme in theological anthropology—the ecstatic characteristic of human persons. Whenever we love another, we are literally an ecstasis, a standing outside of ourselves. Human beings are made for such relationship, for such self-transcendence, for repeatedly feeling drawn beyond ourselves in both our human and divine loving. This human capacity for ecstasy is a normal part of ourselves. We all know that ecstatic sensual experience can be very spiritual. We experience uplifting ecstatic energy in music, in art, in worship, in intense feelings of love, in creativity, in sport, play, and dance, in communion with nature, as well as in our attractions and passions with human or divine lovers. As we all know as spiritual directors, some persons experience intensely erotic, ecstatic energy in their mystical experiences as well.

As spiritual directors, we have no choice but to engage this sexual core in our religious experience and that of our directees. We need to be alert to the ways in which explicit sexual themes and more diffuse sensual-sexual energies and passions emerge in directees' experience.

In my premise that we are personal embodied spirits, I imply as well an important relational aspect to our sexuality. Our sexuality is the instinctual root of our movement toward others. We learn, helpfully or unhelp-fully, from our families of origin how we are to express our sexual selves, or to contain or repress them. We unconsciously assimilate from them how we dare to feel about these powerful energies. Our first bodily experiences of nurture are patterned usually by our parental experience. So, too, psy-chologically are our images for God. Here I want to connect our early atti-tudes toward our body-selves, which originate in our families, and our images of God. They often get mixed up with one another.

Repressive family or religious contexts do not help us to become com-fortable with, familiar with, and accepting of our sexuality, regardless of our orientations. If we are gay, bisexual, or lesbian, we implicitly receive negative and shame-inducing judgments and feelings about our sexuality before we even know clearly what our orientation might be. Repressive approaches to any form of sexuality do not help us learn much about our-selves, nor do they teach us how to adopt spiritual practices that can edu-cate and transform these desires, which we ourselves do not even quite understand.

The psychological characteristics of our sexuality will always have both conscious and unconscious aspects. If Freud has taught us nothing else, he has taught us that sex is almost never only sex, but often a complex symbol for many other things. As spiritual directors we need to be open to the symbolic meanings that sexual behaviors, desires, and images may have within the context of the particular histories of the people who share their sacred stories with us.

LOVE AT THE CORE

The human drive toward self-transcendence in a religion that places divine and human love at the core suggests that our passion, our eros as well as our agape, is ultimately directed toward God. If we do not follow the meanderings of these sometimes wayward and misplaced desires, we also cannot discover whence they originate and whither they lead. Without nonjudgmental attentiveness to these complex and confusing desires, we cannot discover what, as human lovers and companions, each person requires in order to discover the love at the heart of the universe and the life-force that propels us toward it.

This passion is the energy that wise directors enable their directees to endure, suffer, contain, explore, express, surrender to, respect, and rever-ence. Believe me, we will suffer with them as they struggle. Passion and authentic love cannot ultimately be controlled and still be love. Something about these experiences is mysterious. "They are about infatuation and longing, courtship and poetry, passion and friendship."[5]

PARTICIPATION IN MYSTERY

In other words, sexual experience in all its forms—bodily longing, sexual fantasies, relationships which begin in infatuation, response to arousal, and simple offers of loving friendship—are among the core human experiences that participate in surpassing Mystery. These experiences present openings into the Sacred Beloved at the heart of the universe, regardless of our sexual orientations or the choices we or our directees make about forms of sexual expression.

In many cultures of the world, religious traditions treat sexuality as one access to the Sacred. Prior to our technological, scientific, and psychological age, sexuality symbolized life itself. The power to bring human life into the world was a wondrous mystery—one to be reverenced, respected, and even worshiped. Sexuality itself was sacred. The twin mysteries of human existence—life and death—bring us face to face with the divine. Who originates this life in which we participate? Who ends this life of ours or of our beloved's at some moment in time? Primordially in human experience, the life force biologically and instinctively part of our creaturely existence brings us face to face with the even larger Mystery "in whom we live and move and have our very being."

At the same time, passionate love—our erotic attractions toward another—remains both mysterious and fearsome. We encounter this mysterious quality when we surrender to that love—whether in romantic pursuit of another or in response to one who desires us—or welcome its arrival in other ways. Both the joy and ecstasy of self-transcendence may occur in sexual union, in the delight related to childbirth, and in the demands of nurturing young life. Passionate love can also be blind, like a fire moving rapidly across the terrain, leaving destruction in its path. Our love and passion are not always ordered, not always enlightened, not always self-giving and mutually respecting. We often don't know what we are doing. The dangerous aspect of sexuality is no less mysterious than the ecstatic and loving aspects.

Sexuality in its erotic playfulness and passion is inherently mysterious, participating in the deeper Mystery of God's own life for women and men who live in a context of faith and love for God. Paul Ricoeur captures something of this mystery in human sexual love:

————•◆•————

*Ultimately, when two beings embrace, they don't
know what they are doing, they don't know what
they want, they don't know what they are looking for,
they don't know what they are finding. What is the
meaning of this desire which drives them toward
each other? Is it the desire of pleasure? Yes, certainly.
But this is a poor response, for at the same time we
feel that pleasure does not contain its own meaning.
That it is [symbolic]. But of what?*

*We have the vivid and yet obscure feeling that sex
participates in a network of powers whose cosmic
harmonies are forgotten but not abolished; that life
is much more than life—that is, much more than
the struggle against death, or delaying the time
when the debt must be paid; that life is unique,
universal, everything in everyone, and that
sexual joy makes us participate in this mystery. . . .*[6]

————•◆•————

Church teaching recognizes that this mystery "is bound up in the mystery and purpose of God, who is the author of all life, and love itself."[7] It is participation in co-creativity with God, who made us sexual in the first place. God, too, must somehow be passionate and delight in spousal joy. God must somehow be at the root of our desire and longing and want to fill us full of Divine life and love. For the vast majority, marriage or other form of committed partnering is a path of salvation and transformation. Love begets love.

Because sexuality at its core is the "mystery of the human need to reach out for the physical and spiritual embrace of others," our familial relationships and friendships become a school of love. The drive toward sexual union is the source of creativity both biologically and in other ways that serve the common good. Stability of relationship can foster profound growth into love that is faithful in season and out of season. Such relationships, through the joys and challenges of shared life, can serve as crucibles of transformation into greater love. Church teaching has been clear that "the one core universal vocation is to love and be loved."[8] Faithfulness to love becomes revelatory of God. We learn to love, to embody, express, be love in our world as an intrinsic aspect of Christian vocation.

This experience of and desire for love is what James Thurber and E. B. White call "the strange bewilderment which overtakes one person on account of another person."[9] This strange bewilderment is almost always as much about what we mean by God as about human love. We need to feel this bewilderment, because we only become truly ourselves by allowing ourselves to be "carried away"—this is what I referred to above as our ecstatic nature. When we say yes to these experiences, desirous of love, we often discover that there we can abide in God, and God abide in us.

TASK OF SPIRITUAL DIRECTORS

How attuned are we as spiritual directors to receive such revelations from our directees? Only if we are comfortable with the sexual and spiritual and truly appreciate the confusing, troubled, guilt-ridden, intense, ecstatic, deceptive, revelatory, fluid, tender, joyful, powerful, and intimate quality of these stories can we help. Through our embodied and sensitive responses we can slowly help our directees integrate their sexuality and spirituality, both in human relationship and in prayer, when prayer takes the form of complex erotic imagery related to God's intimacy with them.

As I described elsewhere,[10] this comfort is not easily presupposed among spiritual directors shaped by a religious tradition that has variously construed the relationship between sexuality and spirituality. On the one hand, we have consistently taught and defended the goodness of our created world, which includes sexuality and sexual love. We have taught that we as sexual beings are made in the image of God and so partake mysteriously in God's love. We understand the nature of the triune God to be love, which was expressed in God's becoming fully human—incarnate in flesh in Jesus who gifts us with the indwelling Spirit. On the other hand, Christian tradition remains deeply ambivalent about sexuality. For much of our history, we have privileged sexual abstinence as an ascetical means of pursuing holiness, while neglecting forms of asceticism appropriate to sexually bonded relationships as an equally valid path of holiness. We have clearer teaching about sexual morality and sexual sinfulness than we do about sexual holiness, sexuality in the service of love, and sexuality as a privileged locus of ecstatic and mystical experience. We have dignified marriage with its own sacrament. Yet in much of our public discourse and practice, we fail to recognize the primordial sacramentality of all forms of bodily loving. Such sacramentality occurs in the following ways: through interpersonal presence and communion; through the myriad ways of "touching" one another in life-affirming and creative ways; and through all the concrete actions of nurture and care required by our bodily existence. In the mystical tradition, we have reserved spousal symbolism for the purely spiritual domain and neglected the mystical potential of marital sexuality.

Most of us experience anxiety in the face of sexual or mystical experience that appears to deviate from standard heterosexual norms or that conflicts with public church teaching on reproductive issues. We and our directees are programmed more for anxiety than for appreciation—more for controlling sexuality (even in imagined prayer or fantasy) than for wondering about how love is trying to express itself or how God is trying to break through in profound mystery of erotic love and desire. Our response to directees will either open them to further exploration and integration or shut them down. Directees look to us for a safe "holding environment"—a safe place where they can risk voicing and responding to strange solicitations by God in perplexing experiences.

Were we more familiar with the gender-bending and fluid gender identifications of the Christian mystical tradition, we would discover that mystics, regardless of their gender, sexual orientations, or genital behaviors, use a great variety of erotic metaphors to describe their increasing intimacy with God. For instance, women mystics like Julian of Norwich and Teresa of Ávila relate to Jesus as a mother breast-feeding her child, or as a lover nourished by the breasts of the beloved in ecstatic joy and pleasure, receiving divine milk at the same time. Men in the medieval period might have related to Mary as a lover, or, like Francis, espoused Lady Poverty—powerful feminine images of the Divine for heterosexual men. Others related to Sophia—the feminine personification of God from the Book of Proverbs that is now being appropriated by both men and women as a contemporary mixed-gender image for Jesus. There is a long homosexual tradition, especially in religious art, which portrays John as a homosexual in relationship to Jesus.

What I am trying to evoke is a sensibility that our sexuality and our spirituality are deeply interwoven with one another. Our erotic experiences of human lovers as well as our non-genitalized loving relationships become templates of our imagery for God as the divine beloved. In a sense, as goes our sexuality, so goes our spirituality.

This acknowledgment can be extremely confusing and even embarrassing for directees should that imaging take unconventional forms. Some directees are completely unfamiliar with the tradition of love mysticism and become disturbed if their prayer becomes eroticized. In some Christian circles, sexuality lives so far from God that directees cannot even imagine that God or Jesus might express love in a sexualized form. For others, homoerotic imagery in prayer can be profoundly disturbing. For some directees, this may be the first indication that they are, in fact, gay, lesbian, or bisexual; they may not yet be ready to welcome this reality into their lives. Many heterosexual directees may be shocked when imagery for God contradicts their ordinary sense of themselves and their sexuality. They may be unaware that such imagery may be transient and not uncommon. For directees with little exposure to any real spiritual tradition, dream images or prayer images of a sexual nature may be a covert symbol for spiritual desire. For directees who have long been engaged in spiritual life, the emergence of the sexual may be an invitation to integrate these energies in more conscious and explicit ways. One Kundalini teacher I know asserts that spiritual energy is exactly one octave higher than sexual energy. People who have emphasized spiritual energy without integrating sexual energy may become involved with a partner who is more sexual than spiritual, and vice versa. John of the Cross teaches us to expect an upsurgence of sexual energy in the aggression in the *Dark Night of the Senses;* such emergence is typically a midlife phenomenon today.

As directors, we need to attend to our own sexual energies, fantasies, and desires as they emerge in both our prayer and relationships, so that we do not bring unnecessary anxiety or discomfort to our directees. This is a fruitful area in which to work with our own spiritual directors, so that we are not thrown off balance by highly charged material our directees need the freedom and safety to explore.

Cultural Influences

I have discussed some aspects of church culture that may make this a difficult area for directors themselves to gain their own spiritual right relationship to this area of their lives. Yet we also are embedded in and unconsciously influenced by a secular culture that offers tremendous challenge. Cultural definitions of body and sexuality are pervasive, often pornographic and exploitative. Despite our allegiance to gender equality, women continue to be exploited sexually, abused, raped, commodified, and defined by standards of beauty or desirability that lead to anorexia, self-loathing, and disrespect.

Neither are men excluded from such treatment. Body image, sexual conquest, the severance of sexuality from relationships, confusion between love and power, sexual forms of domination, and abuse of power continue to be glorified in the media. Young people by the age of ten, or earlier, have often experimented sexually, and reach young adulthood with a series of unintegrated sexual experiences that leave them confused about sexuality, boundaries, and relationships. Directees of all ages have been shaped by the popular culture of film, television, and pop psychology—poor models for relationships. As a result, many of us are obsessed by sexuality in some form and search for instant intimacy in an individualistic quest to assuage our loneliness. Even technology leads us to relational misunderstandings. The Internet is a new location for sexual predation and inadequate forms of intimacy. This technology, although extremely helpful in some ways, disembodies our relationships. Hours spent at a keyboard or clicking a mouse create greater isolation and decrease the social skills needed to develop healthy face-to-face relationships. Virtual relationships can now supplant real ones.

REFLECTIONS FOR SPIRITUAL DIRECTORS

As spiritual directors we need to ask deeper questions. We need to question our own assumptions and beliefs and ask ourselves and our directees: What might be happening here? Where is this passion or desire leading? Do we have the balance and patience to follow the desire into places of incredible light and incredible confusion? By what are we seduced? In what ways are our directees deceived? In what ways might they be our teachers, making us aware of ways of living and loving we might never know? Do we hold healthy images of embodied loving for all who constitute the Christian community—gays and lesbians, married and unmarried, partnered and unpartnered? How do we experience God revealing God's self to each of them through their unique personalities and lives? How do we deal with the hypocrisy that is displayed in the media and press about political and religious leaders whose sexuality is abusive, exploitative, or contrary to what they profess it publicly to be? Are we open to a broad range of sexual experiences, without being overly moralistic or overly protective? Are we discerning enough to recognize when referral for dysfunctional or self-destructive sexual behavior is appropriate, while staying with our directees in their sacred place with God? Do we believe that all desire can lead to God, if we can help our directees discern among their desires?

If we can remember, as Pattiann Rogers reminds us, that "there's more to flesh than flesh," we might be able to do so.

Maybe it's the pattern of the shattering
sea-moon so inherent to each body
that makes each more than merely body.
Maybe it's the way the blood possesses
the pitch and fall of blooming grasses
in a wind that makes the prairie
of the heart greater than its boundaries.
Maybe it's god's breath swelling
in the breast and limbs, like a sky
at dawn, that gives bright bone
the holiness of a rising sun.
There's more to flesh than flesh.[11]

REFERENCES

Egan, Robert J., S.J. "Experiencing Ourselves as Sexual Beings in the Context of Contemporary American Culture: Some Theological Reflections." 1996.

Nelson, James B. *Between Two Gardens: Reflection on Sexuality and Religious Experience*. New York: Pilgrim Press, 1983.

Norris, Kathleen. *The Cloister Walk*. New York: Riverhead, 1996.

Northrup, Christiane. *Women's Bodies, Women's Wisdom: Creating Physical and Emotional Health and Healing*. New York: Bantam, 1994.

Oliver, Mary. *Selected Poems*. Boston: Beacon Press, 1992.

Ricoeur, Paul. "Wonder, Eroticism, and Enigma." In *Sexuality and the Sacred: Sources for Theological Reflection*, edited by James B. Nelson and Sandra P. Longfellow. Louisville: Westminster/John Knox Press, 1994.

Rogers, Pattiann. *Eating Bread and Honey*. Minneapolis: Milkweed, 1997.

Ruffing, Janet. "Encountering Love Mysticism: Issues in Supervision." *Presence* 1 (January 1995) 20–33.

———. *Spiritual Direction: Beyond the Beginnings*. Mahwah, N.J.: Paulist Press, 2000.

———. "You Fill up My Senses: God and Our Senses." *The Way* 35 (April 1995): 101–10.

United States Catholic Conference. *Human Sexuality: A Catholic Perspective*, 1991.

Chapter Thirteen

A GRAPH OF SPIRITUALITY: UNDERSTANDING WHERE WE ARE GOING BY KNOWING WHERE WE HAVE BEEN

Steven Charleston

———— •◆• ————

AMHERST—Contemplating an agenda for the future, University of Massachusetts at Amherst Chancellor David K. Scott envisions bringing religion back into higher education. He is not talking about a department here or there devoted to the teaching of a particular faith. He wants to infuse spirituality into every part of academic life.
—*Boston Globe,* October 3, 1999

The article in the *Boston Globe* was a surprise. While I had become accustomed to hearing about the influence of "spirituality" in the church, even in business and science, this was the first time I had encountered it so clearly identified in higher education. The *Globe* article described how Dr. Scott, a physicist, believes that we are entering an age of integration, a time when people will need to use spirituality to process the flood of data they receive on a daily basis. Therefore, spirituality will return to the curriculum of major universities, not as a single subject to be taught on its own, but rather as a new way of thinking which underlies and integrates all knowledge.

What struck me about Dr. Scott's bold hope for the future of academic life in America was its location. Our culture has operated under the assumption that segregation must exist between the state university and the denominational church. We have prided ourselves on keeping this boundary clear. Far from the medieval image of the academy as only an extension of the church, we have compartmentalized learning to the point where religion has been relegated to the periphery. We have done so for what we believe are good reasons.

As with the separation of "church and state," we have believed that mixing intellectual formation and spiritual formation is a volatile combination within a democratic society. Fearing the intolerance and demands for religious conformity of the past, a history from which we believed we had escaped, we have maintained careful distance between spiritual viewpoints and the free classroom. In the process, of course, many critics assume that we have so sanitized the university from faith that we have created a value-less learning environment. That the chancellor of a major university would publicly question this assumption makes front-page news. It calls into question one of the fundamental principles of American higher education and raises the issue of denominational influence in education. It challenges us to consider again what we mean by "spirituality" and the role it plays in our postmodern culture.

I cannot predict the outcome of Dr. Scott's vision, but I can take it as a starting point to analyze how pervasive the subject of spirituality has become. If a renewal of interest in spirituality has brought scientists like Dr. Scott to call for a reevaluation of spiritual practice in the formative centers of American learning, then it seems to me that the tide of spirituality has reached a new level in our national consciousness. The concern is no longer for the religious few, but for the spiritual many. In other words, spirituality as a subtext at the start of the twenty-first century has filtered out into so many areas of our awareness that it has begun to erode the bedrock of our traditional assumptions as a culture—the foundation of the European Enlightenment. The assumptions of the Enlightenment, with science at the center and politics enclosed in a "faith-free zone," have gradually been undercut by forces that have brought spirituality back to a place of primacy.

I propose to sketch those forces as they have emerged in recent history and as they will carry us into a new history. I offer a rough graph to delineate how spirituality has come to occupy such an important place in our consciousness. Admittedly, the graph will be drawn only in broad strokes. I do not pretend to be a sociologist of spirituality: the statements in the *Boston Globe* caught my attention as an academic and a practicing Christian. Consequently, I am a stakeholder in the outcome of the history I observe. I am not a neutral party, but a person with both practical experience in the field of the spiritual and with a vested interest in its future. What I share is a practitioner's model. It is not exhaustive or extensive, but a working model for spiritual directors.

There are three simple lines on my rough chart. They begin in the late 1960s and move to the turn of the century. They aim beyond the year 2000, suggesting directions we will follow as spirituality continues to shape the agenda of history. But before I draw them out, I need to say something about background. I need to look at the graph paper itself, the much deeper history of North American religious life from which the three lines emerge.

The Enlightenment as Paradigm (The Graph Paper)

If any area of scholarship could be described as having burgeoned in the last thirty years, it would be cultural studies. Beginning with such seminal figures as Stuart Hall in Great Britain and radiating into a global network of new researchers, cultural studies has radically changed our intellectual worldview. While this boomtown mentality of excitement makes defining cultural studies precarious, there are some definitive threads. Cultural studies as a discipline questions the colonial assumptions that have dominated world history; the gender bias that has been a hidden subtext within that history; and, ultimately, the paradigm of the Enlightenment as the matrix of human thought. Ironically, the spread of spirituality into the academic community has been paralleled by the spread of cultural studies into theological education. The secular and the religious are twin streams of education, both eroding the cultural premise on which they have been built.

If we are to understand the future of spirituality, we must understand its past in terms of the Enlightenment, the era in intellectual European history that has cast such a long shadow. The Enlightenment as global mindset was transported to North America with the colonists. Just as it had altered both social and religious development in the mother countries of Europe, so it altered the new cultures planted in the Americas. Its assumptions about science and government organization were especially important in North America. American spirituality was a European design modified to fit a more democratic body politic.

Looking at American history as a piece of imaginary paper, its texture and color have clearly been imprinted by the Eurocentric vision of the Enlightenment. The institutions we created, the schools we founded, the principles of our governance, the methods behind our technologies, even the social fabric of our attitudes toward race, gender, and class—all derive from our understanding of European philosophy as expressed in the Enlightenment. Our paper is white, etched with the graphic lines of scientific and social theory that we thought normative for all times and places.

This is precisely why people like Dr. Scott catch us off guard. They surprise us with fundamental questions about our background. They question the paper itself even before new lines can be drawn. While to some it may still seem almost sacrilegious to wonder about principles we have been taught to cherish—for example, that science knows best—the rolling back of the Enlightenment, a fixed model for reality, has been the countercurrent to colonialism in creating what we now call the postmodern world.

In describing this complex history through the metaphor of the paper itself, I suggest that if we are serious about spirituality, we need to be aware that its points of origin are deeply influenced by the acceptance of the Enlightenment as the foundation for our cultures. The Enlightenment is the historical reality on which I will trace a few lines of spirituality. Those lines will only make sense if we remember that they are not drawn in thin air, but that there is a philosophical context to what we describe as "spirituality." Spirituality is never culture-neutral, nor does it exist outside the history from which it arises. Any study of contemporary American spirituality is grounded in the colonial experience of the Enlightenment. That's where we begin.

THE PROLIFERATION OF SPIRITUALITY (THE FIRST LINE)

The first line on our graph represents what I call the proliferation of spirituality. The line in some ways begins at the very edge, because the American experience is of a proliferation of spiritualities. It is axiomatic to say that American colonial history was the playing out of European religious history on the shores of North America. Competing denominations found a safe, if temporary, haven in what with casual arrogance they described as a "New World." Religious pluralism has been integral to American spirituality for generations.

However, if we fast-forward to the mid-1960s, we encounter a very noticeable "blip" in the chart. Something spikes in the 1960s. In a climate of drugs and free love, the definition of spirituality gets hazy. What the veterans of World War II had taken for granted in the late 1940s and throughout the prosperous 1950s—a solid Christian spirituality firmly rooted in the comfortable pieties of the institutional church—suddenly starts to unravel when entrusted to their children.

For the postwar generation, spirituality was no longer institutionally based, no longer confined to the church or synagogue. These institutions had always been assumed to be the home of spirituality (neatly compartmentalized by the Enlightenment into the appropriate places for the exercise of religion) were directly challenged as being sterile museums of an outdated religion. Looking for spirituality, a large segment of the population walked out of church and into the streets.

They discovered a supermarket of spiritual possibilities. In the late 1960s and early 1970s, spirituality became like a medieval fair. People could stroll through the carnival, browse esoteric wares, and stop for any guru who cast a spell of hope and wisdom. Some of these encounters, of course, were harmless and diverting; others were disastrous, even terminal.

One element causing the "blip" in this line was connected with the rediscovery of "Eastern" thought. The dialogue among Christianity and Judaism—the "Western" religions—and Buddhism and Hinduism, their "Eastern" neighbors, began a mixed conversation in which spiritual images and practices wove together like strands of religious DNA, producing abundant hybrids and mutations. Native American traditions became popular. The traditional teachings of authentic indigenous leaders were widely circulated and absorbed into the fertile spiritual soil. More dubious claimants to the title of "medicine man" or "shaman" also appeared, adding to the exotic nature of spirituality that was constantly shifting, but endlessly appealing. Finally, a vast area we have often encompassed with the term "New Age" created too many variations to list.

At this time the old models of Enlightenment religion ruptured, and new spiritualities proliferated. This rupture created a new assumption: that religion was no longer institutional. The twin definitions of what constituted religion and spirituality blurred. Religion was often seen as monolithic, reactionary, and enclosed. Spirituality in the popular consciousness became fluid, progressive, and inclusive. Even as the hinge year of 1968 dampened the fervor for change, the belief in a pluralism of religious expression remained. The "hippie" influence of the period might have been shed in the aftermath of assassinations and riots, but spiritual proliferation continued into the following decades and, as I will suggest, beyond.

One other point should be made. What I have sketched as spiritual proliferation includes not only variety, but content. It is important to remember that the proliferation was not just a matter of choice, but of choice that mattered. The political context of spirituality was fundamental and deeply affected American religious life. The civil rights movement was of definitive importance to this historic transition. Liberation theology offered a powerful political and spiritual counterpoint to the gurus of the 1960s. The radicalization of spirituality from the American Black, Latino, Asian, and Native communities provided a charged critique of power and brought new consciousness of the connection between the religious and the political. The Vietnam War and the national struggle over its justification infused American spirituality with a rejection of the status quo. If some Americans partied through the 1960s and early 1970s, many others grew up and were changed forever.

In the end, a major dynamic behind the proliferation of spirituality, whether ephemeral or substantive, has been a trajectory of the *alternative*. In the late 1960s and early 1970s, two discoveries were made: (a) that religion offers many spiritual alternatives, and, (b) that spirituality itself can become its own alternative. What had congealed in national religious life—the church on the corner where religion was business as usual—exploded into a question of the alternative. It became possible to envision an authentic religious life outside the church, to discover hybrid forms of that expression in a wide array of spiritualities. It became possible also to self-identify spirituality as an alternative lifestyle, a personal embodiment of religion that centered reality outside the parameters of the old Enlightenment models and within the individual as the final arbiter of his or her own salvation.

THE PRIVATIZATION OF SPIRITUALITY (THE SECOND LINE)

If the countercultural movements of the 1960s and early 1970s saw institutional religion as suspect, by implication, they saw community religion as suspect. The older models of Christian and Jewish worship—the Norman Rockwell image of religion in America—were always community-based. They were grounded firmly in the traditional liturgies of parish and synagogue. By breaking down the walls of the institution, the counterculture also broke down boundaries that had held individuals within a worshiping community. Religion became more of an individual choice. Spirituality became privatized.

It is not surprising that the group following the Woodstock generation was the much more bland, though still deeply self-indulgent, "me" generation. Scholars have shown how the apparent failures of the countercultural dream (social, political, and spiritual) drove many Americans to reject faith in shared ideals, and to begin an inner search for either pleasure or meaning or both.

The late 1970s and 1980s, as marked by a line on the spirituality graph, show a deep valley of introspection. The personal need for fulfillment replaced the more traditional need for community. In fact, the definitions of community began to fall apart as, in the light of Watergate, people retreated from blind patriotism into cynicism about political institutions in general. The hope of the civil rights movement faded, and the realities of race, class, and gender intensified. Rapid changes in the church (e.g., in liturgy and the ordination of women) rocked many denominations and splintered them into factions. In family life, people claimed a variety of new relationships as constitutive of family. The unifying limits that had always served to define community began to be breached. In reaction, people turned within, seeking validation for the self, which became the true measure of spirituality.

The rise of self-help groups is symbolic of the movement of this line on the graph. The rapid expansion of personal growth industries reflects the movement inward during this period. In the most positive forms, these self-focused strategies improved personal health, increased self-awareness, and opened doors for marginalized persons to claim a sense of dignity. In more negative forms, the strategies were personality cults, phony therapies, and diversions from reality.

The underlying issue, however, is the way in which spirituality became a more private affair. The mega-theories of faith, the calls to a universal consciousness or to institutional solidarity, had to struggle against spiritual privatization, in which individuals could accept or reject any aspect of religion and still claim to be valid practitioners. Those who remained within institutions found themselves in turmoil as splinter groups clamored for power.

The 1980s brought political ferment to every branch of the Christian faith in the United States. Coming out of Vatican II and decisions to ordain women, once-solid institutional veneers cracked into shifting configurations of believers, each claiming some hold on the banner of tradition.

Confidence in the group eroded as reliance on the self increased. Institutional responses to this privatization of spirituality sought to recapture the believer's attention. Among Christian "fundamentalists," for example, the emergence of televangelists provided a subtle twist to the privatization of spirituality. Beneath the anything-but-subtle techniques of many televised ministries was a consistently "private" message: individual healing, individual happiness, individual prosperity, individual salvation. The emphasis is on the word individual, because televised ministries implied that these benefits of faith are guaranteed for the person alone. The spiritual message pointed toward what the viewer could get from religion, not on what he or she might *give*. The aim was to recruit the individual believer by appealing to what he or she wanted, needed, or expected. An entitlement focus runs within this kind of privatization: a feeling that a person deserves these benefits.

It is not accidental that this spiritual entitlement mirrored an increase in litigation. In a society characterized as whining and litigious, the clamor of "what's in it for me" found an echo in the popularity of religious messages that were self-help oriented. Religious television's promise to meet individual needs illustrates the trajectory of this line away from community and toward privatization.

Focusing on Christian fundamentalism allows us to see the privatization of spirituality in places we might otherwise overlook. It is perhaps easier to spotlight New Age philosophies or "therapy spiritualities," which presented spirituality as magic, intended unashamedly for self-benefit, or therapeutic science, in which attention fixed on the person as client or patient. Individualism seeped both into the spas and trailer parks with a spirituality tuned into the electronic hope for health, prosperity, and success.

In the 1980s, the roller coaster of technological change also began. As the institutions of community either collapsed or were shaken, information flooded the home through the personal computer. The information brought a paradox: people felt more isolated just as they became more connected. The phenomenon of privatized spirituality rides this crest of isolation. The individual, who is not physically isolated but spiritually isolated, increasingly is thrown into an interior reality. Human contact is reduced. The privatization of spirituality, therefore, is aided and abetted by isolation.

The irony is that spiritual isolation accompanies entry into a global community. The person in the spa is part of an elite international network that transcends, even supersedes, national frontiers. The person in the trailer park is only a push of a button away from contact with the world. As spirituality in this nation continues to be challenged by privatization, it will also be challenged by globalization.

THE GLOBALIZATION OF SPIRITUALITY (THE THIRD LINE)

Through the 1990s, spirituality has continued to move upward into the international context. In an increasingly permeable global network the boundaries of spirituality have opened: spirituality has been franchised. It is now possible to speak of spirituality from a variety of sources and in a variety of locations.

Developments at the University of Massachusetts are only one example. In the academic, scientific, political, and corporate worlds, we are growing accustomed to spiritual talk. A new language of spirituality speaks in accents unfamiliar to those accustomed to faith in the context of religion. For example, major companies influenced in their business conduct by ecological or social issues use a form of spiritual expression; the practice might be termed "ethical commerce." While the motivation may be either altruistic or promotional, this corporate language helps create an international spiritual vocabulary. As business has become multinational, it has also become multispiritual. Cultural influences, international political realities, and the need to speak to universal values have brought corporations to this point. Spirituality may seem a strange partner in the corporate boardroom, but it has earned a place for its ability to communicate across global frontiers. While the authority of spirituality to change policy within these networks may still be marginal, that more businesses are using spiritual or quasi-spiritual images means that this generic spirituality is expanding globally along with capitalism.

The content of this spirituality is the question. Corporations may assume publicly ethical postures, but is this genuine spirituality? Universities and scientific communities may announce their spiritual connections, but what kind of spirituality are they describing? The globalization of spirituality is evident in the way that the word *spirituality* is being co-opted, integrated into networks that are not only national or denominational, but also global and pan-religious. International business, education, and science are all new conduits for carrying the message of spirituality around the planet. The term is being redefined as it is being disseminated to new audiences. Different amalgamations are forming as local spiritualities, so to speak, are mixed, creating transnational mutations.

Taoism, a form of magical spirituality within traditional Chinese culture, provides one example. The *Tao* was by no means a household word in the spiritual lexicon. At the beginning of the twenty-first century, however, that is no longer true. Through its new connections to science (the Tao of physics), business (the Tao of management), education (the Tao of teaching), and commercialized lifestyles (the Tao of Pooh), this once esoteric spirituality has become a brand name. Its traditional content, of course, has mutated into forms that the Chinese sage Lao-tzu would never have recognized, much less approved. But the fact remains that the spiritual veneer of Taoism has been overlaid on a wide range of institutions and cultures. Whether we perceive this as cheap commercialization or provocative insight, the "Tao" is a new shorthand linguistic symbol recognizable from Taiwan to Tanzania.

Nor is the Tao alone in representing the globalization of spirituality. The crosscurrents of international exchange mean that Western spirituality enters Asian wedding liturgies; that Asian spirituality enters the West through wholistic medicine; that African spirituality travels through a global music market; that the Gregorian chant of a Christian monastic order becomes an international hit as Hollywood celebrities embrace Tibetan Buddhism.

The sources of spirituality have been franchised. Religion is no longer the lone source of spirituality, which has become a free agent, available on the Internet, used to sell fashion and make movies, to instruct corporate retreatants, and to realign education departments. Spirituality is sound bite and logo.

Consequently, the "it" in spirituality, the defining quality, has been submerged. In the 1990s, the United States became used to encountering spirituality in almost every cultural locale. Substance was not always important. Simply the *perception* of the spiritual was sufficient. Spiritual association was enough to communicate reassurance. In whatever form, generic spirituality offered a positive link to the emerging global awareness. Our culture in particular began to be satisfied with the perception that something was spiritual without fussing about the details. Is the Tao a true form of spirituality or a label? What does the Tao mean? With the globalization of spirituality, the answer is: it doesn't matter. It is enough to perceive that the "Tao," a mystical integrating principle linking us to a benign universal reality, is an end in itself. Confronted with multiple choices, we seek comforting images vaguely reminiscent of an older spiritual form, while still acceptable to the new global agenda.

The globalization of spirituality represents the deconstruction of spirituality. Spirituality has infused postmodern life in an instantaneous translation that puts religious, ethical, and moral information into easily transmitted shorthand. Which is not to say that spirituality of this kind is value-less. Only that it is root-less.

At the change in the millennium raw materials are emerging for a new transnational, even transreligious, spirituality. While orthodox centers of religion wage relentless action against such syncretism, the forces of globalization continue to produce new strains of spirituality that both embody and express international culture. Fundamentalism is a powerful opponent, but the populist, hybrid spirituality endures precisely because it is popular. The new missionary movement of world religions rides the Internet. Spirituality bypasses orthodoxy by hitchhiking on the information superhighway.

The question is one of perception versus substance. While many entering the twenty-first century may long for the substance of religious faith that provides a genuinely spiritual life, many more embrace a popular spirituality that keeps them free from commitments. Even more important, given the general loss of grounding in what organized religions would call the "basics," the expanding number of spirituality shoppers is searching more for designer labels than for discipleship. The name will do. What this bodes for both spirituality and religion in the twenty-first century is open to debate, but I believe that the three trends of proliferation, privatization, and globalization are predictive of the future.

THE INTEGRATION OF SPIRITUALITY

What will spirituality be like in the years to come? What should spiritual directors expect? I believe that Dr. Scott, whose surprising announcement opened this essay, offers some answers: in the decades to come spirituality will be an integrative force in religious as well as secular life.

Integrating spirituality into life is the work of future spiritual directors. Trends over the last three or four decades will play themselves out, continuing to weave spirituality into the fabric of American society. The threads of spirituality will appear in all areas. Dr. Scott is right in assuming that higher education will continue to explore spiritual values as a process for collating the intellectual data of higher education. Spirituality will continue to play a role in the debates over ethics in science, medicine, and law. Issues such as euthanasia, capital punishment, genetic research, environmental protection, social engineering, global debt, and political morality will open doors for spiritual talk. International business and communications will globalize (as well as trivialize) spirituality, synthesizing its content in world cultures and reducing it to sound bites to sell ideas and products. Hybrid forms of spirituality will multiply. The gnostic-style spirituality of life management through magic will offer solutions to many persons bewildered by change. The orthodox spirituality of religious fundamentalism will grow as millions from all faiths seek certainty and conformity as answers to their need for security in the faith. The media and the arts will turn increasingly to spiritual subjects. Spiritually based countercultural youth movements will attract a new generation of young men and women wishing to "discover" an alternative to traditional religion. Ultimately, the combination of these many strands will mark the next decades as an era of religious reformation, spiritual renewal, and cultural upheaval. While I do not pretend to predict the future, I do believe that these several trajectories offer spiritual practitioners some helpful clues.

1. We must be aware that the spiritual ground will continue to shift. The reality check for future spirituality is anxiety. As the familiar paradigm

of the European Enlightenment gradually deconstructs, spiritual seekers will be looking for safe ground. In this time of transition, foundations of culture and social institutions will realign like tectonic plates. The changes may be subtle (e.g., the choice of diet); negotiated (e.g., remaining in organized religion but practicing a hybrid spirituality); dramatic (e.g., conversion to faith as the source of integration); or reactionary (e.g., practicing religious fundamentalism over against change perceived as negative). Moreover, spiritual directors will need to be aware that many people who come to them for counsel will be persons seeking redress from spiritual stress. Whether these men and women embrace or reject the transitions in their social environment, the common denominator will be the struggle for balance as old assumptions are replaced. The European Enlightenment will be exchanged for a different paradigm, whose shape we can only now glimpse in outline. Future generations, of course, will inherit the outcome and consider it normative, but those of us living through the birth will be marked by both trauma and liberation.

2. Practitioners will need to be flexible in understanding religion as just one alternative in the spiritual search. Persons will not seek one spiritual path to fulfillment as much as a road map of alternatives. Combinations of spiritual influences will be common. The spiritual director who relies on a formula for guidance may quickly be bypassed by seekers wary of dogma. The challenge will be to chart new directions in spirituality without losing the integrity of the search itself. The concept that "the journey is the destination" will continue to be popular, but the danger will be that the journey is going nowhere. Finding ultimate value will be tricky in a culture that will tend to relativize faith. Like a pharmacist mixing ingredients, the spiritual practitioner will need to understand the core qualities of the alternatives of twenty-first-century spirituality. Some mixtures will be harmful, while others can reinvigorate spiritual health. Like theological education, spiritual direction will become more multicultural. With the backdrop of the Enlightenment removed, the task of spirituality will be to help in constructing a rational worldview with ethical value.

Eventually, the proliferation of spiritualities will begin to narrow into more definable patterns. Integration will occur and, already, connections are being made. What we thought of as exotic "Eastern" spirituality in the late 1960s is emerging as a solid presence in the United States and Canada. This is especially true of Buddhism. "New Age" spiritualities are forming around media and workshop outlets that are becoming part of the commercial landscape. Conservative spirituality has entered the political process and will be a factor in coming elections. As these forms of spirituality merge into stronger definitions, they will affect the organizational church by accelerating institutional change. Issues such as the ordination of homosexuals and the blessing of same-sex unions will move toward resolution under pressure from the consolidating spiritualities, often embodied within denominations in special-interest lobbies, changing the internal nature of the churches themselves. As with the ordination of women, these changes will divide denominations into factions. Ultimately, the internalizing pressure exerted by spirituality will cause some mainline denominations to split, creating synergy for the Second Reformation.

The outcome will be watershed reform of Christianity toward the end of the twenty-first century. Spirituality, the underground river of emotion running beneath the crust of organized denominations, will flow out into the global community with enough force to splinter the church into new denominational configurations. In both Protestantism and Roman Catholicism, this reform will divide persons into the "progressive" and "traditionalist" factions, which will merge into a Christianity in which "Protestant" and "Catholic" have new meanings. As a consequence, the coming Reformation will be a much more important event in the global history of Christianity than the regional shifts of the sixteenth century.

3. The privatization of spirituality will confront spiritual directors with the difficult dilemma of the lonely person. As global communications erases physical isolation, it will create vast areas of emotional isolation. Those seeking the refuge of spirituality will be coming in from the cold, cut off from the warmth of emotional interaction they describe as transcendent and intimate. The longing for this intimacy will drive many out of isolation and into spiritual journeys. Many will find a home after living as strangers, but many will not.

What defines community, therefore, will be a central question. The loss of community through the breakdown of traditional "family" and the fragmentation of religious institutions will create a vacuum, which will be filled by social spirituality. Spirituality will be seen as a catalyst for community. Groups of individuals, to escape the isolation of a highly technological world or the culture shock of being thrust into such a world, will come together as new communities, whose charter will be a shared spirituality.

For example, the next century will see the return of two older forms of community: the monastic tradition and the utopian adventure. While celibacy will be dropped as a requirement for ordination, the attraction of a monastic vocation will increase. Men and women who have felt deep alienation will seek the antidote of intense community experience. The growth of religious orders may be one of the small but significant spikes on the graph of the mid-2000s. Some orders will follow the ancient patterns of a life dedicated to poverty, obedience, and chastity, but others will develop gender-inclusive patterns open to married or even same-sex couples. In a similar way, utopian projects will increase as part of this experimentation in meaningful spiritual community. These New Zions will not just be agrarian cousins to the communes of the nineteenth or twentieth centuries, but new efforts at colonizing urban areas. Cooperative ventures among like-minded spiritual people will create clusters of mini-communities in urban centers. The gentrification of spirituality will occur as suburban spirituality reclaims the city center as a new frontier.

Privatization will also offer spiritual directors increasingly close connection to related sciences and pseudosciences. Spirituality will be interpreted as physicality and more directly associated with issues of health and body image. In coming decades, the grounding of spiritual discipline in exercise, diet, therapy, and lifestyle will become foundational. Future spiritual directors will likely be proponents of a lifestyle rather than a theology. Spirituality will relate less to the "head" than to the "body." Consequently, the *practice* of spirituality will become primary. Meditation, fasting, physical exercise, and group therapies will be seen as integral to a true spiritual life. Nutrition in general and vegetarianism in particular will be rapidly expanding areas of spirituality. Physical programs such as tai chi or yoga will be much more common, especially as Buddhism in North America continues to grow. Future spiritual directors will not be contemplative "couch potatoes" but active men and women who can keep pace with the personal investment people make in their own spiritual well-being. *Wellness* and *wholeness* will cease to be catchphrases, but will describe a profound shift in spirituality from the mind to the body.

4. Finally, the globalization of spirituality will become the immediate concern of spiritual directors as they combat the trivialization of the sacred. On the future's darker fringes, a negative antimatter will develop to spirituality. The counterforce will run parallel to positive spiritual growth, diminishing the spiritual as purely commercial. If the spiritual is everywhere, it may also be nowhere. The suspicion of spirituality as an escape from reality will grow among those raised with conflicting images of the divine, which have caused them to lose respect for anything holy. As they watch older forms of religion crumble or retreat into rigidity, they will feel the sacred has lost its meaning. The supermarket of spiritual alternatives will

not appeal to such persons if they have been convinced that these are shallow options for a bankrupt religion.

Consequently, the field of spiritual practice will be heavily contested by an entertainment industry that globalizes escapism. Imagining Disneyland in China may be a stretch at present, but it will be a natural extension for the generation to come. The worldwide media will become more sophisticated at standardizing images of the good life. The generic expectation of wealth, beauty, and self-indulgence will become a counterpoint to the rise of global spirituality. As more people expect to find fun, rather than purpose, in life, the values of spirituality will be watered down. A kind of cheapening effect of spirituality will occur, allowing people to substitute entertainment for enlightenment.

Even more ominous will be the rise of rage, which will bubble into the next century like magma. The loss of a spiritual value to life, the stress of competing, hostile religious beliefs, the pressure of fundamentalism across all religious frontiers, and the redress to violence by those who feel cheated of the media promise of the good life will result in a backlash against spirituality. Spiritual directors will not just be safe practitioners of fluffy religion, but will be on the front lines of a spiritual struggle. As capitalism divides humanity into winners and losers, as racism intensifies, and as intolerance grows, future spiritual directors may be religious medics on global battlefields.

The ethnic wars of the 1990s will, tragically, play out again and again. This same crisis in the human spirit will begin to erupt within cosmopolitan areas. Nations like the United States, which have been relatively peaceful over the last few decades, will see the resumption of racially fueled urban riots and ethnic clashes. The endemic quality of violence will take on spiritual trappings in the next century as cults flourish. A spiritual community's responses will be severely tested as it seeks to offer reconciliation and hope. Consequently, spirituality will not be the softer reality that it is today, but a hard reaction to an even harder disruption of human life.

In the end, the integration that spirituality offers will be critical, not only for individual well-being, but for the struggle to produce community in the next century. How spiritual practitioners succeed in bringing that integration will affect not only schools like Dr. Scott's, but populations yet unborn. The peaceful transition from the old Enlightenment to the new millennium will fall under the stewardship of religiously minded people who see spirituality as a force for good, not just as a tool for personal salvation. The great-great-grandchildren of those from the 1960s, 1970s,

1980s, and 1990s will inherit a spirituality that is diverse, multicultural, intimate, and tough. In the community centers that will be the churches of their time, they will practice a physical spirituality. In an America that will speak Spanish as often as it speaks English, and that will be heavily Asian, spirituality will serve as a bridge to a global network made possible by a technology that allows face-to-face conversation from any point on the globe. Urban missionaries will plant monastic orders in cities with triple-digit populations. The regreening of the earth will be the debate of the moment. In this brave new world, spiritual directors will not graph their vocation on paper of one color—paper will be an artifact—but on multicolored holograms that reflect the light of a deeply integrated faith.

Notes

CHAPTER TWO:
SPIRITUAL DIRECTION WITH TRAUMATIZED PERSONS

1. Bureau of the Census, *Statistical Abstract of the United States, 1998* (118th ed.) (Washington, D.C., 1998), table 373.
2. Judith Lewis Herman, *Trauma and Recovery* (New York: Basic Books, 1997), 101.
3. Diana Sullivan Everting and Louis Everting, *Sexual Trauma in Children and Adolescents: Dynamics and Treatment* (New York: Brunner/Mazel, 1989), 155.
4. Herman, *Trauma and Recovery,* 111.
5. Ibid., 99.
6. Ibid., 111.
7. Eliana Gil, *Outgrowing the Pain: A Book for and about Adults Abused as Children* (New York: Dell, 1983), 35, 62.
8. Herman, *Trauma and Recovery,* 101. Parenthetical page references that follow are to Herman's book.
9. Sheila A. Redmond, "Christian 'Virtues' and Recovery from Child Sexual Abuse," in *Christianity, Patriarchy, and Abuse,* ed. Joanne Carlson Brown and Carole R. Bohn (New York: Pilgrim Press, 1990), 72.
10. Gil, *Outgrowing the Pain,* 39.
11. Herman, *Trauma and Recovery,* 113; cf. Gil, *Outgrowing the Pain,* 60–61.
12. Herman, *Trauma and Recovery,* 111.
13. Redmond, "Christian 'Virtues,'" 74.
14. Gil, *Outgrowing the Pain,* 59.
15. Marie M. Fortune, "The Transformation of Suffering: A Biblical and Theological Perspective," in *Violence against Women and Children: A Christian Theological Sourcebook* (New York: Continuum, 1995), 85–91.
16. See Carol Gilligan, *In a Different Voice: Psychological Theory and Women's Development* (Cambridge: Harvard University Press, 1982); Mary Pipher, *Reviving Ophelia: Saving the Selves of Adolescent Girls* (New York: Ballantine Books, 1995).
17. Kathleen Fischer, *Women at the Well: Feminist Perspectives on Spiritual Direction* (New York: Paulist Press, 1988), 157.

18. Ibid., 164.

19. Carol Lee Flinders, *At the Root of This Longing: Reconciling a Spiritual Hunger and a Feminist Thirst* (San Francisco: HarperCollins, 1999), 83–98.

20. For a recent treatment of the importance of voice for women see Mary Donovan Turner and Mary Lin Hudson, *Saved from Silence: Finding Women's Voice in Preaching* (St. Louis: Chalice Press, 1999).

21. Redmond, "Christian 'Virtues,'" 75.

22. Marie Fortune, *Sexual Violence: The Unmentionable Sin* (New York: Pilgrim Press, 1983), 209. See also idem, "Forgiveness: The Last Step," in *Violence against Women,* ed. Carol Adams and Fortune, (New York: Continuum, 1995) 201–5.

23. Flora Wuellner, *Release: Healing from Wounds of Family, Church, and Community* (Nashville: Upper Room, 1996); *Prayer, Fear, and Our Powers: Finding Our Healing, Release, and Growth in Christ* (Nashville: Upper Room, 1989). Also, *Depth Healing and Renewal through Christ: Guided Meditations for Inner Healing* (Nashville: Upper Room, 1992), URC 664, audiocassette.

CHAPTER THREE:
SPIRITUAL DIRECTION WITH AN ADDICTED PERSON

1. Alcoholics Anonymous, *The Big Book: The Basic Text of Alcoholics Anonymous* (New York: 1976), 58.

2. Ibid., xx.

3. The spiritual director should be aware that the addictive personality gravitates toward compulsive behavior and that some recovering persons get as addicted to the twelve-step program as they were to their former self-destructive activities. Experienced twelve-step members often encourage newcomers to prioritize the program above family, work, and church. Their rationale is a good one—"If you cannot stop this addictive behavior, sooner or later you will die, and none of the rest will matter. So do what the program suggests first. Do not miss meetings on the account of other priorities." Later in recovery, the director may suggest attention to balance. The problem is that twelve-step members have found a spirituality and spiritual disciplines that are far more rigorous than those found in most fellowships within the church. They may not want to trade what has worked for what formerly left them freer to practice their addiction and deception.

4. The twelve steps are frequently divided into three spiritual aspects. Steps 1–3 are to find God; steps 4–10 are to clean house and make amends; steps 11 and 12 are to serve others. The spiritual-direction process can be tremendously useful in all phases, but in step 11 one needs help improving conscious contact with God and in praying for God's will to be manifest. AA literature states specifically that it cannot tell one how to accomplish this and that the assistance of understanding clergy may be helpful. "Suggestions about these may be obtained from one's priest, minister, or rabbi. Be quick to see where religious people are right. Make use of what they offer" (*Alcoholics Anonymous, The Big Book*, 87).

5. Gerald May, *Addiction and Grace* (San Francisco: Harper, 1988), 38–39.

CHAPTER FIVE:
GENERATIONS, OUR DIFFERENCES AND SIMILARITIES

1. William Strauss and Neil Howe, *Generations: The History of America's Future, 1584 to 2069* (New York: Morrow, 1982).

2. Gary L. McIntosh, *Three Generations: Riding the Waves of Change in Your Church* (Grand Rapids, Mich.: Fleming H. Revell, 1995).

3. Mike Regele with Mark Schulz, *The Death of the Church* (Grand Rapids, Mich.: Zondervan, 1995).

4. Ibid., 118.

5. Ibid., 121.

6. Ibid., 123.

7. Ibid., 132.

CHAPTER SIX:
SPIRITUAL DIRECTION WITH LESBIAN, GAY, BISEXUAL, AND TRANSGENDERED PERSONS

1. Larry Graham, *The Journal of Pastoral Care* 50, no. 1 (spring 1996).

2. James Nelson and Sandra Longfellow, *Sexuality and the Sacred: Sources for Theological Reflection* (Louisville: Westminster/John Knox Press, 1994), xiv and following.

3. I have drawn also from Peg Thompson, "The Coming-Out Process in Spiritual Direction," *Presence: The Journal of Spiritual Directors International* 4, no. 3 (September 1998).

4. For information, call (213) 486–4497.

5. For an excellent treatment of spiritual direction with the l/g/b/t person at different stages of adult development, read chapters 7, 8, and 9 of James L. Empereur, S.J., *Spiritual Direction and the Gay Person* (New York: Continuum, 1998).

CHAPTER SEVEN:
CAN I GET A WITNESS? SPIRITUAL DIRECTION WITH THE MARGINALIZED

1. Cathy J. Cohen, *The Boundaries of Blackness: AIDS and the Breakdown of Black Politics* (Chicago: University of Chicago Press, 1999), 38.

2. Patricia Hill Collins, *Fighting Words: Black Women and the Search for Justice* (Minneapolis and London: University of Minnesota Press, 1998), 3–11.

3. James Baldwin, "The Devil Finds Work," in *The Price of the Ticket: Collected Nonfiction, 1948–1985* (New York: St. Martin's Press, 1985), 606.

CHAPTER EIGHT:
COMPANIONS AT THE THRESHOLD: SPIRITUAL DIRECTION WITH THE DYING

1. Informal presentation at the hospice she directed in Sydenham, England, January 1984.

2. Quotations from the Psalms are from the 1979 *Book of Common Prayer.*

3. Henri J. M. Nouwen, *The Living Reminder: Service and Prayer in Memory of Jesus Christ* (New York: Seabury Press, 1981), 44–45.

CHAPTER NINE:
"LET THE OPPRESSED GO FREE": SPIRITUAL DIRECTION AND THE PURSUIT OF JUSTICE

1. F. W. Faber, *Growth in Holiness* (Rockford, Ill.: Tan Books Publishers, 1990, reprint), 239.

2. Marcia Griffiths, "Steppin' Out of Babylon" was top of the pop charts in Jamaica in the early 1980s. It entered into various books as a title for chapters. See for example, Paul Gilroy, "Steppin' out of Babylon: race, class and autonomy" in *The Empire Strikes Back: Race and*

Racism in '70s Britain (London: Centre for Contemporary Cultural Studies, 1982), 276–314; David Nicholls, "Stepping Out of Babylon: Sin, Salvation, and Social Transformation in Christian Tradition," in *Essays Catholic and Radical,* ed. Kenneth Leech and Rowan Williams (London: Bowerdean Press, 1983), 38–51; and Kenneth Leech, "Stepping Out of Babylon: Politics and Christian Vision," chap. 3 in *The Eye of the Storm: Spiritual Resources for the Pursuit of Justice* (London: Darton, Longman and Todd, 1992), 91–139.

3. Dietrich Bonhoeffer, *Letters and Papers from Prison* (New York, Macmillan, 1972), 300. I am sure that Kathleen Fischer is right to insist that spiritual direction "involves a commitment to creating communities of mutuality and justice" (*Women at the Well* [London: SPCK, 1989], 46).

4. Theodore Roszak, *Where the Wasteland Ends* (London: Faber, 1972), xxii.

5. For the term *growth industry* in relation to spiritual direction, see William A. Barry, S.J., *Spiritual Direction and the Encounter with God* (New York: Paulist Press, 1992), 7; and Gordon Oliver, "Counseling, Anarchy, and the Kingdom of God," Frank Lake Memorial Lecture, 1990 (Oxford: Clinical Theology Association, 1991), 5. Gordon H. Jeff (*Spiritual Direction for Every Christian* [London: SPCK, 1987], 1) adds another word, calling this ministry "a fashionable growth industry."

6. On the danger of cultural captivity, see Bruce H. Lescher, "The Professionalisation of Spiritual Direction: Promise or Peril?" *Listening* 32, no. 2 (spring 1997): 81–90.

Not all the current literature has succumbed uncritically to the professional model. Thus Jerome M. Neufelder and Mary C. Coelho, eds., *Writings on Spiritual Direction* (New York: Seabury Press, 1982), xv: "The evidence of history challenges those efforts which reduce spiritual direction to a kind of counseling with directors claiming a type of trained professional authority in matters of prayer and meditation and the stages of spiritual growth." Or Peter Selby, *Liberating God* (London: SPCK, 1983), 12: "It is perhaps the inevitable consequence of the increased interest that there should be established institutes and programs of training to foster it. One wonders what the wise counselors and confessors of earlier generations would have thought had they dreamt that in the future spiritual direction might turn into a professional discipline with a diploma to ensure standards."

7. Daniel Berrigan, "Contemplation and Resistance," *Peace News,* 18 May 1973.

8. R.A. Lambourne, *Contact* (Spring 1974): 38.

9. Peter Selby, *Grace and Mortgage* (London: Darton, Longman and Todd, 1997), 6.

10. See Chris Rowland and John Vincent, eds., *Liberation Spirituality* (Sheffield: Urban Theology Unit, 1999), especially Bridget Rees's essay, "Liberation Spirituality," 10–16.

11. David Nicholls, in *Christianity Reinterpreted?* ed. Kenneth Leech (London: Jubilee Group, 1978).

12. Alasdair MacIntyre, "Social Structures and the Threat to Moral Agency," annual lecture, Royal Institute of Philosophy, London, 24 February 1999.

13. Lambeth Conference, Canterbury Press Release no. 48 (1998): 3.

14. Theodore Roszak, *Unfinished Animal* (London: Faber, 1976), 31.

15. Alasdair MacIntyre, *Marxism and Christianity,* 2d ed. (London: Duckworth, 1995), xiii–xiv.

16. See R. H. Tawney, *Religion and the Rise of Capitalism* (Penguin, 1938), 289; Selby, *Grace and Mortgage.*

17. Alasdair MacIntyre, in *Philosophers in Conversation,* ed. Andrew Pyle (New York, Routledge, 1999), 83.

18. Denise Levertov, *Light Up the Cave* (New York: New Directions, 1981), 96.

19. The notion of a "correct line" had its origins in Stalinism and was heavily criticized by those to the left of the Communist parties, not least by Trotskyists. However, today, the apparently similar notion of "political correctness" is promoted by the right-wing media as a way of trivializing and distracting attention from real issues of justice and equality. When I speak here of a "correct line," I have in mind positions which are ruled as correct by a centralized bureaucratic elite, leaving no space for creative thought and dissidence. It goes without saying that religious institutions are very prone to this syndrome.

20. James W. Douglass, *Resistance and Contemplation* (New York: Doubleday, 1972), 139.

21. Daniel Berrigan, *America Is Hard to Find* (London: SPCK, 1972), 77–78: "The time will shortly be upon us, if it is not already here, when the pursuit of contemplation becomes a strictly subversive activity. . . . I am convinced that contemplation, including the common

worship of the believing, is a political act of the highest value, imply-
ing the riskiest of consequences to those taking part." See also
Kenneth Leech, "Contemplation as a Subversive Activity," chap. 5 in
The Social God (London: Sheldon Press, 1981), 51–56.

22. Robert McAfee Brown, *Spirituality and Liberation* (Philadelphia:
Westminster Press, 1988), 94.

    A number of writers have pointed out that, within Anglicanism, a
key text for spiritual direction is the *Book of Common Prayer* itself. See
Gordon Mursell in *The Way*, April 1991, 163; and Bede Thomas
Mudge, cited in Peter Ball, *Journey into a Truth: Spiritual Direction
in the Anglican Tradition* (London: Mowbrays, 1996), 45. It is
worth commenting that much, perhaps most, in the current interest
in spiritual direction in the West—its individualistic focus, its discon-
nectedness from sacramental life, its tendency to follow a psy-
chotherapeutic model, and so on—is in sharp contrast to Anglican
tradition. Harvey Guthrie is therefore right to say that "spiritual direction is, in Anglicanism, a broad-based thing, and the term itself, in
the sense in which it is presently so widely used, is not native to
Anglicanism" (in *Anglican Spirituality*, ed. W. J. Wolf [Wilton,
Conn.: Morehouse-Barlow, 1982], 12).

23. Michael Ramsey, *The Gospel and the Catholic Church* (1936; London:
Longmans, Green, 1956), 38.

24. Brian Griffiths, in *The Kindness That Kills*, ed. Digby Anderson
(London: SPCK, 1987), 113. Rowland and Corner point out that
"individual champions of sacred causes who feel the need to leave
behind the critical support of the people of God are peculiarly vulnerable to self-deception" (Christopher Rowland and Mark Corner,
Liberating Exegesis [London: SPCK, 1990], 138).

25. *Faith in the City*, Report of the Archbishop's Commission on Urban
Priority Areas (London: Church House Publishing, 1985), 56.

26. I have been much helped in my thinking in this area by an unpub-
lished dissertation by Linda M. Unger, "The Ministry of
Reconciliation and the Gifts of Spiritual Direction," M.A. diss.,
General Theological Seminary, New York, 1999.

27. Don Cupitt, *The Meaning of It All in Everyday Speech* (London:
SCM, 1999), 4.

28. Martin Thornton, *English Spirituality* (London: SPCK, 1963), xiii;
idem, *Spiritual Direction* (London: SPCK, 1984); John A. T.

Robinson, *On Being the Church in the World* (London: SCM, 1960); idem, *The Body* (London: SCM, 1961); and idem, *Honest to God* (London: SCM, 1963).

CHAPTER TEN:
TENDING THE COMMUNAL SOUL
IN A CONGREGATIONAL SETTING

1. "A Conversation with Walter Wink," *Alive Now*, November/December 1996, 25.
2. Walter Wink, *Engaging the Powers* (Minneapolis: Fortress Press, 1992), 3, 6.
3. Flora Wuellner, "Prayer and Our Communal Body," in *Prayer and Our Bodies* (Nashville: Upper Room, 1987); idem, *Release: Healing from the Wounds of Family, Church, and Community* (Nashville: Upper Room, 1996).
4. Wink, *Engaging the Powers*, 66.
5. Brother John H. Mostyn, C.F.C., has worked with groups for twenty years and wrote his dissertation about how to evaluate training programs for spiritual directors with a view toward transforming social structures.
6. Walter Burghardt, "Contemplation: A Long, Loving Look at the Real," *Church* (Winter 1989).
7. Parker Palmer, *To Know as We Are Known: A Spirituality of Education* (San Francisco: Harper & Row, 1983), 31–32.
8. Mostyn.
9. Andrew Dreitcer, co-pastor of Sleepy Hollow Presbyterian Church, a ninety-five-member congregation, and director on staff at San Francisco Theological Seminary, comments that he experiences the necessary freedom as pastor/spiritual director because the role is to facilitate discovery of the relationship with God. While he recognizes some potential "hooks," like board control over the pastor's salary, he believes there are benefits to such interrelationships that were classically a part of monastic communities. He cautions that attributing "too much formalized preciousness" to spiritual-direction relationships can be counterproductive to the very Spirit we seek to foster.
10. Ellen Morseth, B.V.M., staff mentor, Worshipful-Work Center for Transforming Church Leadership, Kansas City, Missouri, in her pre-

sentation, "The Selection of Church Leaders Using Spiritual Discernment," in Davis, Calif., spring 1999.

11. Annette Simmons, *A Safe Place for Dangerous Truths: Using Dialogue to Overcome Fear and Distrust at Work* (New York: Amacom, 1999).

12. Morseth, "Selection of Church Leaders."

13. Simmons, *Safe Place for Dangerous Truths*, 30.

14. Charles M. Olsen, *Transforming Church Boards into Communities of Spiritual Leaders* (Washington, D.C.: Alban Institute, 1995).

15. Wink, *Engaging the Powers*, 10.

CHAPTER ELEVEN:
NOT WORDS ALONE: SPIRITUAL DIRECTION
WITH VISUAL IMAGES

Special thanks to three who have influenced this essay: Tom Hedberg, for twenty years of shared brainstorming and support; Alexander Shaia, fellow seeker and external examiner of my dissertation, from which this material is excerpted; and Jim Neafsey, who lives the integration of imagery and the spiritual life.

1. See, for example, Leonard Shlain, *The Alphabet versus the Goddess: The Conflict between Word and Image* (Viking, 1999).

2. Jacques Barzun, *Teacher in America* (Little, Brown, 1945), 130.

3. See Maria Gimbutas, *The Goddesses and Gods of Old Europe* (Los Angeles: University of California Press, 1974).

4. See his *Becoming Adult, Becoming Christian* (Harper & Row, 1984).

5. An excellent treatment of Tillich's 1956 ideas appears in Doug Adam's essay "Theological Expressions through Visual Art Forms," in *Art, Creativity, and the Sacred,* ed. Diane Apostolos-Cappadona (Crossroad, 1992). This volume also contains Tillich's 1961 article, "Art and Ultimate Reality." See also Diane Apostolos-Cappadona and Doug Adams, eds., *Art as Religious Studies* (Crossroad, 1990). Just a few of the many other provocative writers on sacred art are Jane Dillenberger, Jacques Maritain, Margaret Miles, Ananda Coomaraswamy, Hans Küng, Bernard Cooke, and, much earlier, Bernard of Clairvaux.

6. In *Psychological Types,* vol. 6 of *The Collected Works of C.G. Jung* (Princeton University Press, 1971), par. 414.

7. This has been an especially strong theme in the work of French feminists. Gayle Green and Coppelia Kahn, eds., *Making a Difference: Feminist Literary Criticism* (Methuen, 1985), offers several slants on this topic.

8. Translated from German with the original title of *The Art of Spiritual Harmony* (Dover, 1977).

9. See Eugene Honee's essay in *The Art of Devotion in the Late Middle Ages in Europe,* by Henk Van Os (Merrell Holberton, 1992).

10. Julia Cameron, *The Artist's Way* (Jeremy Tarcher, 1992).

11. Frederick Franck, *Art as a Way* (Crossroad, 1981).

12. Chogyam Trungpa, *Dharma Art* (Shambhala, 1996).

13. Henri Nouwen, *Behold the Beauty of the Lord: Praying with Icons* (Ave Maria Press, 1987).

14. See *St. John of Damascus: On the Divine Images* (St. Vladimir's Seminary Press, 1980).

15. The simple reflections in Sister Wendy Beckett's *A Child's Book of Prayer in Art* (Dorling Kindersley, 1995) are suitable for all ages. See also her *The Gaze of Love: Meditations on Art and Spiritual Transformation* (HarperCollins, 1993). She reminds us that art was once considered one of the four bridges to God (the other three: philosophy, religion, and science).

16. Sylvia Shaw Judson, *The Quiet Eye* (Henry Regnery, 1954).

17. Titus Burckhardt, *Sacred Art in East and West* (Perennial Books, 1967), 12.

18. Betsy Caprio and Thomas M. Hedberg, *Coming Home: A Manual for Spiritual Direction* (Paulist Press, 1986), contains details on the Jungian style of direction, and specifics about the sand tray. Sandplay Therapists of America can be contacted for information on training (P.O. Box 4847, Walnut Creek, CA 94596).

19. Readers will recognize the translation of the old Greek ideas into Christian thought as one aspect of neo-Platonism. Pseudo-Dionysius spoke of the "Divine Benignant Rays" which draw us back to their source. While these early dualistic views of creation separated matter from spirit (with resulting heresies), today we can revisit Plato and other philosophers from a more unitive perspective, which acknowledges the oneness of all. See Robert Lawlor's *Sacred Geometry* (Crossroad, 1982) for a good introduction to this complex topic.

20. This chart is reproduced in my book *The Mystery of Nancy Drew* (Source Books, 1992).

21. Then there is the rarely seen *dextrarum iunctio,* or joining of right hands, in which Jesus and Mary are the spousal couple. The Museum of Fine Arts in Boston has such an artwork in the gable of a painting by the fourteenth-century Master of the St. George Codex. Iconographically, such imagery comes from Mary's conflation with the bride of the Canticles and then with Ecclesia, who is often embraced by Christ in art.

22. Jung's painting can be found in Gerhard Wehr, *An Illustrated Biography of C. G. Jung* (Shambhala, 1989).

23. For altarpiece pictures, try used bookstores for Sarel Eimerl, *The World of Giotto* (Time-Life Books, 1967), which is not hard to find. It contains several pictures of exquisite altarpieces that could be used as examples.

24. *Psychology and Religion,* vol. 11 of Jung's *Collected Works* (Princeton University Press, 1958), par. 146. See also the late Edward Edinger's treatments of scripture in *The Bible and the Psyche* (Inner City Books, 1986) and *The Christian Archetype* (Inner City Books, 1987).

25. *Psychology and Alchemy,* vol. 12 of Jung's *Collected Works* (Princeton University Press, 1953), par. 119

26. *America,* 18 May 1996 (emphasis mine).

CHAPTER TWELVE:
"FLESH IS MORE THAN FLESH":
SEXUALITY AND SPIRITUALITY IN SPIRITUAL DIRECTION

1. Kathleen Norris, *The Cloister Walk* (New York: Riverhead, 1996), 124.

2. James Nelson, *Between Two Gardens: Reflection on Sexuality and Religious Experience* (New York: Pilgrim Press, 1983), 5–6.

3. Christiane Northrup, *Women's Bodies, Women's Wisdom: Creating Physical and Emotional Health and Healing* (New York: Bantam, 1994), 227.

4. Ibid., 236.

5. Robert J. Egan, S.J., "Experiencing Ourselves as Sexual Beings in the Context of Contemporary American Culture: Some Theological Reflections," 1996, 5.

6. Paul Ricoeur, "Wonder, Eroticism, and Enigma," in *Sexuality and the Sacred: Sources for Theological Reflection,* ed. James B. Nelson and Sandra P. Longfellow (Louisville: Westminster/John Knox Press, 1994), 83. Ricoeur's essay originally appeared in 1964.

7. United States Catholic Conference, *Human Sexuality: A Catholic Perspective* (1991), 5.

8. Ibid.

9. Quoted in Egan, "Experiencing Ourselves as Sexual Beings," 18.

10. Janet K. Ruffing, "Encountering Love Mysticism: Issues in Supervision," *Presence* 1 (January 1995): 20–33.

11. Pattiann Rogers, *Eating Bread and Honey* (Minneapolis: Milkweed, 1997), 9.

Contributors

Tom Cushman is an Episcopal layman whose energies go into management of a technology team in the Silicon Rainforest of Seattle, as well as into the world of the Spirit. Tom has worked in electronic media for more than forty years, and has been doing spiritual direction—primarily with clergy and corporate managers—since 1986, following certification in the Northwest Spiritual Directors Training Program. Closely related is his mentoring work as a corporate coach, mentoring those already successful and competent, but who want something more. Cashman is passionately committed to reclaiming the values of Celtic Christian Spirituality by teaching, writing, speaking, and leading retreats and workshops; he also enjoys fly fishing, music, and cooking. He and wife, Lin Houston Cashman, who is a spiritual director and healer, have four grown children.

Steven Charleston currently serves as president and dean of the Episcopal Divinity School in Cambridge, Massachusetts, and was previously the diocesan bishop of the Episcopal Church for Alaska. Bishop Charleston is a graduate of Trinity College, Connecticut, and received his M.Div. from the Episcopal Divinity School in 1976. He is a citizen of the Choctaw Nation of Oklahoma, one of the original five tribes removed to Oklahoma on the "Trail of Tears." He has spent most of his adult ministry working within multicultural communities. A collegial member of the House of Bishops, Charleston currently chairs the Justice, Peace, and Integrity of Creation Task Force. He travels and speaks internationally on issues relating to people of color, especially indigenous people's rights and spirituality.

Joseph D. Driskill is associate professor of spirituality and Ronald D. Soucey Lecturer at the Pacific School of Religion, and the assistant dean of the Disciples Seminary Foundation's Berkeley office. A third-generation minister in the Christian Church (Disciples of Christ), Driskill also maintains ministerial standing with the United Church of Canada. He served as a pastor and university chaplain in the United States and Canada before pursuing doctoral studies in spirituality and pastoral care at the Graduate Theological Union. A spiritual director and pastoral counselor with the Lloyd Center of San Francisco Theological Seminary, he is the author of a number of articles, as well as the recently released *Protestant Spiritual Exercises: Theology, History, and Practice* (Harrisburg, Pa.: Morehouse, 1999).

Margaret Guenther is an Episcopal priest, currently serving as Associate Rector for Spiritual Formation at St. Columba's in Washington, D.C. She is professor emerita of the General Theological Seminary and retired director of the Center for Christian Spirituality there, which includes among its programs the training of spiritual directors. Guenther's publications include *Holy Listening: The Art of Spiritual Direction; Toward Holy Ground: Spiritual Directions for the Second Half of Life;* and *The Practice of Prayer* (all published by Cowley).

Betsy Caprio Hedberg, D.Min., A.T.R., from the Roman Catholic tradition, is the director of the Center for Sacred Psychology in Culver City, California. She sees others for spiritual direction and art therapy, as well as supervision and educational consultation. Over the years, Betsy has increasingly valued visual adjuncts to spiritual direction and psychotherapy, and she continues to explore ways to include imagery in individual and group sessions. Betsy is the author of several books, including *Coming Home* (Paulist, 1986) and its accompanying spiritual-direction manual, both written with her husband, Thomas M. Hedberg. They are also coauthors of *A Code of Ethics for Spiritual Direction* (Dove, 1992).

Kenneth Leech is community theologian at St. Botolph's Church, Aldgate, East London, England. An Anglican priest, he has spent most of his ministry in the East End of London, where he has been heavily involved in issues of homelessness, racial justice, drug abuse, and socialist politics. Thirty years ago Leech founded Centrepoint, the center for homeless young people in London. He is the author of *Soul Friend, Subversive Orthodoxy, True Prayer, The Eye of the Storm, The Sky Is Red,* and many other works.

Sandra (Pickens) Lommasson is founding director of the Bread of Life Center for Spiritual Formation, a mission outreach of Davis Community Presbyterian Church in Davis, California. Prior to this appointment, she served the church as lay minister of Christian formation, in which her primary role was as spiritual director to individuals and groups in the congregation. In addition to her ministry of spiritual direction, she teaches in programs for the formation of spiritual directors, and is a member of the Coordinating Council for Spiritual Directors International.

Juan Reed is vicar of St. Martin's Episcopal Church in Chicago. Located on the far West Side of Chicago, St. Martin's is in transition, like many urban communities. However, Reed and his vestry have actively sought to build a vibrant congregation among the local community. Fr. Reed is nurtured by monastic patterns, and is a regular retreatant. He is a candidate in the D.Min. program with a concentration in spirituality at the Catholic Theological Union in Chicago. Reed's interests are in spirituality and social justice and gender issues.

Howard Rice is a lifelong Presbyterian, having attended McCormick Theological Seminary in Chicago and served two inner-city churches as pastor, one in Minneapolis and the other in Chicago. In 1968, Rice was called to San Francisco Theological Seminary, where he served as professor of ministry, director of field education, and chaplain of the Seminary, and was instrumental in developing that institution's emphasis in spiritual formation and direction. Having retired in 1997, Rice is now theologian in residence at the Presbyterian Church of the Roses in Santa Rosa, California. His books include *Reformed Spirituality, A Book of Reformed Prayers* (both published by Westminster/John Knox), and *The Pastor as Spiritual Guide* (Upper Room).

Rich Rossiter, D.Min., is a pastor, spiritual director, bodyworker, author, and retreat leader. An ordained pastor in the Universal Fellowship of Metropolitan Community Churches, Rossiter is presently pastor of Holy Covenant Metropolitan Community Church in Hinsdale, Illinois. In addition to his theological degree from Iliff School of Theology in Denver, Rossiter has a D.Min. in spiritual direction from the Graduate Theological Foundation in Donaldson, Indiana. Rich lives with his life-partner, Perry Wiggins, in Oak Park, Illinois, and is author of the newly released *Out With a Passion: A United Methodist Pastor's Quest for Authenticity* (Alamo Square Press).

Janet Ruffing, R.S.M., is associate professor in spirituality and spiritual direction in the Graduate School of Religion and Religious Education at Fordham University in New York. She was one of the founding members of the Coordinating Council of Spiritual Directors International and a founder of the Internship in the Art of Spiritual Direction at Mercy Center in Burlingame, California. She is author of *Uncovering Stories of Faith: Spiritual Direction and Narrative* (Paulist, 1989), *Spiritual Direction: Beyond the Beginnings* (Paulist, 2000), and *Essays on Mysticism and Social Transformation* (Syracuse University Press, 2000), as well as more than fifty essays in various journals and collections.

Norvene Vest is a spiritual director, author, and workshop leader, well known especially for her books on Benedictine spirituality for the common life. She is an Episcopal laywoman, oblate of a Roman Catholic monastery (St. Andrew's, Valyermo, California), and graduate of a Protestant seminary (Fuller Theological Seminary, Pasadena, California). With her priest husband, Douglas, Norvene leads regular pilgrimages to Britain and Italy as opportunities for deepened faith formation. Her books include *Preferring Christ* (a devotional commentary on Benedict's Rule, published by Source Books), *Gathered in the Word* (Upper Room), *No Moment too Small,* and *Friend of the Soul* (Cowley).

Barry Woodbridge, Ph.D., is the President of Woodbridge and Associates in Rancho Cucamonga, California, and is active in the twelve-step movement. Woodbridge received his doctorate in philosophical theology and hermeneutics from Claremont Graduate School, as well as a D.Min. degree from Claremont School of Theology. He has been actively pursuing work on process hermeneutics and spirituality at the Center for Process Studies in Claremont, and has worked in spiritual direction for nearly twenty years. Woodbridge's books include *A Guidebook for Spiritual Friends* (Upper Room, 1984).